IOWA
BIOGRAPHICAL
DICTIONARY

IOWA
BIOGRAPHICAL
DICTIONARY

PEOPLE OF ALL TIMES AND PLACES
WHO HAVE BEEN IMPORTANT TO THE HISTORY
AND LIFE OF THE STATE

———

SOMERSET PUBLISHERS, INC.
521 Fifth Ave., 17th Floor
New York, N.Y. 10175

Library of Congress Cataloging-in-Publication Data

Iowa biographical dictionary : people of all times and all places who
have been important to the history and life of the state.
    p.   cm.
  ISBN 0-403-09919-6 : $79.00
  1. Iowa--Biography--Dictionaries.   2. Iowa--History.   I. Somerset
Publishers.
CT234.I59 1993
920.0777--dc20   93-36120
                                                                   CIP

FOREWORD

"All History is Biography."
—Samuel Johnson

Events have importance to the extent that they affect or are affected by *people.*

Places, too find their relevence to the extent that people were from there, died there or distinguised themselves in the area.

This State has boundries. Within those boundries people have related to its attributes in many ways.

It is our purpose, in this Biographical Dictionary to detail the lives and activities of those persons, past and present, who have made history or news here, even if only by the possible coincidence of birth or death.

Virtually every sphere of human activity is represented. Government figures dominate because they are most clearly defined within the area. Entertainment, sports, the arts-the famous and infamous alike are included when they have been deemed newsworthy.

LIST OF PERSONS

ALDRICH
  BESS STREETER,
ALLISON
  FRAN,
ANSON
  ADRIAN CONSTANTINE,
ARMSTRONG
  HERBERT,

BALL
  GEORGE WILDMAN,
BANDSTRA
  BERT ANDREW,
BARRY
  LYNDA JEAN,
BAY
  HOWARD,
BEARDSLEY
  WILLIAM S.,
BECKER
  CARL LOTUS,
BEDELL
  BERKLEY WARREN,
BEIDERBECKE
  LEON BISMARCK,
BIRDSALL
  BENJAMIN PIXLEY,
BLACK-HAWK,
BLIVEN
  BRUCE,
BLUE
  ROBERT DONALD,
BOIES
  HORACE,
  WILLIAM DAYTON,
BORLAUG
  NORMAN ERNEST,
BRANSTAD
  TERRY E.,

BRIGGS
  ANSEL,
BROMWELL
  JAMES EDWARD,
BURDICK
  EUGENE LEONARD,
BURNQUIST
  JOSEPH ALFRED ARNER,

CAMPBELL
  ED HOYT,
CANUTT
  YAKIMA,
CAROTHERS
  WALLACE HUME,
CARPENTER
  CYRUS CLAY,
CARROLL
  BERYL FRANKLIN,
CARSON
  JOHNNY,
CARTER
  STEVEN V.,
CASSILL
  R.V.,
CAYTON
  HORACE ROSCOE,
CESSNA
  CLYDE VERNON,
CHAMBERLAIN
  SAMUEL,
CHAMBERS
  JOHN,
CHILDS
  MARQUIS WILLIAM,
CLAMPITT
  AMY,
CLARK
  JAMES,

LIST OF PERSONS

LIST OF PERSONS

LIST OF PERSONS

KYL
  JOHN HENRY,

LANDERS
  ANN,
LANE
  JOSEPH REED,
LANGDON
  HARRY,
LARRABEE
  WILLIAM,
LE COMPTE
  Karl Miles,
LEACHMAN
  CLORIS,
LEAHY
  WILLIAM DANIEL,
LEEDOM
  BOYD (STEWART),
LEFFLER
  SHEPHERD,
LEOPOLD
  ALDO,
LEWELLING
  LORENZO DOW,
LEWIS
  JOHN LLEWELLYN,
LIEURANCE
  THURLOW,
LIGHTFOOT
  JAMES ROSS,
LOGAN
  JOHN BURTON,
LOVELESS
  HERSCHEL C.,
LOWE
  RALPH PHILLIPS,

MAHASKAH,
MAHTOIOWA,
MANFRED
  FREDERICK,
MARTIN
  GLENN L.,
  THOMAS ELLSWORTH,
MAXWELL
  ELSA,

MAYNE
  WILEY,
MAYTAG
  ELMER HENRY,
MCCAIN
  JOHN SIDNEY, JR.,
MCCREE
  WADE H., JR.,
MERRILL
  SAMUEL,
MEZVINSKY
  EDWARD MAURICE,
MILLER
  GLENN,
  MERLE,
MOREY
  WALT,
MORRIS
  MARK,
MOTT
  FRANK LUTHER,

NAHPOPENAHPOPE,
NAREY
  HARRY ELSWORTH,
NEWBOLD
  JOSHUA G.,

PARETSKY
  SARA,
PEPPER
  IRVIN ST. CLAIR,
PICKETT
  CHARLES EDGAR,
PUSEY
  NATHAN MARSH,

RAWSON
  CHARLES AUGUSTUS,
RAY
  ROBERT D.,
REASONER
  HARRY,
ROBINSON
  THOMAS JOHN BRIGHT,
ROSS
  LAWRENCE S.,

LIST OF PERSONS

ROWE
  LEO STANTON,
RUML
  BEARDSLEY,
RUMPLE
  JOHN NICHOLAS WILLIAM,
RUTLEDGE
  WILEY (BLOUNT, JR.),

SANDBERG
  RYNE DEE,
SCHERLE
  WILLIAM JOSEPH,
SCHULLER
  ROBERT,
SCHWENGEL
  FREDERICK D.,
SEBERG
  JEAN,
SHAW
  LESLIE MORTIER,
SHERMAN
  BUREN ROBINSON,
SMITH
  COURTNEY (CRAIG),
  JEFF,
  WALTER INGLEWOOD,
SPEDDING
  FRANK H.,
STECK
  DANIEL FREDERIC,
STEELE
  THOMAS JEFFERSON,
STEGNER
  WALLACE,
STEWART
  DAVID WALLACE,
STONE
  WILLIAM MILO,
STROUSE
  NORMAN HULBERT,
STRUBLE
  ISAAC S.,
SUCKOW
  RUTH,

SUNDAY
  BILLY,
SWANSON
  CHARLES EDWARD,
SWEET
  BURTON ERWIN,

TAGGARD
  GENEVIEVE,
TAIMAH,
TAUKE
  THOMAS JOSEPH,
THOMPSON
  SADA CAROLYN,,
THURSTON
  LLOYD,
TOWNER
  HORACE MANN,
TURNER
  DANIEL W.,

UTTERBACK
  HUBERT,

VAN BUREN
  ABIGAIL,
VAN DUYN
  MONA,
VAN VECHTEN
  CARL,

WADE
  MARTIN JOSEPH,
WALLACE
  HENRY AGARD,
WAYMACK
  WILLIAM WESLEY,
WAYNE
  JOHN,
WEAVER
  JAMES BAIRD,
WILCOX
  FRANCIS (ORLANDO),
WILLIAMS
  ANDY,

xi

LIST OF PERSONS

WILLSON
  MEREDITH,
WILSON
  GEORGE ALLISON,
  MARGARET WILHEMINA,
WOOD
  GRANT,
WOODS
  FRANK PLOWMAN,

YOUNG
  LAFAYETTE,

A

ALDRICH, BESS STREETER, (1881-1954) — was a writer noted for her historical accuracy.

Born in Cedar Falls, Iowa on February 17, 1881, she was graduated from Iowa State Teachers College in 1901. From then until 1906, Aldrich taught in public schools in Iowa and Salt Lake City, Utah. For a year, she was assistant supervisor of primary training at Iowa State Teachers College.

Aldrich began writing in 1911 using the pen name of Margaret Dean Stevens, but after 1918 she wrote using her own name. Aldrich published about 160 short stories, many of which were syndicated and resold to British magazines. Her stories were published in such popular magazines as *Saturday Evening Post, Good Housekeeping, Harper's Weekly* and *Ladies Home Journal.* She also published numerous books. A collection of her work was produced in 1950 and was titled "The Bess Streeter Aldrich Reader."

Much of Aldrich's writing was based on the theme of the settling of the midwest and drew upon the details of her own pioneer ancestry. Many of her stories emphasized the resourceful optimism of the Midwestern women of the 1800s. Her novel, "A Lantern In Her Hand," which had a Nebraska background, sold consistently long after its publication and was eventually printed in an edition designed for use in schools.

Throughout her work, Aldrich preserved historical accuracy. Her books often served as supplemental reading in history classes. Various books were translated into Dutch, Danish, Swedish, Hungarian, French, Chinese and Spanish. Her novel, "Miss Bishop," was made into a movie under the title of "Cheers for Miss Bishop."

Aside from her professional writing, Aldrich was a director of the American Exchange Bank in Elmwood, Nebraska from 1909 until 1938. She served as a member of numerous associations and organizations. In 1929, she received the Kiwanis Medal for distinguished service in citizenship in Lincoln, Nebraska and in 1934, received an honorary LL.D. degree was conferred on her by the University of Nebraska.

Aldrich married Charles Sweetzer Aldrich in 1907. The couple had four children. She died on August 3, 1954.

ALLISON, FRAN, (1907-1989) — television personality, was born in La Porte City, Iowa. Even as a youngster, Fran was predisposed to be on stage as she made her singing debut at the age of four. She later attended Coe College in Cedar Rapids and earned degrees in music and education. Afterward she worked for awhile as a fourth-grade teacher, a producer of amateur contests, and a singer on small Iowa radio stations.

In 1937, Miss Allison moved to Chicago and worked as a vocalist on the *Breakfast Club* radio programme. While she was with the Iowa radio stations, she had created several characters: Aunt Fannie, Bert Beerbower, Orphie Hackett and Ott Ort. Now, at the Chicago station, she continued to develop those characters.

During the war, in 1942, Miss Allison met Burr Tillstrom, a puppeteer. At that time, he was in need of someone who could help him with his puppet show and Miss Allison agreed to be that person. On

October 13, 1947, Tillstrom's show and Miss Allison, went on television on WBKB-TV (now WMAQ) for one-half hour, five days a week. The show was called *Kukla, Fran and Ollie* and consisted of Fran Allison interviewing guests, singing and interacting with several puppet personalities. One unique fact about the show is that it was unscripted and Allison and Tillstrom would come up with the format and dialogue only one- half hour before air time. The show ran until 1957 and then went off the air. During the time it was on the air, it won several Emmy and Peabody awards for excellence in children's programming.

After the show ended, Fran Allison hosted an Emmy award- winning variety show which was dubbed as "the most ambitious show in Chicago's decade of television." She also appeared in plays, commercials and television features and later hosted the CBS Saturday and Sunday *Children's Film Festival* with Tillstrom and his puppets.

In 1942, Fran Allison met and married Archie Levington, a representative for a music publisher. In the 1980's, after Levington's death, Allison moved to Los Angeles and hosted a talk show about aging and senior citizens' issues. She died of leukemia in Sherman Oaks, California on June 13, 1989. She was eighty-one years old.

ANSON, ADRIAN CONSTANTINE, (1852-1922) — baseball player and manager also known as "Cap," was born in Marshalltown, Iowa to Henry and Jeannette (Rice) Anson. He could probably be considered the first superstar of baseball and definitely one of the greatest first basemen. In 1871, the Philadelphia Athletics of the National Association acquired him from a baseball team in Rockford, Illinois and he was on his way to a fantastic baseball career. He played every position except pitcher for the Athletics. In 1876, his friend, Albert G. Spalding, who had just become manager of the Chicago Whitestockings, signed Anson on as player and captain. Anson eventually succeeded Spalding as Manager in 1879 and won league batting championships in 1879, 1881, 1887, and 1888. He compiled a lifetime batting average of .339, but twice hit over .400, with over 3500 hits total at the end of his career. He was the first player in history to go over the 3000 mark. Under his direction, the Chicago club won five pennants: 1880, 1881, 1882, 1885, and 1886. He also took the team on a world tour in 1889-1890.

In the winter of 1885, Anson decided that the team needed to get in shape a couple of months before the season started. The men had a bad habit of coming back and starting the season in a fat and unfit condition. So Anson started spring training for his men. In spite of grumbling and complaining from them, Anson whipped his team into shape and went on to win the pennant in 1886. Anson was also noted for his strict discipline when it came to alcoholic beverages. In an age where the players drank too much and behaved in a rowdy manner, Anson set a different standard. He believed in sobriety for himself and his players and was known for enforcing the rules with his fists when his words didn't work. He had a rather aggressive manner and a booming voice that demanded attention. He also was genial with a good sense of humor and was deeply loved by those who knew him.

After retiring from the Chicago Whitestockings in 1897, Anson managed the New York Giants for a year until he retired altogether in 1898. From 1905 to 1907 he was clerk of the city of Chicago, and died on April 14, 1922. He was posthumously elected to the Baseball Hall of Fame in 1939. It has been said that he desired his epitaph to say, "Here lies a man that batted .300."

ARMSTRONG, HERBERT, (1892-1986) — evangelist and author, was born in Des Moines, Iowa to Horace and Eva Armstrong. He started out in the advertising business as a copywriter and salesman. In 1934, he left the advertising business and became a minister in the Church of God. He had his first pastorate in Eugene, Oregon and while there started preaching on the radio, naming his show "World Tomorrow," under his new found sect, The Radio Church of God. In 1947, Armstrong moved his ministry to California where he incorporated and named his church the Worldwide Church of God. His church, while claiming some fundamentals of Christianity, also mixed in Judaism, rejected the Holy Trinity and taught that worldly wealth was a sign of divine favor. The ministry publishes the magazines *Quest* and *Plain Truth,* and there are television and radio broadcasts which are syndicated to hundreds of television stations throughout the world. Armstrong also established the Ambassador College, the Ambassador International Cultural Foundation, the Everset House publishing firm and the Ambassador Auditorium. The Worldwide Church of God had 80,000 members at the time of Armstrong's death.

Armstrong's writings include *The Book of Revelation at Last!, Just What do You Mean, Born Again?, The Missing Dimension in Sex, The United States and British Commonwealth in Prophecy, The Incredible Human Potential,* and *A Voice Cries Out Amid Religious Confusion.*

Armstrong's ministry, while rich with worldly wealth, was also filled with controversy. In the 1970's, he and his son Garner Ted Armstrong, who was the president of Ambassador College, had a falling out over the senior Armstrong's remarriage in 1977. It seems that the church had a strong rule against remarriage of any kind but Herbert Armstrong broke that rule by marrying Ramona, a divorci, after his first wife died in 1967. The second marriage ended in divorce in 1984, but the rift between father and son was never healed. A short while later, in 1979, the Attorney General's office placed the church in receivership saying that the church officials had misappropriated funds. After consulting an attorney, Armstrong dissolved the church and set up a one man corporation, making him virtually untouchable by the law. After a law was enacted that protected churches from the rules that applied to other businesses and charities, Armstrong re-established his church and sued the state for damages.

Herbert Armstrong died on January 16, 1986 at the age of 93. He is survived by his daughters, Beverly Gott and Dorothy Mattson, his son, Garner Ted, eight grandchildren, and four great-grandchildren.

B

BALL, GEORGE WILDMAN, (1909-1994) — lawyer, United States Under Secretary of State, was born on December 21, in Des Moines, Iowa to Amos and Edna (Wildman) Ball. He attended primary school in Des Moines and at the age of eleven, moved with his parents to Evanston, Illinois where he received his secondary education. In 1926, he started attending Northwestern University and graduated in 1930 with a B.A. degree. Next, he attended law school at Northwestern and earned his J.D. degree in 1933. In that same year, when Professor Herman Oliphant was appointed general counsel for the Farm Credit Administration, Ball and several other young law graduates accompanied him. In 1935, Ball left Oliphant and went back to Chicago. He worked for the next seven years successively for two law firms in order to gain more experience.

In 1942, with experience in federal taxation, corporate reorganization, and the reorganization of major railroads, Ball returned to government service. He started out on the staff of the general counsel of the Office of Lend-Lease Administration and advanced to associate general counsel.

In 1943, he became associate general counsel for the Foreign Economic Administration and in 1944, became the civilian member of the Air Force Evaluation Board. Later, he was appointed director of the United States Strategic Bombing Survey and, in 1945, took part in a seven-day interrogation of the former German minister of armaments, munitions, and production, Albert Speer. A report of this interrogation, written by Ball and John Kenneth Galbraith was printed in *Life* magazine on December 17, 1945.

From 1945 to 1946, Ball served as general counsel for the French Supply council and in 1946, helped found the law firm of Cleary, Gottlieb, Steen and Ball with offices in New York, Brussels, Paris, and Washington, D.C. The firm represented American companies and individuals doing business in foreign countries. Working with Jean Monnet, originator of the European Unification movement, Ball became involved in 1945 with establishing the coal and steel community in Europe. For years he made monthly trips to Paris and altogether crossed the Atlantic approximately 155 times by air and twenty times by ship.

In 1952, Ball was national director of volunteers for Adlai E. Stevenson in his presidential campaign that year. Ball and Stevenson had become friends in 1935, as they worked together in a law firm in Chicago. In 1961, impressed with a study on foreign affairs that Ball took part in, John F. Kennedy designated him as Under Secretary of State for Economic Affairs. As such, Ball received assignments in problem areas of the world including the Congo (Zaire), the Dominican Republic, Korea and Ghana. He also sat in on cold-war strategy talks with the president and West German Chancellor, Konrad Adenauer.

Ball was active in the Council of Foreign Relations and was part owner of the *Northern Virginia Sun,* a newspaper in Arlington County, Virginia. Awards he received throughout his career include, the French Legion of Honor and the United States Medal of Freedom.

George Ball married Ruth Murdoch of Pittsburgh on September 16, 1932. They had two sons, John Colin and Douglas Bleakly.

Ball's writings include, *The Discipline of Power, Diplomacy for a Crowded World, The Past Has Another Pattern, Error and Betrayal in Lebanon,* and *The Passionate Attachment: America's Involvement with Israel 1947 to Present.*

George Ball died on May 26, 1994.

BANDSTRA, BERT ANDREW, (1922-   ) — a U.S. Representative from Iowa; born on a farm between Eddyville and Albia, Monroe County, Iowa, January 25, 1922; in 1925 moved to a farm in Mahaska County near Taintor; attended Taintor Independent School and New Sharon High School; enlisted as a seaman in the United States Navy in March 1942, served in the Solomon Islands and Okinawa campaigns, and was honorably discharged as a second- class petty officer in December 1945; received the Presidential Unit Citation; resumed education and graduated from Central College at Pella in 1950 and from the University of Michigan at Ann Arbor in 1953; was admitted to the bar in 1953 and began the practice of law in Pella, Iowa; as Marion County attorney, January 1955 to June 1959; assistant to Congressman Neal Smith, January 1959 to February 1964; elected as a Democrat to the Eighty-ninth Congress (January 3, 1965-January 3, 1967); unsuccessful candidate for reelection in 1966 to the Ninetieth Congress; resumed the practice of law in Knoxville, Marion County, Iowa; is a resident of Pella, Iowa.

BARRY, LYNDA JEAN, (1956-) — is a popular cartoonist and author.

Born in Richland Center, Wisconsin in 1956, she was four years old when her family moved to Seattle, Washington. Growing up in a family that was half Norwegian-Irish and half Filipino gave Barry a lot of material about the sometimes frightening world of childhood, recalling one time that she sometimes experienced "emotional flipouts." Some of those times came from her often feeling "completely different." "I never felt completely Filipino and I never felt completely white," she once told an interviewer, "I didn't even feel like a girl; I didn't feel like a boy, either. I could not find a peer." Later on, when she was using her childhood experiences to create her work, she noted: "I think about my own childhood all the time. It's the only place to go if you're looking for answers. It's where all our motivations, feelings and opinions come from."

Barry began attending Olympia's Evergreen State College in 1974, and it was there that she met another cartoonist, Matt Groening, the creator of the *Life is Hell* comic strip, and the cartoon family, *The Simpsons*. Groening recognized Barry's talent immediately when she showed him cartoons she had drawn, calling them "the wildest cartoons (he had) ever seen," and "funny," but with a "very strong point of view." Her first comic drawings came from a night of no sleep after a boyfriend had broken up with her. Called *Spinal Comics,* the initial strips portrayed men as being, according to one source, "spiny cacti attempting to seduce weak-willed women." Groening printed the comic strip in the college's campus newspaper, and another friend helped to get her work published in the University of Washington's school paper, the *Daily.*

Barry received her B.A. degree from Evergreen in 1978, and, having convinced herself that cartooning would not provide her with a living, tried to support herself with freelance artistic work such as illustrating and painting. Once again, her good friend Matt Groening came to the rescue in a roundabout way when he wrote an article about the group he dubbed the "Evergreen mafia," mentioning Barry as one of the talented artists he knew. Because of that article, Chicago *Reader* publisher Bob Roth hired her at eighty dollars a week to submit her comic strips, which Roth described as "a hipper kind of strip that you couldn't find anywhere else...She was addressing adult concerns in a way that comic strips almost never do." Several other publications picked up the comic including *New Times,* and England's *New Musical Express.* After going through several name changes, Barry settled on *Ernie Pook's Comeek,* for the name of the strip, Ernie Pook being a name one of her brothers had often used for his pets. As of 1994, her work appeared in over sixty newspapers in the U.S. and several other countries such as Russia and Canada.

Collections of her works began to get published in 1981, starting with *Girls and Boys.* The following compilation, *Big Ideas,* was described by writer Tom Robbins as "wonderfully funny, true, and disturbing stuff...Lynda Barry's pen goes from zero to sixty in two seconds flat, and when it gets there it is sweaty with genius."

In 1984 Barry was hired by *Esquire* magazine to draw a color cartoon which was first named *Modern Romance,* then *On the Home Front,* making her the first woman to have a cartoon series in that publication. Proud of that fact at first, she later had creative differences with editors who wanted her perspective to resemble that of the "Esquire Man." In 1989 she left the magazine, later bluntly telling one writer that it was because she was unable to "see the world through the eyes of a successful, thirty-year-old white guy." Through the years, her work has appeared in several other publications such as *Newsweek, Seventeen, Entertainment Weekly,* and *Mirabella.*

Subsequent compilations of her work were *Naked Ladies! Naked Ladies! Naked Ladies!* (1984); *Everything in the World* (1986); *The Fun House* (1987); and *Down the Street* (1988).

BARRY

Barry once admitted to a reporter that she gets many of her ideas by simply eavesdropping on people, calling the technique "inspirational, not only for subject matter but for actual dialogue." Other material is sometimes derived from handwritten notes that she comes across.

Barry had the idea for her next artistic project while on a Hawaiian vacation in which she envisioned a series of portraits "in funky metal frames, of my favorite musicians--most of them black, most of them dead." Eighteen portraits came out of her idea, some of which included such soul music pioneers as Otis Redding and Gertrude ("Ma") Rainey. When a Seattle gallery was getting ready to exhibit her work, she was asked to write a short paragraph for the show's catalog. It was when she began to investigate the lives of the musicians she had portrayed that she learned of the deep racial prejudice and poverty many of them had to endure--along with many other African-Americans--and realized that racism is "bound up in the fabric of everything." It was from this project that she got the idea for what would be her most compelling work, her first novel, *The Good Times Are Killing Me* (1988)--a story about a young white girl who becomes friends with a spirited black girl and how, due to social conditions regarding racial hostilities, the two girls end up enemies.

In the *New York Times Book Review,* critic Deborah Stead, impressed with Barry's writing style, noted thatshe "has an impeccable ear, and this funny, intricate, and finally heartbreaking story exquisitely captures an American childhood." In 1989 Barry was honored with a Washington State Governor's Writers Award, and that same year, worked in tandem with Arnold Aprill, artistic director of Chicago's City Lit Theater Company, writing a musical adaptation for the stage. A second adaptation was written by Barry for its debut at New York City's Second Stage Theater in 1991. *Newsweek's* David Gates noted that the latter work tuned into "one of America's central anxieties: that the interracial utopia imagined in the 1960s was an illusion." Another critic wrote that Barry had "distilled the essence of being young--specifically, how children deal with fantasy and reality, good and evil, boredom and just plain fun...The result is positively rejuvenating."

Later cartoon compilations include *Come Over, Come Over* (1990); *My Perfect Life* (1992); and *It's So Magic* (1994). Awards Barry has received include a Seattle Design and Advertising Silver Award for Illustration (1985), and the Excellence in Journalism Award for Cartooning in Non-Daily Publications, bestowed by the Society of Professional Journalists (1986).

In summing up the impact of Lynda Barry's work, a critic for *Washington Book World* wrote admiringly: "To call Barry a cartoonist is to diminish her work...the best of (her) four- and six-panel stories are almost literature, literature that culminates in an unbearably poignant insight."

BAY, HOWARD, (1912-1986) — was once described as the dean of American stage designers.

Born in Centralia, Washington on May 3, 1912, he attended several colleges, including: the University of Washington, Seattle, 1928; Chappell School of Art, 1928; University of Colorado, 1929; Marshall College, 1929-30; Carnegie Institute of Technology (later Carnegie-Mellon University), 1930-31; and Westminster College (1931-32). Also, in 1939, Bay spent some time studying his craft in Europe.

Bay designed either lighting or sets, or both, for a large number of stage productions, some of which include: *Morning Star* (1940); *The Corn is Green* (1940); *Johnny 2X4* (1942); *The Merry Widow* (1943); *Carmen Jones* (1943); *Show Boat* (1946); *The Big Knife* (1949); *Come Back Little Sheba* (1950); *Two on the Aisle* (1951); *Tevya and His Daughters* (1957); *Carmen* (1959); *Toys in the Attic* (1960); *Pal Joey* (1961); *The Music Man* (1965); *Man of La Mancha* (1965); *Equus* (1974); and *The Utter Glory of Morrissey Hall* (1979); among several others.

Bay won *Variety's* New York Drama Critics Poll in 1942 for his set designing in *Brooklyn, U.S.A.* In 1944 and 1945 he won a Donaldson Award for sets and lighting for *Carmen Jones* and *Up in Central Park,* respectively. He also received Tony Awards for his sets and lighting for *Toys in the Attic* (1960), and *Man of La Mancha* (1966).

The designer created sets in other venues as well, including for operas at Carnegie Hall, and for several television productions, such as: *The Fred Waring Show, Somerset Maugham Theatre, Mr. Broadway,* and *The Pueblo Incident.*

Amidst all his other work, Bay was a set designing instructor at Brandeis University for fourteen years, and also gave lectures on the subject throughout his career. He was named Alan King Professor of Theatre Arts in 1966, and served as head of that department until 1969. During 1966-67 he was also visiting professor at Yale University.

Bay was married to Ruth Jonas and the couple had two children. He died on November 21, 1981.

BEARDSLEY, WILLIAM S., (1901-1954) — was Governor of Iowa from 1948 to 1954.

Born in Beacon, Iowa on May 17, 1901, he attended the Bowen Institute of Pharmacy, graduating in 1921. The following year he began what would be a sixteen year career in the retail drug business. In 1938, he retired from that line of work and began farming on a parcel of land that he had purchased.

During his years as a pharmacist, he ran for the Iowa State Senate on the Republican ticket, and after winning his campaign, served from 1933 to 1941. Six years later, he began serving in the Iowa House of Representatives (1947- 49). In 1948, he ran for Governor of Iowa and won, beating the incumbent governor, Robert Blue in the primary, and his Democratic opponent, Carroll O. Switzer, in the general election. Beardsley went on to win two more terms for the gubernatorial office.

While governor, Beardsley worked hard to balance the state budget. He used funds he had appropriated in order to upgrade schools and roads, and also added more officers to the highway patrol, made gambling illegal, and gave the workmen's compensation a much-needed raise.

Beardsley intended to retire from office after his third term, but he was killed in a car accident, and died on November 21, 1954. He was buried in New Virginia, Iowa, and was survived by his wife, Charlotte Manning, and their four children.

BECKER, CARL LOTUS, (1873-1945) — historian, was born on a farm in Black Hawk County, Iowa. His Christian name was Lotus Carl, but while in school, he changed it to Carl Lotus because his friends thought his name was strange. He attended high school at West Side in Waterloo and after graduating in 1892, attended Cornell College in Mount Vernon. After a year at Cornell, he transferred to the University of Wisconsin in Madison. It was around that time that he decided to become a writer of history. He spent two years in graduate work at Wisconsin and in 1898 went to Columbia University to study for another year.

After completing his graduate work at Columbia, Becker taught for two years at Pennsylvania State College and one year at Dartmouth College before going to the University of Kansas in 1902 where he stayed until 1916. In 1907, he completed his doctorate from the University of Wisconsin. In 1916, he left Kansas for the University of Minnesota where he stayed for only one year. In 1917, he became a professor of history at Cornell University in Ithaca, New York where he taught until his retirement in 1941.

Becker was known as an historian of history. His ideas of "historical relativism," "detachment," "objectivity," and "fact" were pioneering efforts of his that were often criticized by his contemporaries. Nevertheless he was able to influence his contemporaries and successors and persuade them to look again at the history of history. Becker was an historian who was concerned with the possible uses and abuses of history. His address, "Everyman His Own Historian," before the American Historical Association, in 1931, appealed to those who embraced "historical relativism," the idea that history is subject to the influence of the historian's own environment and rejects the idea that history is merely objective truth.

Becker wrote 16 books, 75 articles and approximately 200 book reviews on history. His books include: *The History of Political Parties in the Province of New York, 1760-1776, The Beginnings of the*

American People, The Eve of the Revolution: A Chronicle of the Breach with England, The United States: An Experiment in Democracy, The Declaration of Independence: A Study in the History of Political Ideas, Modern History; the Rise of a Democratic, Scientific, and Industrialized Civilization, The Heavenly City of the Eighteenth-Century Philosophers, Everyman His Own Historian, Progress and Power, The Story of Civilization, Modern Democracy, New Liberties for Old, Cornell University: Founders and the Founding, How New Will the Better World Be?, Freedom and Responsibility in the American Way of Life, and *Detachment and the Writing of History: Essays and Letters.* The subjects of his writings were political history, intellectual history, biographies, college and high school textbooks, historiographical essays, essays of contemporary opinion, reviews, and review essays.

In spite of his achievements, Becker seemed at times unsure of his own knowledge of history and on some occasions his behavior was rather ambiguous in nature. He himself declared that his knowledge of history consisted "in having thought a good deal about the meaning of history rather than having achieved erudition in it." Once, when asked to speak at an American historical Association session on the social studies, he refused, stating that he had "no ideas on the subject of history teaching in the schools." On another occasion, he turned down a nomination for the prestigious Harmsworth visiting professorship of American history at Oxford University, saying that he had never taught American history and did not know enough about it to teach it. Nevertheless, by 1931, Becker had become known as one of the most distinguished American historians, mostly because his challenges to those who wrote

BEDELL

American history rather than for his contributions to it.

Carl Lotus Becker married Maude Hepworth Ranney on June 16, 1901. Miss Ranney was a widow who was seven years his senior and who had a seven year old daughter.

Carl Lotus Becker died of uremia in 1945. His body was cremated and his ashes buried in Pleasant Grove Cemetery in Ithaca, New York.

BEDELL, BERKLEY WARREN, (1921-   ) — a U.S. Representative from Iowa born in Spirit Lake, Dickinson County, Iowa, March 5, 1921 educated in Spirit Lake public schools; graduated, Spirit Lake High School, 1939; attended Iowa State University, Ames, 1940-1942; engaged in fishing tackle business; founder and chairman of Berkiey & Co., Spirit Lake; served in United States Army, first lieutenant, 1942-1945; member, Spirit Lake Board of Education, 1957-1962; unsuccessful candidate for election in 1972 to the Ninety-third Congress; delegate to Iowa State Democratic conventions, 1972- 1974; elected as a Democrat to the Ninety-fourth and to the five succeeding Congresses (January 3, 1975-January 3, 1987); was not a candidate for reelection in 1986; is a resident of Spirit Lake, Iowa.

BEIDERBECKE, LEON BISMARCK, (1903-1931) — known as "Bix" to his friends, was a jazz musician born in Davenport, Iowa. As a child, he taught himself to play the piano and coronet. He attended Lake Forest Academy for one year and then joined a jazz group by the name of the Wolverines with whom he played all over the Midwest and in New York. He played jazz with other bands such as Frankie Trumbauer's, Jean Goldkette's, Paul Whiteman's, and Glen

Gray's. He also had the opportunity to play with some of the top jazz musicians such as Joe "King" Oliver and Louis Armstrong. He was the first important white jazz artist, though he was little known outside certain circles. He also composed several songs that contained his distinctive style of rhythmic lyricism, such as "Singin' the Blues," "I'm Comin' Virginia," "Fidgety Feet," "Since My Best Girl Turned Me Down," "The Love Nest," and "I'm a Mist."

After his death in 1931 of pneumonia complicated by alcoholism, a semi-fictional biography was written about Beiderbecke by Dorothy Baker, entitled, *Young Man With a Horn*(1938). Later, in the 1970's, two factual biographies were written: *Remembering Bix: A Memoir of the Jazz Age,* and *Bix: Man and Legend.*

BIRDSALL, BENJAMIN PIXLEY, (1858-1917) — a U.S. Representative from Iowa; born in Weyauwega, Waupaca County, Wis., October 26, 1858; attended the common schools of Iowa and Iowa State University, Iowa City; studied law; was admitted to the bar in 1878 and practiced; served as district judge of the eleventh judicial district of Iowa from January 1893 to October 1900; elected as a Republican to the Fifty-eighth, Fifty-ninth, and Sixtieth Congresses (March 4, 1903-March 3, 1909); resumed the practice of law in Clarion, Wright County, Iowa, where he died May 26, 1917; interment in Evergreen Cemetery.

BLACK-HAWK, or **KARA-ZHOUSEPT-HAH,** (1767-1838) — Indian chief was born in the present limits of Randolph County, Illinois, in 1767. He was the adopted brother of the chief of the Foxes, and although by birth a Pottawattomie, was brought up by the Sacs. He bore several names; at the time of the

BLACK-HAWK

treaty at Prairie du Chien his name was *Hay-rayptshoan-sharp,* but later, when he was taken prisoner, it was *Muscata-mish-kia- kiak.* At the age of fifteen, already rated as a warrior, he was a leader amoung his people, and at twenty-one he became head chief of the Sacs.

His course from the start was one of opposition to the whites, and the assertion of the rights of his people even to lands sold by them. It is probable that his policy was shaped by the false information that the Americans were few and could not fight. In 1804 the Sacs and Foxes signed a treaty in St. Louis with General Harrison, in which, for an annuity of $1,000, they transferred to the United States their lands along the Mississippi River. Alleging that the chiefs were drunk at the time of signing, Black-Hawk for several years successfully resisted the ratification of its provisions. A second treaty was made, however, in 1816, he himself being a party, by which the cession of lands was completed. Seven years later the main body of both tribes migrated to their new reservation under the leadership of Keokuk, but Black-Hawk still remained behind.

In 1830 the chiefs of the Foxes were invited to a treaty at Prairie du Chien for a settlement of their difficulties with the Sioux. On the way to attend the treaty meeting, nine Foxes were killed by the Sioux, and next year a band of Sioux, within a mile of Prairie du Chien were attacked by Black-Hawk's party and twenty-eight were killed. The Americans demanded the murderers, but Black-Hawk refused to deliver them up.

By the treaty of 1830 the Sacs and Foxes had sold their country to the U.S. government. Black-Hawk had nothing to do with this sale, and the attempt to ratify it displeased him. When he heard, the following year, of his people having to move from his village, by the advice of the trader, to take up a residence elsewhere, he became the leader of those who were opposed to removal. The Sacs were then on the Rock River, and Black-Hawk agreed to deliver up their lead mines if allowed to hold their village. Their women and children, dispossessed, were on the banks of the Mississippi, without lodges, while the Sacs were camped on the west bank of that river. They decided to repossess their lands.

The whites agreed to let them plant together, but had secured the best grounds. The women were badly treated, but the Indians did not resort to retaliation until they were cheated out of their guns. Finally they were told not to come to the east side of the river, but Black-Hawk, refusing to obey, recrossed and took possession. Governor Reynolds declared Illinois invaded by hostile Indians, although they were only on U.S. lands, and six companies of regulars and 700 militia were ordered there under General Gaines. Black-Hawk met the general in council and declared he would not move, but when all the troops had arrived the Indians fled, returning only to take corn from their own lands. General Atkinson met them at Fort Madison, but they retreated up the Rock River to plant on the lands of Black-Hawk's son, the Prophet. Major Stillman followed them; a flag of truce was sent in, but its bearers were taken prisoners; five messangers sent by Black-Hawk were pursued and killed.

The war cry was then raised, and the Indians rushed on with guns, knives and tomahawks. Stillman ordered a retreat, which became a rout. Black-Hawk, with seventy men, had put to flight a detachment of 270. The chief then proceeded to Four Lakes, at the head of the Rock River. Atkinson pursued, and on

BLACK-HAWK

June 18th, 3,000 whites brought face to face with 500 Indians were defeated after a difficult fight. General Scott was then ordered to the frontier with nine companies of artillery, but his troops were struck down with cholera. General Dodge fell on Black-Hawk's trail on Ouisconsin, and Black Hawk, deceived in his support, was forced to retreat, crossing the river in the night with much suffering and disaster.

At Blue Mounds, Dodge and Atkinson united forces in pursuit. While descending the Ouisconsin, Black-Hawk's forces were upset in their boats. Many drowned and others were captured. A steamboat overtook Black-Hawk's forces on August 1st, and the chief sent two white flags for surrender. A company of 150 of Black-Hawk's men, unarmed, approached the river, but the captain of the boat fired into them. The next morning General Atkinson's whole army was upon them, and Black-Hawk's forces were defeated and driven into the river, to their total destruction.

Black-Hawk again escaped, but this fight ended the war. The Sioux, with 100 men, pursued the flying Sacs, and murdered another 120 of them. Two young Winnebagoes brought Black-Hawk into camp, dressed in white deer skin clothes made for him by squaws. When taken before the commander he said: "You have taken me prisoner; I am grieved. I tried to bring you into ambush. I saw my evil day was at hand. Black-Hawk's heart is dead, but he can stand torture; he is no coward "he is an Indian who fought for his squaws, against those who came to cheat. You know the cause of this war, and you ought to be ashamed of it. We looked up to the Great Spirit. Farewell, my nation."

Black-Hawk, with eleven chiefs and fifty warriors, was landed at the lower rapids. His two sons, Prophet and Naopope, and five principal warriors, were given up as hostages to be held during the pleasure of the president, at Jefferson Barracks, Missouri. Black-Hawk was then about 63 years of age. Not a chief by birth, he had acquired his position by bravery and wisdom. In his interview with President Jackson, he said, with true dignity: "I am a man; and you are another." The president directed that articles of dress intended for his party be exhibited and distributed, and commanded him to go to Fort Monroe. Black-Hawk replied: "If I had not struck for my people they would have said I was a woman. Black-Hawk expects to return to his people." The president replied: "When all is quiet you may return," and assured him that his women should be protected.

On June 5, 1833, they were set free. President Jackson again met Chief Black-Hawk in Baltimore, and all along the return route crowds greeted him. In New York he visited the Seneca Reservation. He arrived at Fort Armstrong in August, 1833. Indians met him there with bands of music. Keokuk was then the acknowledged chief of his tribe, and Black-Hawk, declaring that he would not conform to anyone, departed in silence, downcast and broken. Black-Hawk died in Des Moines, Iowa, October 3, 1838. He was buried according to the custom of the Sacs; his body seated on the ground; his cane between his knees, grasped in his hands, with slabs or rails then piled about him.

BLIVEN, BRUCE, (1989-1977) — magazine editor, was born in Emmetsburg, Iowa on July 27, 1889 to Charles F. and Lilla C. (Ormsby) Bliven. He attended Stanford University and completed his B.A.

degree in 1911. During that time he was a member of the editorial staff of the San Francisco *Bulletin* and also contributed several articles to different publications.

In 1914, Bliven became director of the Department of Journalism of the University of Southern California. Two years later, he joined the editorial staff of *Printer's Ink* and later went to work for the New York *Globe.* At the *Globe,* he started out as chief editorial writer, then moved into the position of managing editor and finally became associate editor.

In 1923, Bliven accepted the position of managing editor of the *New Republic* and seven years later became its president and editor. When he took charge of the editorial policy after becoming president, the paper became noticeably more liberal. He came to be considered one of the most respected instruments of the moderate left and was also looked upon as an intellectual godfather of the New Deal.

From 1925 to 1947, Bliven became the New York correspondent for the Manchester *Guardian*. Later, he lectured on subjects of communications and journalism at Stanford University. He also spent some time doing his own writing and authored several essays including, *Public Opinion, the Case of Citizen Jones, America Now, an Inquiry into Civilization in the United States by Thirty-Six Americans;* and several books including *The World Changers.*

Bruce Bliven married Rose Emery of San Jose, California in 1913. The couple had one son, Bruce Bliven, Jr. who became a contributor of articles to the *New Republic* as well as other magazines.

Bruce Bliven died on May 27, 1977 in Palo Alto, California.

BLUE, ROBERT DONALD, (1898-) — thirtieth governor of Iowa (1945-49), was born on September 24, 1898 in Eagle Grove, Iowa. Blue attended Des Moines's Capital City Commerical College for a year, then studied forestry at Iowa State College, during which time he also served in the student army training corps. Deciding to pursue a law career, Blue attended Drake University, taking his LL.B. degree in 1922.

Going into private practice, Blue teamed up with his brother to establish Hobbet, Blue, and Blue, then from 1924 to 1931, served as attorney for Wright County. In 1932 he was named city attorney for Eagle Grove, and starting in 1934, he served for four terms in the Iowa House of Representatives, which ended in 1942. The following year he was elected lieutenant governor of Iowa, and in 1944, he secured the governorship. When he ran for reelection in 1946, the campaign was somewhat peculiar, in that it was, according to one source, "marked by indifference on both sides." To prove the point, Governor Blue was quoted as saying: "There is no public interest in the campaign, so why should I stir it up?" Even with the apathy surrounding the entire affair, Blue won a second term by over 95,000 votes.

During his tenure, Blue pushed for a County Assessor Law, which the state legislature passed in 1947. Created to standardize property assessments, it was described as "one of the most forward-looking pieces of legislation adopted in years." Blue also lobbied for more aid to cities and towns throughout the state. In addition, Blue "secured two hundred new factories in Iowa through the Iowa Development Commission; extended the hospital program to local communities; started a new program for the care and rehabilitation of mental patients; (and) inaugurated a retirement program for public employees."

After being defeated for a third term in the 1948 primary, Blue retired from public life and returned to his law practice and farming interests. Blue is married to Cathleen Beale and the couple have two children.

BOIES, HORACE, (1827-1923) — fourteenth governor of Iowa (1890-94), was born near Aurora, Erie County, New York on December 7, 1827. He was brought up on his father's farm, attending school during the winter seasons. As soon as his own earnings enabled him to pay the necessary fees, he began the study of law, and was admitted to the bar in 1849, in Erie County, New York. He began his practice in Buffalo, where he continued to reside until 1867. Early on, he identified himself with the Republican Party, which elected him in 1857 to the lower house of the New York Assembly. In 1864 he was a candidate for district attorney for Erie County, but was defeated by two votes, after which he retired from politics for some time. In 1867 he moved to Iowa, settling in Waterloo, Black Hawk County. He was soon recognized as one of the ablest lawyers in the state. When not actively engaged in his professional duties, he devoted himself to the cultivation of a farm in Grundy County.

He opposed the prohibition movement in the ranks of the Republican Party from the start, finding in this a reason for once more entering the political arena. With regret he severed his connection with that party and supported Presidential candidate Grover Cleveland in 1884, his convictions on the tariff issue being quite as pronounced as on the temperance question. Having fully identified himself with the

Democratic Party, in 1889 he received the Democratic nomination for governor of Iowa. The campaign that followed centered on the state prohibition law. Boies attacked the existing statute from the platform in every section of the state. He was elected by a plurality of 7,000 votes, and was the first Democrat to be elected to the governorship in thirty-five years. He was reelected in 1891, but was defeated for a third term in the election of 1893. During his administration, in regards to the affairs of the state, he won the confidence of the people, and his energy and sincerity secured him the respect of even his political opponents.

Boies also contributed extensively to agricultural literature. He died on April 4, 1923.

BOIES, WILLIAM DAYTON, (1857-1932) — a U.S. Representative from Iowa; born on a farm in Boone County, Ill., January 3, 1857; moved with his parents to Buchanan County, Iowa, in 1873 and settled near Suasqueton; attended country schools and the public schools of Belvidere, Ill.; was graduated in law from the State University of Iowa at Iowa City in 1880; was admitted to the bar in 1881 and commenced practice in Sanborn, O'Brien County, Iowa; moved to Sheldon, Iowa, in 1887 and continued the practice of law; unsuccessful candidate for election as judge of the district court in 1890; member of the school board of the independent school district of Sheldon 1900-1912; appointed judge of the district court of the fourth judicial district of Iowa January 1, 1913; on a division of this district became judge of the twenty-first judicial district of the State and in 1914 was elected for a term of four years, which position he resigned on March 31, 1919, to become a candidate for the Republican nomination for Con-

gress; elected as a Republican to the Sixty- sixth and to the four succeeding Congresses (March 4, 1919- March 3, 1929); one of the managers appointed by the House of Representatives in 1926 to conduct the impeachment proceedings against George W. English, judge of the, United States District Court for the Eastern
District of Illinois; was not a candidate for renomination in 1928; died in Sheldon, Iowa, May 31, 1932; interment in Eastlawn Cemetery.

BORLAUG, NORMAN ERNEST, (1914 -) — scientist and agriculturalist, was born in Cresco, Iowa on his father's farm on March 25, 1914. His parents were Henry O. and Clara (Vaala) Borlaug. Borlaug graduated from his town's high school and at the urging of his grandfather, enrolled at the University of Minnesota, earning his B.S. in forestry in 1937.

While still earning his degree, Borlaug worked for the United States Forestry Service as a field assistant. In 1937, he worked in the Idaho National Forest and in 1939 was a junior forester in Massachusetts. In 1940, he returned to the University of Minnesota and worked as a research assistant. The following year his promotion to instructor coincided with his earning a doctor of philosophy degree in plant pathology.

After graduate school, Borlaug worked for three years with the E. I. du Pont de Nemours and Company as a plant pathologist to study the effects of the new chemicals on plants and plant diseases. In 1944, he was included on a team of American agricultural scientists sent by the Rockefeller Foundation to Mexico to start an "agricultural revolution" in that country. The other men that he accompanied were George Harrar, who headed up the team, Edward

Wellhouse, a corn breeder, and William Colwell, an agronomist.

In Mexico, Borlaug set out to develop a hearty strain of wheat using Gaines seeds -- derived from the Japanese Norin dwarf known for it short, sturdy stalk and heavy head -- and mixing them with the Mexican varieties. He came up with a high-yield, highly adaptable dwarf wheat which has won him international acclaim. On October 21, 1970, he also won the $78,400 Nobel Peace Prize for his outstanding work. Because of his renowned work, he has been called upon for advice to West Pakistan, India, Turkey, Afghanistan, Tunisia, and Morocco. Using his superior knowledge, these countries were able to produce a crop fifty- percent larger than before within two years.

Borlaug believes that high population growth is the biggest of the world's problems and that man is on a self-destructive course if he continues with what he terms "irresponsible population growth." He thinks of his work, along with that of his colleagues, as only temporarily abating the hunger and deprivation in the world.

Norman Borlaug married Margaret G. Gibson on September 24, 1937 and had two children, Norma Jean and William Gibson.

Borlaug has won several other awards in addition to the Nobel Peace Prize. Those awards include, a citation and award from the government and farmers of Tlaxcala, Mexico; a diploma of honor from the wheat farmers of Queretaro, Mexico; the outstanding achievement award of the University of Minnesota; the national award of the Agricultural Editors' Association; the International Agronomy Award of the American Society of Agronomy; the Distinguished Service Medal of Pakistan; and an honorary doctorate from the University of Punjab, India. There is also a street named after him in Obregsn, Mexico.

BRANSTAD, TERRY E., (1946-) — became Governor of Iowa in 1983.

Born on November 17, 1946 in Leland, Iowa, he attended the University of Iowa, earning a B.A. degree in 1969. He went on to Drake University Law School, receiving his J.D. degree in 1974.

Branstad became involved in politics in 1968 when he served as a delegate to various Republican conventions. His first political office was in the Iowa House of Representatives in 1972, and he was reelected to his seat two more times. He became lieutenant governor in 1978, serving under incumbent governor, Robert Ray during the latter's last term in office. After Ray resigned in 1982, Branstad was elected as governor.

During his first term, Branstad was faced with a crippling farm crisis, during which he made budget cuts of over 90 million dollars, feeling it was important that the state government join the farmers and "pare back and adjust to the economic realities of today." Other programs he supported had to do with a bigger fund for highways, the increase of teachers' salaries, and the upgrading of academic and research programs at colleges throughout the state.

Branstad served as chairman of the Midwestern Governor's Association, the Committee on Agriculture of the National Governors' Association, as well as the Task Force of the NGA's Committee on International Trade.

He is married to Christine Ann Johnson and the couple have three children.

BRIGGS, ANSEL, (1806-1881) — first state governor of Iowa (1846-50), was born in Vermont on February 3, 1806, son of Benjamin Ingley and Electa Briggs. His early education was acquired in the schools of his native town, and he afterwards spent three years at the Norwich (Conn.) Academy. In 1830, he moved with his parents to Cambridge, Guernsey County, Ohio, where he engaged in commercial pursuits. He was twice elected sheriff of Guernsey County, and competed with John Ferguson for the office of county auditor, but was defeated.

In 1836, he moved to Iowa, settling first at Davenport, where he contracted with the post office department for establishing mail routes and conveying the U.S. mails between Davenport and Dubuque and Iowa City, the latter at the time, being the capital of Iowa. Later he moved to Andrew, became deputy treasurer of Jackson County, and in 1842, represented it in the Territorial House of Representatives. At the state convention held in Iowa City on September 24, 1846, he was nominated for governor on the Democratic ticket, and was the first to be elected by the people. Under his administration, the state government was organized, the boundary line between Iowa and Missouri was established, and the free and normal school system was put in operation. So ardent was he in the support of the school measure, that in order to put the system in operation, he advanced out of his own pocket about $2,000, which was afterwards repaid to him by the state. He served as chief executive of Iowa until December of 1850.

In 1854, he established himself as one of the founders of Florence, and a member of its land company. This town, situated six miles above Council Bluffs, on the Nebraska side of the Missouri, was a successful rival of Omaha. He also had large property interests in Council Bluffs, Columbus and Bellevue, the latter being another rival of Omaha. Here Governor Briggs was one of the founders of Nebraska Lodge No. 1, Free and Accepted Masons, which was moved from Bellevue to Omaha in 1888. From 1860 until 1865, he and his son, John Shannon, engaged in overland freighting to Colorado and Montana.

From 1876 to 1879, he resided at Council Bluffs, and for the remainder of his life, at Omaha. He was dedicated to his work as soon as he set foot upon the soil of Iowa, and the beginning of his term of office marked an epoch in the state's history. In all departments of life, he aimed to be true to his convictions of truth and right. He was a wise counselor, a man of strong will, but not tyrannical, plain and unostentatious, and of great kindness and benevolence. A writer at the time of his death said: "In honorable old age he lived to see the full realization of the desire he had expressed in his retiring message to the general assembly in 1830, that this, his adopted state, might ever be distinguished for virtue, intelligence and prosperity.

Governor Briggs was married twice: to Nancy M. Dunlap, with whom he had eight children (only two of whom reached adulthood, John, and Ansel, Jr.), and Mrs. Frances Carpenter (no children). Governor Briggs died in Omaha, Nebraska on May 5, 1881.

BROMWELL, JAMES EDWARD, (1920-   ) — a U.S. Representative from Iowa; born in Cedar Rapids, Linn County, Iowa, March 26, 1920; attended Johnson School; graduated from Franklin High School in 1938 and from the University of Iowa in 1942; during the Second World War entered the United States Army as a private, was assigned to the European theater with

Headquarters Information and Education Division, served four years, and was discharged as a captain; graduated from the Harvard University School of Business Administration in 1947; returned to the University of Iowa to study law and was graduated in 1950; was admitted to the bar and began practice in Cedar Rapids; elected as a Republican to the Eighty-seventh and Eighty- eighth Congresses (January 3, 1961- January 3, 1965); unsuccessful candidate in 1964 for reelection to the Eighty-ninth Congress; unsuccessful candidate for the Republican nomination for United States Senator in 1968; resumed the practice of law until 1974, and practiced again from 1979 to 1986; is a resident of Cedar Rapids, Iowa.

BURDICK, EUGENE LEONARD, (1918-1965) — political theorist and writer, was born in Sheldon, Iowa to Jack D. Burdick and Marie Ellerbroek. His father died when he was four and his mother married a cellist with the Los Angeles Philharmonic. After the family relocated to Los Angeles, Burdick attended Santa Monica Junior College and Santa Barbara Junior College before transferring to Stanford as a sophomore. He completed his degree in psychology in 1941. In 1948, he became a Rhodes scholar at Oxford University in England where he earned a D.Phil. degree in 1950.

Around 1945, Burdick wrote his first short story while spending three years in the Navy. After returning to civilian life, he attended graduate school at Stanford and studied writing under Wallace Stegner. In 1948, he was awarded a Breadloaf Writer's Fellowship and then a major short story prize. In 1952, he became a professor of political science at the University of California at Berkley.

Burdick's first book, *The Ninth Wave,* was published in 1956. It was very successful, becoming a best-seller and a Book-of-the-Month Club selection. His second book, *The Ugly American,* made him famous while it stirred up much controversy. This novel was about a fictionalized Southeast Asian country and the inept administration of the United States aid programs. It was considered so offensive that Senator J. William Fulbright denounced it on the Senate floor and the informational Media Guaranty program banned its sale overseas. It was rumored, however, that President Eisenhower, being "strongly impressed" by the book, appointed the nine- member Draper Committee to review the whole sphere of American foreign aid and it's administration. Burdick's third book, *Fail-Safe,* stirred up almost as much controversy as his first one. Also fiction, this second novel dealt with the possibility of a breakdown in the Strategic Air Command's ground- to-air communications which leads to a group of American planes unloading their nuclear bombs on Moscow. Both *The Ugly American* and *Fail-Safe* were made into major motion pictures.

Other novels Burdick wrote after those already mentioned include, *The 480, Nina's Book,* and *Sarkhan.* Eugene Burdick married Carol Warren on July 3, 1942 and had three children. Burdick died on July 26, 1965.

BURNQUIST, JOSEPH ALFRED ARNER, (1879-1961) — nineteenth governor of Minnesota (1915-1921), was born in Dayton, Iowa on July 21, 1879, the son of John and A. Louise (Johnson) Burnquist. He attended Carleton College (B.A., 1902), Columbia University (M.A., 1904), and the University of Minnesota (LL.B., 1905). After graduation, he began to practice law in Minneapolis and St. Paul. In 1906, he married Mary Louise Cross. They had four children.

Burnquist was elected to the Minnesota House of Representatives in 1908 and 1910. In 1912, and again in 1914, he won election as Lieutenant Governor of the State. When Governor Hammond died in office on December 30, 1915, Burnquist succeeded him in the office. He was elected in his own right in 1916, and again in 1918. Much legislation was passed during Governor Burnquist's terms, including the equal suffrage amendment; a uniform sales act to break up monopolies; and a World War I soldier's bonus act. A new public safety commission was created; improvements were made to highways; and a special power to vote was given to state soldiers serving on the Mexican border.

Burnquist left office in 1921 and returned to his law practice in Minneapolis. From 1938 to 1955, he was State Attorney General, and from 1956 to 1958, he was Court Commissioner. He also served on the Land Exchange Commission, the State Executive Commission, and the State Pardon Board. He died on January 12, 1961.

C

CAMPBELL, ED HOYT, (1882-1969) — a U.S. Representative from Iowa; born in Battle Creek, Ida County, Iowa, March 6, 1882; attended the public schools of his native city, and was graduated from the law department of the State University of Iowa at Iowa City in 1906; was admitted to the bar the same year and commenced practice in Battle Creek; mayor of Battle Creek 1908-1911; member of the State house of representatives 1911-1913; during the First World War served as a private in Company Six, First Officers Training School, Fort Snelling, Minn.; member of the State senate 1920- 1928, serving as president pro tempore 1924-1926; elected as a Republican to the Seventy-first and Seventy-second Congresses (March 4, 1929-March 3, 1933); unsuccessful candidate for reelection in 1932 to the Seventy-third Congress; resumed the practice of law; died in Battle Creek, Iowa, April 26, 1969; interment in Mount Hope Cemetery.

CANUTT, YAKIMA, (1895-1986) — was an actor who later became one of Hollywood's busiest stuntmen.

Born in Colfax, Washington on November 29, 1895, his birth name was Enos Edward Canutt. At the age of 17 he hooked up with a Wild West show, garnering several titles for his roping and riding abilities. After winning a rodeo world championship, a newspaper writer dubbed him "The Cowboy from Yakima," thus giving him his lifelong nickname.

Canutt's rodeo work eventually led to his getting bit parts in a number of silent westerns, in which he also did his own stunts. Like many actors in those films, his voice did not impart well to "talkies," and he began making his living as a full-time stuntman, occasionally playing a villain. But it was his stunt work that impressed Hollywood insiders and soon he was considered the town's top stuntman, performing what became known as the "transfer" stunt--making dangerous leaps between horses and wagons, or vice-versa. He served as a double for some of Hollywood's top motion picture stars including John Wayne, Clark Gable, Gene Autry, and Errol Flynn.

With his stunt work being so respected, Canutt was eventually asked to become a second unit director, which often entailed creating stunt and battle scenes, including the one representing Custer's Last Stand in the western, *They Died with Their Boots On.* Beginning in 1944 he directed a number of B-Westerns by Republic, then in 1948, was hired by major movie studio MGM as a second unit director.

It was during his years at MGM that he directed action sequences for some of Hollywood's most classic movies, including *Spartacus; El Cid; Where Eagles Dare; How the West Was Won;* and *Cat Ballou. Ben Hur* was perhaps his greatest accomplishment; he started his part of the project two years before production on the film began, training 80 horses for the famous chariot race scene. Canutt's last directing chore was for the movie *Breakheart Pass,* in 1976.

In 1967 Canutt received a Special Academy Award for "creating the profession of stuntman as it exists today and for the development of many safety devices used by stuntmen everywhere." He published his memoirs in 1979, entitled *Stunt Man: The Autobiography of Yakima Canutt.*

He died at the age of 91 on May 24, 1986; he was survived by two sons.

CAROTHERS, WALLACE HUME, (1896-1937) scientist, was born in Burlington, Iowa on April 27, 1896 to Ira Hume and Mary Evalina (McMullin) Carothers. His father was a teacher and later vice-president at the Capital City Commercial College where young Carothers attended for a year after high school. In 1915, he began attending Tarkio College in Missouri where he received his B.S. degree in

1920. He did his graduate work at the University of Illinois, receiving an M.S. degree in 1921. Afterward, he was an instructor in chemistry for a year at the University of South Dakota.

It was while he was teaching at the University of South Dakota that Carothers began to develop ideas in regards to the application of the new electronic concepts of valence to organic molecules. In 1922, he returned to the University of Illinois to work on his doctorate in organic chemistry. His thesis was on the subject of catalytic hydrogenation of aldehydes over a platinum catalyst, particularly with effects of catalyst promoters and poisons. In 1926, he went to Harvard as an instructor, but left after two years when he was invited to direct and develop a program of research in organic chemistry in a new laboratory at the Experimental Station of E. I. du Pont de Nemours & Company in Wilmington, Delaware. While with du Pont, Carothers jammed a lifetime's worth of work into ten years. He drove himself with high expectations for achievement, to the point where, after ten years, neither his mind nor his body could take it any longer. He was, however, extremely successful in his work at du Pont and was responsible for a great number of experiments that resulted in marketable substances including a synthetic rubber known as neoprene and the first usable synthetic fiber known as nylon. During that time, he and his associates had published more than thirty papers in this field and after his death, du Pont named its new large laboratory for the study of synthetic fibers in his honor.

Because of bouts with deep depression, especially after the death of his sister in 1936, Carothers ended his own life in April of 1937. He had been a quiet, unassuming man, who did not like large crowds of people, but was friendly within his own group of peers. In 1936, he had been elected to membership in the National Academy of Sciences. On February 21 in that same year, he had married Helen Everett Sweetman of Wilmington, Delaware and had a daughter, Jane. After his death, his ashes were buried in the Glendale Cemetery in Des Moines, Iowa.

CARPENTER, CYRUS CLAY, (1829-1898) — eighth governor of Iowa (1872-76), was born in Harford, Susquehanna County, Pennsylvania on November 24, 1829, son of Asahel and Amanda (Thayer) Carpenter. Through his mother, he was descended from General Sylvanus Thayer, "Father of West Point Military Academy," and founder of the Thayer School of Civil Engineering at Dartmouth College. Cyrus was left an orphan before he was twelve. In 1852, he started for the West, teaching for a time in Licking County, Ohio, and arriving in Des Moines, Iowa in 1854. He taught the first school opened in Fort Dodge, and devoted much time to land surveying for the general government. He also opened a land agency on his own account, locating land- warrants, paying taxes for non-residents, and buying, selling and surveying lands. He was chosen to the Iowa House of Representatives for the session of 1858. At the start of the Civil War, he enlisted as a private, but was at once commissioned as captain and commissary of subsistence, continuing in this office until the close of the war, in the meantime being advance to the rank of lieutenant-colonel, and receiving a colonelcy by brevet. He served mostly on the staffs of Generals Rosecrans, Thomas, Dodge and Logan.

In 1866, he was elected register of the state land office in Iowa, and was reelected two years later. At the Republican State Convention, in 1871, he was nominated for governor on the first ballot. He was elected by a large majority, and was reelected in 1873. His administrations were distinguished by his support of the state university and the agricultural college. In his first inaugural address, he advanced the proposition that the rates for freight and passenger fares on the railroads should be subject to state control, and this came more conspicuously to the front in the "granger law," which was affirmed by the Supreme Court of the United States in a suit carried up from Iowa. The legislature placed $10,000 at the disposal of Governor Carpenter for the prosecution of this suit; however, he employed competent counsel and accomplished the work with an expenditure of only $2,000. Carpenter appointed the first visiting committee to the hospital for the insane, and although this measure was bitterly fought in the legislature, it afterward became very popular. After completing his second term, he was appointed second comptroller of the United States Treasury department, and remained for fifteen months, resigning when appointed by Governor Gear to the first board of railroad commissioners. Being elected to Congress soon after, he resigned his office, and two years later, he was reelected.

His congressional career was very successful, meeting the highest expectations of his constituency. He originated the policy of establishing experimental stations in connection with the agricultural colleges, but his bill did not pass until the next session, when the proposition was reintroduced by his successor. He also secured the passage of the bill dividing the state into two districts for the Federal courts. He was again chosen to the lower house of the Iowa state legislature in 1883. After returning from the army, he devoted many years to cultivating his farm on the Des Moines River near Fort Dodge.

Carpenter was married, in 1864, to Susan C. Burkholder, who survived him when he died at Fort Dodge on May 29, 1898.

CARROLL, BERYL FRANKLIN, (1860-1939) — twentieth governor of Iowa (1909-13), was born on March 15, 1860 in Salt Creek Township, Davis County, Iowa, the son of Willis and Christena (Wright) Carroll. He first attended the Southern Iowa Normal and Scientific Institute at Bloomfield, then enrolled at the North Missouri State Normal School where he received a B.S. degree in 1884. He worked as a teacher for the subsequent five years, served as principal of a school in Missouri during 1886- 87, and during 1887-89, was superintendent of schools in Rich Hill, Missouri.

Deciding to join his brother in a business venture, Carroll returned home to Iowa. After two years, he bought the Davis County *Republican,* a newspaper for which he also served as publisher and editor. It was around this time that he became involved in politics, as a member of the Republican Party, and in 1892, served as a presidential-elector. Carroll next ran for, and won, a seat in the state senate, serving in that post for two years (1896-98). In the latter year, he resigned to serve as postmaster of Bloomfield, Iowa.

From 1903 to 1909 he served as state auditor, then secured the governorship, making him the first native of Iowa to be elected to the position; he was reelected for a second term in 1910. During his tenure as governor, Carroll initiated various new programs and departments such as the Office of Commerce Counsel, which was established to represent the citizens of Iowa in business matters. Other departments included a new state fire marshal division, a State Board of Education, which helped consolidate the state's numerous educational facilities under one source, and a new highway improvement and construction division.

After leaving the governor's office, Carroll returned to his business interests, creating, and serving as president of, the Carroll Investment Co., and the Provident Life Insurance Co. Carroll was married to Jennie Dodson, and the couple had two sons. He died on December 16, 1939 in Louisville, Kentucky.

CARSON, JOHNNY, (1925-) — television personality, was born in Corning, Iowa to Homer Lloyd and Ruth (Hook) Carson. When Johnny was still a little boy the family moved to Norfolk, Nebraska where he grew up. At twelve years of age, he discovered magic when he sent away for a book on the subject. Ever since then he was enthralled with performing before an audience, his first paid performance being a magic show for which he earned $3. At his high school in Norfolk, he appeared in many plays and wrote a humor column for the school newspaper. After serving for the duration of World War II on a ship in the Pacific, he earned his B.A. degree from the University of Nebraska, in 1949.

While he was still in college, Carson took his first professional radio job at KFAB in Lincoln, Nebraska in 1948. After graduation, he landed a job at another radio station, WOW, in Omaha. He then worked for awhile at the WOW-TV station before moving to California and taking a job at KNXT-TV in Los Angeles. He started out at that station as an all-purpose announcer and a short while later was given his own half-hour comedy show on Sunday afternoons. Even though the show closed after only thirty weeks, it had attracted the attention of the likes of Groucho Marx, Red Skelton, and Fred Allen. Skelton gave Carson a job as a writer on his show on CBS-TV and in August of 1954, when Skelton was injured during a rehearsal just before show time, Carson was called upon to fill in. That was the break he needed. Carson so impressed the critics that he was offered his own primetime show. Unfortunately, the show only lasted thirty-nine weeks and then closed.

After the disappointing flop of his show, Carson moved to New York and hosted the quiz game show *Who Do You Trust?* for five years. He then accepted the position of host on the *Tonight Show* when the current host, Jack Paar quit. Carson did so well that six months after his debut on the show, he had the commercial revenues back up to where they were at the peak of Paar's career.

Carson's manner on the *Tonight Show* greatly differed from that of Parr's. He had a non-emotional and somewhat distant personality and treated his guests respectfully, never trying to one-up them or cut them down. Because of this, he was able to attract such guests to his show as John F. Kennedy and Nelson A. Rockefeller. He is also known for the ability to recover after a bad joke and to gracefully turn a boring guest into good material. Because of Carson, the *Tonight Show* became the largest-grossing entertainment program on television by 1967. In 1962, his average audience was 7,500,000; by 1972, 11,000,000; and by 1978, 17,300,000. Carson's salary was also in the millions. In 1977, his contract with NBC gave him an annual salary of almost $3,000,000 and according to the December 7, 1981 issue of People Magazine, his annual salary for the *Tonight Show* in that year was $8,000,000.

Carson made other television appearances as well such as hosting the Emmy Awards ceremony in 1972 and other television specials. He even branched out into other business ventures such as a restaurant franchise which failed, and a line of clothing which proved rather successful. However, his most notable work was always the *Tonight Show.* Carson has also written two books of cartoons for which Whitney Darrow Jr. drew the illustrations: *Happiness Is...A Dry Martini,* and *Misery Is...A Blind Date.*

Carson has been married four times, most recently to Alex Maas, whom he married in 1987. His three former wives are: Jody Wolcott with whom he had three sons, Joanne Copeland, and Joanna Holland.

Johnny retired from the *Tonight Show* on May 22, 1992 ending and era in late-night television.

CARTER, STEVEN V., (1915-1959) — a U.S. Representative from Iowa; born in Cartellrille, Utah, October 8, 1915; at the age of 14 years moved with his parents to Lamoni, Decatur County, Iowa, and attended the public schools; graduated from Graceland College, Lamoni, Iowa, in 1934, University of Iowa in 1937, and State University of Iowa College of Law in 1939; was admitted to the bar in 1939 and commenced the practice of law in Leon, Iowa; county attorney, Decatur County, 1940-1944; served as a supply officer in the United States Navy 1943-1946, with service in the South Pacific Theater; city attorney, Leon, Iowa, 1946-1948; unsuccessful Democratic candidate for election to the Eighty- fifth Congress in 1956, and later unsuccessfully contested the election; elected as a Democrat to the Eighty-sixth Congress and served from January 3, 1959, until his death in

Bethesda, Md., November 4, 1959; interment in Leon Cemetery, Leon, Iowa.

CASSILL, R.V., (1919-) — writer, was born in Cedar Falls, Iowa while his parents were students at Iowa State Teachers College. He grew up in Iowa farm communities and as a teenager during the Depression, hitchhiked around the countryside. He later attended college at the University of Iowa and graduated with a B.A. in 1939. In 1947, after serving a stint in the Army, traveling Europe and studying at the Sorbonne, he completed his M.A. degree at the University of Iowa. In the same year he received his first award for writing when he won an *Atlantic* "Firsts" for his short story, "The Conditions of Justice."

For the next several years, Cassill held several different positions. He was a lecturer at Columbia University from 1957 to 1959. He then taught the Writer's Workshop at the University of Iowa from 1960 to 1965. From 1965 to 1966, he was writer in residence at Purdue University, and beginning in 1966, became an associate professor of English at Brown University. From 1967 to 1971, he was president of the Associated Writing Programs also at Brown University.

In 1950, Cassill had his first novel, *The Eagle on the Coin,* published. This book about a liberal young professor entrapped in a racial-sexual-political dilemma in a small, midwestern industrial town, did not fair well with critics. Not discouraged by the lack of succeess of his first effort, he subsequently wrote the novels *Pretty Leslie, La Vie Passionie of Rodney Buckthrone, Clem Anderson, The President, On an Iron Time, Doctor Cobb's Game,* and a host of others including his latest work, *The Unknown*

Soldier. He also wrote a "how to" book called *Writing Fiction,* and a number of short stories including, "The Father," "Larchmoor is Not the World," "This Hand, These Talons," "The Biggest Band" and others.

Other awards Cassill received for his work include, the O. Henry short-story award for the "The Prize" in 1956, a Rockefeller Foundation in 1954 and a Guggenheim Fellowship grant in 1968.

Ronald Cassill married Karilyn Kay Adams on November 23, 1956 and had three children, Orin, Erica and Jesse.

Cassill is a writer of extraordinary awareness and varying talent. Although much of his work suggests the transcendent craftsman without much confidence, his best work-- the stories and the novel *Clem Anderson*-- deserve more recognition than they have received.

CAYTON, HORACE ROSCOE, (1903-1970) — was a respected sociologist and author.

Born in Seattle, Washington on April 12, 1903, Cayton, an African-American, received his first taste of racial prejudice when he began attending Franklin High School, and by the time he was a junior, he decided he'd had enough and quit school. Soon after, he was headed for Alaska as a messman on a steamer he had signed up with. With that job he got to see various parts of the U.S. such as Wyoming, California, Mexico, and Hawaii.

By the age of twenty, Cayton decided he wanted to reach out to young people who were experiencing the same bigotry that he had, and returned home to continue his schooling. After studying at a YMCA preparatory school, he enrolled at the University of Washington, majoring in sociology. When sociologist

Robert E. Park, an educator at the University of Chicago, met Cayton, he convinced the young man that he should transfer to that school, which Cayton did after garnering his B.A. degree in 1932. After working as a research assistant at the university for two years, he was named special assistant to the United States Secretary of the Interior. A year later he traveled to Nashville, Tennessee to take the post of economics and labor instructor at Fisk University. The following year, Cayton was appointed as overseer of a research project for the Works Progress Administration in Chicago; the project entailed research into the lives of African- Americansliving in the Windy City.

In 1939 Cayton was awarded with a Rosenwald Fellowship, which he used to travel to Europe. That same year he also published his first book, co-written with George S. Mitchell, entitled *Black Workers and the New Unions.* The book's subject was about African-Americans in industry and how "prejudice forms and is formed by economic relationships." At the end of 1939, Cayton was appointed director of the Parkway Community House in Chicago, a post he held until 1949.

During 1950-51, his research involved the study of the Jewish family for the American Jewish Committee. Between 1952 and 1954 Cayton served as a correspondent to the United Nations for the Pittsburgh *Courier* newspaper. From 1954 to 1958 he was a research associate with the National Council of Churches, and during 1957-58, lectured in sociology at New York's City College. During 1958-59 Cayton served as special assistant for the Commissioner of Welfare in New York City, then went to San Francisco where he was a research assistant for studies in geriatric mental illness at Langley Porter Clinic during 1959-60. In 1960-61 he was overseer for an international survey of correction at Berkeley, California's Institute for the Study of Crime and Delinquency. Remaining in Berkeley, Cayton worked as the program coordinator of university extension at the University of California (1963-64), then from 1965 to 1970, was project director at the Institute of Business and Economic Research.

Cayton's best known and most admired work was his book *Black Metropolis* (1945), which he co-wrote with anthropologist St. Clair Drake. A treatise on what life is like for African-Americans living in the United States, the book received unanimous praise, and was considered "a landmark in American social history." *Nation* reviewer Bucklin Moore wrote: "It offers no short cuts or magic solutions, but it contains the clearest picture of what it means to be a Negro in America that I have ever encountered. It is realistic and far- reaching, probing where other books have glossed over, interpreting where others have merely stated generalities." In the *Saturday Review of Literature,* Harry A. Overstreet called the tome "a book for all Americans to read, since the facts it presents--unfavorable though they are to most of us--are essential to a full, critical knowledge of ourselves." Thomas Sancton concurred in his *New Republic* review, stating: "From cover to cover, this is a book of intellectual discipline and talent. It towers high above the slight, journalistic volumes that have been written in recent years..."

Later writings by Cayton included *Social Work and the Church,* co-written with S.M. Nishi (1945), and his autobiography, *Long Old Road* (1965). In addition, he also contributed numerous articles to such publications as *Nation, American Journal of*

Sociology, New Republic, Chicago *Sun-Times,* Chicago *Tribune,* and the New York *Times.*

Cayton was married four times (twice to his second wife). He died in Paris on January 22, 1970.

CESSNA, CLYDE VERNON, (1879-1954) — was a manufacturer of airpanes.   Born in Hawthorne, Iowa on December 5, 1879, he attended publi schools in Kingman County, Kansas. He displayed a marked mechanical aptitude as a youth. Cessna's first employment was as a serviceman for an automobile and farm implement dealer in Harper, Kansas.

In 1910, Cessna attended an air show in Oklahoma City and from that time on, his interest was devoted entirely to airplanes. He built his first plane, a wooden monoplane with spruce wings, in the winter of 1910-11 and flew it at an exhibition in Jet, Oklahoma. From 1911 until 1925, he supported his family by farming and making exhibition flights in the summers.

Having become a skilled builder in the airplane field, Cessna joined Walter H. Beech in organizing the Travel Air Company in 1925 in Wichita. He served as president of the organization for two years. During that time, he also worked privately to develop and build a four-place cabin plane. He and Beech flew the plane to Kansas City, Missouri, where they won a contract from an air transport line. That same plane was flown from San Francisco to Honolulu in 1927.

In later years, Cessna sold his interest in Travel Air and with that money built the first cantilever plane in the country. The cantilever was a plane that did not have struts or wires to anchor the wing to the fuselage. Encouraged by the successful trial runs of the new plane, he organized the Cessna Aircraft

CHAMBERLAIN

Company in Wichita and in 1928 began building cantilever monoplanes. The planes were entered in a succession of races during the next two years and won every race, frequently flying over planes with greater horsepower.

Curtiss Flying Service, which was operating airlines and a sales service from coast to coast, contracted to take all the planes Cessna built. Accordingly, the plant was expanded to meet the need. However, the Great Depression of 1929 put Curtiss Airlines into bankruptcy and Cessna was able to collect only a portion f the money owed to him. By 1931, his plant had to be closed down. In January 1934, members of the Cessna Aircraft Company Board of Directors decided to resume operations. Shortly thereafter, Cessna sold the major part of his interest in the company and retired from active participation in the business, devoting his efforts to his farm near Rago.

Cessna was married in 1905 to Europa Elizabeth Dotzour. The couple had two children. He died in Rago, Kansas on November 20, 1954.

CHAMBERLAIN, SAMUEL, (1895-1975) — was a photographer, artist and author.

Born on October 28, 1895 in Cresco, Iowa, he entered the Univesity of Washington in 1913 and transferred to the Massachusetts Institute of Technology in 1915 to study architecture. Two years later, Chamberlain enlisted in the American Field Service of the French Army and later served with the United States Army Ambulance Service. As a specialist in photo intelligence during World War II, Chamberlain held the rank of major with the U.S. Army Air Force. The Legion of Merit and Bronze Star were conferred upon him in 1944 and he was made chevalier of the Legion of Honor in 1949.

Although he returned to M.I.T. after World War I, Chamberlain, stimulated by the architecture of France, decided to capture its beauty with pictures, rather than design it. He eventually returned to France where he became a travel writer and illustrator. His articles and accompanying sketches appeared in numerous national and international magazines.

An American Field Service traveling fellowship was awarded to Chamberlain in 1923. He studied in Paris under Edouard Leon. In 1925 and 1926, he was an assistant professor of architecture at the University of Michigan. Near the end of 1926, a Guggenhiem fellowship provided him with the opportunity to study etching at the Royal College of Art in London.

The artist's interest in Early Americana led him to Virginia when Williamsburg was recreated as the 18th century colonial capital. Chamberlain's work on the project was selected for exhibition at the Grand Central Galleries in New York. He was eventually named official etcher for colonial Williamsburg.

Portraying with his camera the native charm of the American countryside, Chamberlain has photographed many beautiful and famous scenes which have been collected in more than 40 books.

Chamberlain married Narcissa Gellatly in 1923. They had two daughters. He died on January 10, 1975.

CHAMBERS, JOHN, (1780-1852) — second territorial governor of Iowa (1841-45), was born in Bromley Bridge, New Jersey on October 6, 1780, son of Roland and Phoebe (Mullican) Chambers. In 1794, when John Chambers was thirteen years old, his father moved his family to the state of Kentucky, which was then sparsely settled, and, owing to the conflicts which were constantly taking place between the settlers and the Indians, every cabin was a little fort. Here young Chambers grew to manhood, and no doubt at an early age became familiar with the weapons of defense, as every man and boy learned to use a rifle, not only to hunt game in the forests, but to hunt and fight the Indians as well. He was educated in part at Transylvania Seminary, Lexington, Kentucky, but it is probable that he received his early training for the most part from his parents, and was otherwise self-taught.

He read law and eventually entered into the profession. That he was successful and rapidly rose in the estimation of the public was demonstrated by the fact that he was appointed or elected prosecuting attorney of his district. At this period the state was overrun by lawless characters, who were terrorizing people, but by teaming up with other prosecuting officers, Chambers soon established a vigorous system of enforcing the criminal laws, which made safe the lives and property of the citizens.

Early on he enlisted in the service of his country, and participated in the Indian war of 1811, and the War of 1812 with Great Britain, as well as in the battle of the Thames, serving on the staff of General William Henry Harrison, who then commanded the American forces. As Chambers advanced in years he became an active politician, and was part of that galaxy of Whig statesmen and orators which, headed by Henry Clay and John J. Crittenden, so long controlled the politics and swayed the destinies of Kentucky. While not the equal of those leaders as an orator, Chambers was a strong and forcible speaker. In 1812, 1815, 1830, and 1832, he served in the Kentucky House of Representatives. In 1827 he was elected to Congress, serving only one term. In 1835, he was again sent to Congress, where he served for four years and became the respected colleague of Thomas Corwin, ex-Gov. Vance, of Ohio, and others.

Colonel Chambers was a great admirer of Henry Clay and a devoted friend of General Harrison. When, in 1839, the latter was nominated for the Presidency, Chambers took an active part in his support and was one of those who escorted the President-elect from his home to the capitol of the nation, and witnessed his inauguration. Short as was the period of President Harrison's administration, he was not forgetful of his friends, and one of his earliest appointments was that of John Chambers as governor of Iowa and superintendent of Indian affairs in that territory. Chambers took the oath of office before Judge McLean of the United States Supreme Court, and that oath is now on file in the collection within the historical department of Iowa.

Although Governor Chambers had passed the age of sixty when he became governor, and was frail of health, his constitution having been impaired by his many previous hardships and experiences, he was faithful in the discharge of his duties and watched with dedicated care over the interests of the territory. He remained in the office throughout the administration of President Tyler, but did not desert his principles for the sake of office as too many Whigs did. After James K. Polk became President in 1845, Governor Chambers returned to his home. In 1849 he was appointed by the Taylor Administration as a commissioner to negotiate a treaty with the Sioux Indians, in which he was successful. Governor Chambers was an intense Whig and a bitter partisan, and although he made political enemies, the hostility was partisan, not personal. He was described as a courteous, affable Kentucky gentleman of the old school, and was famous for his hospitality.

Governor Chambers was married to Margaret Taylor, and later to Hannah Lee Taylor; his children came from his second union. He died in Paris, Kentucky on September 21, 1852.

CHILDS, MARQUIS WILLIAM, (1903-1990) — journalist and author, was born in the Mississippi River town of Clinton, Iowa to William Henry and Lilian Malissa (Marquis) Childs. In spite of the fact that his father was a lawyer and his grandfather was a farmer, Childs had set his heart on being a newspaper man by the time he was thirteen or fourteen. He received his B.A. degree from the University of Wisconsin in 1923 and went to work for the United Press for a short period of time. He then came back to Iowa to teach English and work on his M.A. which he received in 1925. That same year, he went to New York and picked up his work with the United Press once again, but not for long.

After a year with the United Press, Childs went to work for the St. Louis *Post-Dispatch* as a feature writer. In 1930, he went to Sweden on a leave of absence and wrote a series of articles on Sweden's social and economic progress. In 1934, he took a position on the *Post-Dispatch's* Washington staff, but eventually came back to St. Louis. Although he travelled much, the St. Louis *Post-Dispatch* remained, for the most part, his home base throughout the majority of his career. In the prime of his career, a column that he wrote for that newspaper became syndicated to more than 200 newspapers throughout America ranging from the *Washington Post,* to small newspapers in the middle of nowhere.

Childs prided himself on the fact that he had interviewed many presidents from Franklin Roosevelt to Ronald Reagan. One that would not give him the time of day, however, and had in fact black listed him from the White House, was Richard Nixon. He had also interviewed a number of leading statesmen from other countries including Pandit Nehru, Zhou Enlai, Konrad Adenauer, Anthony Eden, and the Shah of Persia.

Childs wrote much more than job as a reporter required and in 1936, his first literary project was published. *Sweden: the Middle Way,* which became a best-seller, was born out of his visit a few years earlier to that country to attend a housing exposition. The book not only received critical acclaim, but served as inspiration to President Roosevelt to send out a special commission to study cooperative systems in Europe. His next work, *This is Democracy; Collective Bargaining in Scandinavia,* was a result of another trip to Europe. In 1937, he wrote his first novel, entitled *Washington Calling,* which also received critical acclaim and a short while later visited Spain to write several articles on the Spanish War for the St. Louis *Post-Dispatch.* The following year he journeyed into Mexico to write about the oil lien and the social- economic status of that country. In 1942, he wrote another non- fiction piece entitled *This is Your War,* and went on to write several other books, fiction and non-fiction, including, *I Write From Washington; Toward a Dynamic America: The Challenge of a Changing World; The Cabin,* (fiction); *The Farmer Takes a Hand: The Electrical power Revolution in Rural America; The Ragged Edge: The Diary of a Crisis; Eisenhower, Captive Hero: A Critical Study of the General and the President; The Peacemakers,* (fiction); *Taint of Innocence,* (fiction); *Wit-*

ness to Power; and several others including articles for journals and publications such as *Saturday Evening Post, Life, New Republic, Yale Review,* and *Reader's Digest.* When he was almost eighty years old, Childs picked up and finished writing a book that he had started in his late twenties. *Mighty Mississippi* was a work that, according to Childs, was written to "reflect the vigor, the passion, the love of life" of that river.

Marquis William Childs married Lue Prentiss in 1926. The marriage ended when Mrs. Childs died in 1968. In 1969, he was married to Jane Neylan McBain. He had two children, Prentiss and Malissa.

Childs died at the age of eighty-seven, the cause of death is unknown.

CLAMPITT, AMY, (1920-) — poet, was born in New Providence, Iowa to Roy Justin Clampitt and Pauline (Felt) Clampitt. She has four siblings, all younger than herself. She grew up on her father's 125-acre farm which, according to her, gave her a sense of isolation as well as an appreciation of nature. After high school, Clampitt attended Grinnell College in Iowa and majored in English. During that time, she gave no consideration to a career as a writer and had no idea that much later in life, she would have several successful books of poetry published. She graduated in 1941 with a B.A. degree and received a graduate fellowship to go to Columbia University in New York City. She dropped out, however, after a year and took a job as a secretary for the University Press.

After the second of two trips to England, Miss Clampitt returned to New York. She wrote a novel, but was unsuccessful in the marketing of it. She then took a job as a reference librarian at the National Audubon Society in 1952. She continued to write novels throughout the 1950's failing, however, to find a publisher. She did not write any poetry during that time.

In the early 1960's, Clampitt became a free lance editor in New York and found some success at it. She began writing poetry and tried to get some published but failed at every attempt. In 1974, she finally published a collection of poems called *Multitudes, Multitudes* but it was at her own expense. Finally, in 1978, her worked was noticed. The poetry editor of the *New Yorker* became intensely interested in her poetry and saw to it that it was soon being printed regularly in the *New Yorker.* Other publications such as the *Atlantic Monthly,* the *Kenyon Review, Prairie Schooner,* and the *Yale Review* picked up her work as well. Success seemed to finally find her. In 1981, she had her book *The Isthmus* published and two years later, her first major collection of poetry, *The Kingfisher* was published. By this time Clampitt was in her sixties.

Aside from *The Kingfisher,* which was nominated for a National Book Critics Circle Award, Clampitt has had five other collections published: *The Summer Solstice, A Homage to John Keats, What the Light was Like, Archaic Figure,* and *Westward.*

Amy Clampitt's poetry has been known to test those with even the most developed vocabulary, since she uses words that are largely unfamiliar. It has been said that one should keep a dictionary handy while reading her poetry. This and her use of several dependent clauses has been a source of irritation to some. Still, her work has been highly praised by many and has been compared to that of Marianne

Moore, Elizabeth Bishop, and Gerard Manley Hopkins.

In 1982, Amy Clampitt received a Guggenheim Fellowship. She has also received an honorary doctorate from Grinnell College, an award in literature from the American Academy and Institute of Arts and Letters, and a Lila Wallace-Reader's Digest Writer's Award. Her success as a writer was a long time coming, but her perseverance paid off.

Amy Clampitt currently resides in New York City, although she travels quite extensively and enjoys her nomadic lifestyle.

CLARK, JAMES, (1811-1850) — third territorial governor of Iowa (1845-46), was born in Greensborough, Westmoreland County, Pennsylvania in 1811, son of John Clark, who was chief clerk of the county. When quite young, he was apprenticed to the printing trade at Harrisburg, Pennsylvania. After mastering the art of printing and learning how to publish a paper, he traveled west in 1835, and was made territorial printer of the first legislature of Wisconsin, which met at Belmont, Wisconsin in the fall of 1836. He established the *Gazette* in the town of Burlington, Iowa in 1837. Clark was appointed secretary of the Territory of Iowa by President Van Buren, and was later named governor by President Polk in 1845, being the last territorial governor of Iowa. Iowa was admitted into the Union on December 28, 1846, and the first governor elected by the people was Ansel Briggs.

Governor Clarke edited the oldest and leading Democratic paper of the state, and thus exerted a commanding influence. He was married, in 1840, to Christiana, daughter of the late General Henry Dodge, who occupied a number of positions of honor and responsibility. In 1850, the town of Burlington was visited by the fearful epidemic of cholera brought by the boats up the Mississippi River from New Orleans. Governor Clark's wife and child were two of the victims, and he was so completely devastated by grief that he died two weeks after their death, at the age of thirty-nine. At the time of his death, he was just entering into the full maturity of his powers, and having honorably discharged all the high trusts that had been committed to him in the past, was eminently qualified to fill any other stations of honor to which he might have been called. He left three children.

CLARK, LINCOLN, (1800-1869) — a U.S. Representative from Iowa; born in Conway, Franklin County, Mass., August 9, 1800; attended the district and private schools; was graduated from Amherst (Mass.) College in 1825; studied law; was admitted to the bar in 1831 and commenced practice in Pickensville, Pickens County, Ala.; member of the State house of representatives in 1834, 1835, and 1845; moved to Tuscaloosa in 1836; elected attorney general by the legislature in 1839; appointed by Governor Fitzpatrick circuit judge in 1846; moved to Dubuque, Iowa, in 1848; elected as a Democrat to the Thirty- second Congress (March 4, 1851-March 3, 1853); unsuccessful candidate in 1852 and 1854 for reelection to the Thirty-third and Thirty-fourth Congresses; resumed the practice of law in Chicago, Ill.; appointed United States register in bankruptcy in 1866; retired from active business and returned to Conway, Mass., in 1869; died in Conway, Mass., September 16, 1886; interment in Howland Cemetery.

CLARK

CLARK, RICHARD CLARENCE (DICK), (1928-) — a U.S. Senator from Iowa; born in Paris, Linn County, Iowa, September 14, 1928; attended the public schools; attended the University of Maryland, Wiesbaden, Germany, and the University of Frankfort, Germany, 1951-1952; served in the United States Army 1950-1952; graduated from Upper Iowa University, Fayette, 1953; completed graduate work at the University of Iowa, Iowa City, Iowa, 1959; teaching assistant and professor of history and political science 1959-1964; administrative assist-ant to United States Representative John C. Culver 1965-1972; elected as a Democrat to the United States Senate in 1972 and served from January 3, 1973, to January 3, 1979; unsuccessful candidate for reelection in 1978; appointed by President Jimmy Carter to be Ambassador at Large and United States Coordinator for Refugee Affairs 1979; senior fellow at the Aspen Institute for Humanistic Studies 1980 to present; is a resident of Washington, D.C.

CLARK, SAMUEL MERCER, (1842-1900) — a U.S. Representative from Iowa; born near Keosauqua, Van Buren County, Iowa, October 11, 1842; attended the public schools and the Des Moines Valley College, West Point, Iowa; studied law; was admitted to the bar in 1864, but did not engage in extensive practice; editor of the Keokuk Daily Gate City for thirty-one years; delegate to the Republican National Conventions in 1872, 1876, and 1880; appointed commissioner of education to the Paris Exposition in 1889; postmaster of Keokuk from 1879-1885; member of the Keokuk Board of Education 1879- 1894, serving as president 1882-1894; elected as a Republican to the Fifty-fourth and Fifty- fifth Congresses (March 4, 1895-March 3, 1899); was not a candidate for renomination in 1898 to the Fifty- sixth Congress; resumed editorial duties; died in Keokuk, Lee County, Iowa, on August 11, 1900; interment in Oakland Cemetery.

CLARKE, GEORGE WASHINGTON, (1852-1936) — twenty-first governor of Iowa (1913-17), was born on October 24, 1852, in Shelby County, Indiana, the son of John and Eliza Jane (Akers) Clarke. He grew up on a farm near Drakesville, Iowa after his family moved there when he was four. He attended Oskaloosa College, receiving an A.B. degree in 1877. He continued his education at the State University of Iowa, garnering an LL.B. degree in 1878. He began practicing law in the town of Adel, and served as justice of the peace there for four years. In 1882, Clarke teamed up with John Bushrod White to create the company of White & Clarke, which became a prominent law firm.

Clarke entered the political arena in 1899 when he was elected to the lower house of the State General Assembly on the Republican ticket; he was reelected for three subsequent terms. In 1908 he was elected lieutenant-governor of the state, and in 1912, he secured the governorship, winning a second term in 1914. During his two terms, he helped push through such legislation as: stopping unfair discrimination regarding trade; curtailing false advertising; the expansion of the state capitol grounds, the latter of which he had virtually no support on; the upgrading of schools; the building of highways; and workmen's compensation.

After leaving office in 1917, Clarke spent a year at Drake University as Dean of the College of Law. Beginning in 1918, he once again practiced law as a private citizen, and was involved in public affairs only once in 1926, when he headed the campaign team for the reelection of Albert B. Cummins to the United States Senate.

According to one source, Clarke "...possessed outstanding ability as a public speaker and was universally esteemed for his high character and his honesty in politics, as well as in all other activities of life." He was married to Arletta Greene and the couple had four children. He died on November 28, 1936, in Adel Iowa.

CODY, WILLIAM FREDERICK, (1845-1917) — known throughout the world as "Buffalo Bill," was an Indian scout and a showman.

Born in Scott County, Iowa on February 26, 1845, his fathe, Isaac Cody, was one of the early pioneers of Kansas, having emigrated West. The elder Cody took an active part in making Kansas a free state at a period when the political situation was heated and bitter. After being stabbed at a meeting, he was obliged to flee from his home and family, sheltering himself where he could, and eventually dying from exposure in March of 1957.

At this time, Russell, Majors & Waddell were employed by the government to establish stores across the plains, and young Cody was hired by the company. His job was to visit every military fort and post West of the Missouri River. He became a great favorite among the plainsmen and soldiers, and it was during this period that he had his first experience of Indian fighting, having killed an Indian when he was only eleven years old.

After the Civil War began, Cody was employed as an Indian scout, and served until the end of the war with the 7th Kansas Cavalry. Cody had become an expert marksman with a rifle, and after the war, when he was employed as a hunter by the builders of the Kansas Pacific Railroad, he showed remarkable skill and dexterity in killing buffaloes. He entered into a contract with that company, Shoemaker, Miller & Co., for a monthly compensation of $500, to supply their force of laborers with buffalo meat, and in eighteen months he killed over 4,000 buffaloes which garnered him the nickname "Buffalo Bill."

In the spring of 1868, he reentered army life and was appointed by General Sheridan as chief of scouts for the department of the Missouri and the Platte, and was scout and guide for the 5th Cavalry against the Sioux and Cheyennes. He then served with the Canadian River Expedition during 1868-69, and continued to act in the capacity of scout until 1872, making his headquarters at Fort McPherson, Nebraska. It was at this time that he was elected representative from the twenty-sixth district of Nebraska in the state legislature.

After his term of office expired, Cody was offered the position of guide for the Russian Grand Duke Alexis and his party, who were going out on the plains on a hunting expedition. He accepted the offer and piloted the entire party through their excursion, bringing them safely back without a single accident and loaded down with game. Cody was richly rewarded, receiving in particular from the grand duke, a scarf-pin of precious stones as a souvenir.

In 1876, the Sioux war began and Cody, who by this time had begun his theatrical experience with a company of Indians and scouts, disbanded them, joined the 5th cavalry, and in the battle of Indian Creek, killed, in a hand-to-hand fight, Yellow Hand, a Cheyenne chief. Cody had been initiated into the art of stage performance by Ned Buntline, the well-known author, and, after the Indian war was over, he again turned his attention to the possibility of creating a show which would encompass his experience and be profitable. He proceeded to gather Indians, cowboys, scouts, trappers, buffaloes, etc., and produced the Wild West show for the first time in Omaha, Nebraska on May 17, 1883. It is said that over 5,000 people paid to witness the mimic representation of scenes and incidents which a few years before, they could have witnessed in reality. The great success of his show and its original character soon gave it a tremendous vogue and he was besieged by offers from all the principal cities of the country. After teaming up with Nate Salsbury who was already experienced and successful in theatrical production, he continued to enlarge his exhibition and improve on it.

After performing throughout the United States, the American Exhibition Company, which was then exhibiting American products in London, England, made an offer to Cody and Salsbury in 1887, who took their show to England and produced the Wild West in connection with the American exhibition, or "Yankeries," as it was called. If it had not been for the Wild West show, the American exhibition would have been a complete failure. The show was patronized by the royal family, including the queen, and became the rage in London, with the entire experiment proving to be a great success. After the London exhibition closed, Cody continued his success in France, Spain, Italy, Austria, Germany Belgium, returning to America some months later and making a tour across the country. He was at this time worth nearly a million dollars, most of which he invested in western real estate. Cody subsequently visited Europe once more and performed with success in every principal city as far south as Rome.

Cody was married to Louisa Frederici and the couple had two children. He died on January 10, 1917 in Denver, Colorado.

COFFMAN, L. DALE, (1905-   ) — lawyer and educator, was born in Delta, Iowa, to Ralph Gideon and Georgia Green Coffman and received his B.A. (1926) and J.D. (1928) from University of Iowa. He also received an LL.M (1929) and an S.J.D. (1935) from Harvard University. Admitted to practice law in Iowa (1928), New York (1938) and Tennessee (1946), Coffman was hired as a professor of law at University of Nebraska in 1931. He remained in that position until 1937, when he became counsel for the General Electric Company. Nine years later he left General Electric to become dean of Vanderbilt University Law School. In 1949 he was appointed dean of the law school at the University of California, Los Angeles, and from 1957 to 1973, Coffman worked as a professor of law at the university. Then in 1973, he was made professor emeritus. A member of the American Judicature Society, Seldon Society, and the American Bar Association, he has written numerous articles for professional journals. He married Helen Crouch in 1925.

COLE, CYRENUS, (1863-1939) — a U.S. Representative from Iowa; born on a farm near Pella, Marion County, Iowa, January 13, 1863; attended the public schools, and was graduated from Central University, Pella, Iowa, in 1887; engaged in newspaper work, and was connected with the Des Moines Register from 1887 to 1898, serving seven years as editorial writer; acquired an interest in the Cedar Rapids Republican in 1898, and was connected with that paper until 1921, during which period he founded the Times as an evening edition of the Republican; author of many publications; elected as a Republican to the Sixty- seventh Congress to fill the vacancy caused by the resignation of James W. Good; reelected to the Sixty-eighth and to the four succeeding Congresses and served from July 1921, to March 3, 1927; was not a candidate for renomination in 1932; engaged as an author and resided in Washington, D.C., until his death there on November 14, 1939; interment in First Dutch Reform Church Cemetery near Pella, Marion County, Iowa.

CONNOLLY, MAURICE, (1877-1921) — a U.S. Representative from Iowa; born in Dubuque, Iowa, March 13, 1877; attended the common schools; was graduated from Cornell University, Ithaca, N.Y., in 1897 and from the law department of New York University, New York City, in 1898; was admitted to the bar in 1899; did postgraduate work at Balliol College, Oxford, England, and the University of Heidelberg, Germany; engaged in the insurance business and banking; elected as a Democrat to the Sixty-third Congress (March 4, 1913-March 3, 1915); unsuccessful candidate for election to the United States Senate in 1914; chairman of the Iowa State Democratic convention in 1914; was a delegate to the Democratic National Convention in 1916; major in the Aviation Corps during the First World War; died in an airplane accident near Indian Head, Md., May 28, 1921; interment in Mount Olivet Cemetery, Dubuque, Iowa.

COOVER, ROBERT, (1932 -) writer, was born in Charles City, Iowa to Grant Marion Coover, a newspaper editor and Maxime (Sweet) Coover. While Coover was still young, the family moved to Bedford,

Indiana and then to Herrin, Illinois, a small mining town. While living in Herrin, he witnessed a traumatic situation that later spawned a novel. Coover attended the Southern Illinois University at Carbondale and then Indiana University at Bloomington where he received his B.A. degree in 1953. The same day he graduated, he received his draft notice and joined the United States Naval Reserve. He spent three years in Europe and after coming back began to write, first short stories and then novels.

Coover's first published work was "One Summer in Spain: Five Poems," which appeared in the Canadian journal, the *Fiddlehead.* During the next several years in the 1960's, he published several short stories while studying philosophy and history at the University of Chicago where he earned an M.A. degree in 1965. He also studied painting at the Art Institute of Chicago and in 1969, wrote, directed, and produced a film entitled *On a Confrontation in Iowa City.* His first novel was *The Origin of the Brunists* which was a twist of the imagination about a fictitious only survivor of a mining accident that in reality happened in his home town of Herrin, Illinois where he worked at his father's newspaper. The novel won critical acclaim and the William Faulkner Award for the best first novel of 1966. His second novel was based on table-top baseball games that he played as a child. It was entitled *The Universal Baseball Association, J. Henry Waugh, Prop.* His next work was a collection of twenty-one stories entitled *Pricksongs and Descants.* Other novels and short story collections he went on to write include *A Theological Position, The Public Burning, In Bed One Night and Other Stories, Gerald's Party, A Night at the Movies; or, You Must Remember This, Whatever Happened to Gloomy Gus of the Chicago Bears?,* and

Pinocchio in Venice. Short works he did include *Hair o' the Chine, After Lazarus, A Political Fable, Charlie in the House of Rue,* and *Spanking the Maid.*

Robert Coover has a reputation as one of the most original and versatile prose stylists in America. In his works he uses such subtle subject matter such as science, mathematics, historical and political perspectives, and myth. His major subject matter may be religious or political or social. For instance, in *The Origin of the Brunists,* he writes about the creation of a fictitious religious cult, its originator and its followers, while making several obvious comparisons to Christianity; in his controversial *The Public Burning,* he poses Richard Nixon as narrator and a public execution as the main attraction. The book's subject matter was so controversial that Coover had a hard time finding a publisher to take it.

Coover has taught at several universities and colleges in the United States including Bard College, Brown University, the University of Iowa, Princeton University, Columbia University, the Virginia Military Institute in Lexington and Brandeis University. On June 3, 1959, he married Marma del Pilar Sans-Mallafre whom he had met in Spain while he was in the Navy, and had three children: Diana Nin, Sara Chapin, and Roderick Luis. He has received awards including a Rockefeller Foundation Fellowship and two Guggenheim fellowships.

COWLES, GARDNER "MIKE" A. JR., (1903-1985) — was a media execuive, publisher and journalist.

Born on January 31, 1903 in Algona, Iowa, he received his B.A.degree from Harvard in 1925. Upon graduation, Cowles joined the family newspaper business as city editor of the Des Moines *Register and*

Tribune, which was the nucleus of his father's newspaper empire, the Des Moines Register and Tribune Company.

By 1931, Cowles was executive editor of the *Register* and chairman and editor in chief of Cowles Communications. In the 1930s, Cowles added radio interests to the company. Two years later, he launched *Look,* a photo-oriented magazine known for its influential positions on such controversial topics as American foreign policy, race relations and birth control. The first issue of *Look* debuted in 1937 with 400,000 copies. Demand increased the printing order to 835,000 copies just 10 days later. By the mid-1960s, *Look* surpassed its Time Inc. rival, *Life,* in circulation, boasting 8.5 million readers.

Cowles was well-known for his leadership abilities. His business interests grew to encompass television and additional radio concerns, book and magazine publishers -- including *Family Circle* -- and other newspapers. He owned the Minneapolis *Star and Tribune* and the *San Juan Star,* which won a Pulitzer Prize in 1959, the year it was founded by Cowles.

In 1971, due to increased postal costs and a loss of advertising to television, *Look* was forced to cease publication. It was briefly revived in 1974 under different ownership. Cowles directed the New York Times company from 1971 until 1974, remained chairman of the Des Moines *Register* until 1973, and dissolved Cowles Communications in 1978. In the 1940s, he embarked on a world tour with Wendell Willkie, the 1940 Republican candidate for president. It was thought that Cowles helped Willkie write his bestseller, *One World.*

COWLES

Cowles was married twice. First to Helen Curtiss and then to Lois Thornburg in 1933. The couple had three children. Cowles died on July 8, 1985.

COWLES, JOHN SR., (1898-1983) — newspaper publisher born in Algona, Iowa December 14, 1898, the son of Gardner Cowles, Sr and his wife Florence (Call). Cowles graduated from Phillips Exeter Academy in New Hampshire in 1917 and entered Harvard University. He served as a private in the United States Army during World War I and received his A.B. from Harvard in 1921. Cowles married Elizabeth Morley Bates July 18, 1923, they had four children.

The newspaper business was a Cowles' family affair. A banker and real estate investor, Cowles father purchased the *Des Moines Register and Leader* in 1903. A clever businessman, he increased the paper's circulation and made it a profitable entity in less than a year. Over the next 30 years the publication grew to become Iowa's premiere newspaper.

After his graduation from Harvard, Cowles returned to Des Moines joining the staff of the *Register,* he served an apprenticeship that exposed him to all areas of newspaper publishing. Cowles worked both sides of the fence, first as a reporter and later as the paper's general manager. In 1929 Cowles began a four-year term as director of the Audit Bureau of Circulations and was elected the second vice-president of the Associated Press. He became a first vice-president of the Associated Press in 1930 and served as a member of the board of directors from 1934 to 1943.

Cowles and his brother Gardner "Mike," also a staff member of the *Register* persuaded their father in 1935 to allow the purchase of the then struggling

Minneapolis *Star.* Mike remained in DesJMoines with their father and the *Register* while Cowles moved to Minneapolis. Under his direction the *Star* more than doubled its circulation from 1935 to 1939. Cowles broadened not only the coverage but also the range of political opinion of the publication known, at the time, as a Farmer-Labor paper. Cowles brought to the *Star* features and formats that had been part of the success story for the *Register.* However, the paper's true commercial success was realized when Cowles family in 1939 bought and merged with the *Register,* rival newspaper, the Minneapolis *Journal.* Two years later the Cowles family completed a sweep of the Minneapolis newspaper business with their purchase of their only competitor, the *Tribune* The cities' only two newspapers were now owned by the Cowles family. This technique proved so success-ful for the Cowles' empire that is was duplicated in Minnesota, North Dakota, South Dakota. and western Wisconsin. As Cowles continued building his empire, his younger brother Mike launched the picture maga-zine *Look* and created his own publishing enterprise, Cowles Communications.

Cowles philosophy was one that a newspaper had a duty to educate and a responsibility to lead its readers on civic and political matters. He contended that news should be delivered as news without bias or inference from the publisher. At a time when the majority of newspapers relied exclusively on news agencies for non-local information, Cowles main-tained a highly- respected Washington bureau and sent correspondents abroad providing the kind of in-depth coverage he thought his readership deserved. A liberal republican, he championed a number of social causes including more money for schools, higher quality facilities for the arts and actively fought against an anti- Semitic wave in Minneapolis.

An early advocate of the Lend-Lease program that funneled American aid to Britain prior to Pearl Harbor, the newspaper publisher was appointed in 1943 as special assistant to Lend- Lease Administrator Edward R. Stettinius, Jr. Cowles conducted a survey mission that took him to North Africa and England and upon his resignation the following year was awarded the Presidential Certificate of Merit.

One of the first Republicans to urge recognition of mainland China, Cowles consistently counseled his party to be flexible in world affairs and solicited for U.S. aid to developing nations. He was said to have been a major influence in Wendell L. Willkie's decision to run for president in 1940 and in 1952 helped persuade Dwight D. Eisenhower to seek the nations' highest office. In addition, Cowles was a member of the Hoover Commission's Committee on the National Defense Establishment in 1948.

Despite his management responsibilities, Cowles continued to write and produced several politically focused articles and essays. including *America Now* (Scribner, 1938), and "The Future America Faces" (*Proceedings of the Academy of Political Science,* 1941), and wrote a number of articles that appeared in *Look.* He served as a member of the board of directors for General Mills, Inc., Equitable Life Insurance Company of Iowa, and First National Bank of Minneapolis. The newspaper executive also served as a member of the several boards including the Carnegie Endowment, Board of Overseers of Harvard University, and was president of the Harvard Alumni Association in 1953. A trustee of the Ford Foundation, Gardner Cowles Foundation and Eisenhower Exchange Fellowships, Inc. Cowles was the recipient of honorary degrees from Boston University, Jamestown College, and a centennial award from Northwester University.

He retired as chairman of the board of his newspaper company in 1973 turning the title over to his son, John Cowles, Jr., but continued an active interest in its operation. When his eyesight began to fail, he had the paper read to him daily and up until a month before his death, was in his office at the paper twice a week.

Cowles died in his Minneapolis home on February 25, 1983 after a long illness. He was 84 years old.

CROSTEN, WILLIAM LORAN, (1909-   ) — musician and educator, was born in Des Moines, Iowa, to Sidney F. and William T. Crosten and was educated at Drake University where he received his B.A. in music, the University of Iowa (M.A.) and Columbia University (Ph.D). From 1942 to 1946, he served in the U. S. Navy and was discharged with the rank of Lt. Commander. He was an associate professor and later a full professor at Stanford University from 1946 to 1973. At the same time, he served as Executive Head of the Department of Music. In 1954, he was awarded a Guggenheim Fellowship, and in 1964, he received the Distinguished Alumnus Award from Drake University and the Steinway Award for Service to Music. A member of the American Musicological Society and the College Music Society, Crosten published *French Grand Opera* and contributed numerous articles and reviews to leading music journals. He is married to Mary E. Perry.

CULVER, JOHN C., (1932-) — United States Senator from Iowa, was born in Rochester, Minnesota on August 8, 1932, and was raised in Cedar Rapids, Iowa. He attended Harvard University, where he became friends with another first year student, Edward M. Kennedy, and earned a B.A. degree I cum laudeD in 1954. A talented football player, he was good enough to be a draft choice for the pro teams; however, he bypassed a football career and instead traveled to England to study at Cambridge University's Emmanuel College on a Lionel de Jersey Harvard Scholarship (1954-55). Culver then returned home and served a three-year stint in the United States Marine Corps. After his discharge, he continued his studies, graduating from Harvard with a law degree in 1962.

That same year, Culver worked behind the scenes to help his friend, Edward Kennedy, get elected to the Senate, and joined the new Senator in Washington, D.C. to work as his legislative assistant. He later returned to Iowa to practice law for a time, then pursued a seat in Congress on the Democratic ticket in 1964, winning the campaign for Second District Representative. Culver was reelected to four subsequent terms in Congress.

A liberal, Culver's opposition to the Vietnam War grew stronger as the war escalated. His voting record supported such issues as programs for the poor, monies earmarked for cities, and civil rights. He was also the architect for a program that, encouraged Congressmen from urban and rural districts to exchange visits in order to learn more about each other's problems.

As a member of the House Un-American Activities Committee (HUAC), Culver offered the only liberal opinion on HUAC bills, pointing out periodically that civil liberties were often being pushed aside by the committee in their quest to hunt Communists. When HUAC wanted to revive the Subversive Activities Control Board, Culver gave a passionate speech denouncing that possibility, prompting Ohio Representative Thomas L. Ashley to say admiringly: "This is one of the most courageous statements I have ever heard on the floor of this House during the thirteen years I have served in this body. Our colleague from Iowa...represents a district which is anything but secure politically. Nevertheless, he has chosen to speak out forcefully on an issue and to take a position which can easily be misconstrued, misrepresented, and misunderstood. This is an act of statesmanship and courage."

During his tenure in Congress, Culver served on the Foreign Affairs Committee, was chairman of the Foreign Economic Policy Subcommittee, and was also a member of the Select Committee on Committees, whose intent it was to streamline certain aspects of the House.

In 1974, Culver successfully ran for the United States Senate. In keeping with his more liberal stance, during his term, he supported, and voted for such issues as federal subsidization of abortions, repeal of the Hatch Act, cuts in defense spending, no-fault car insurance, and sanctions against Rhodesia. His voting record shows that he opposed the selling of arms to Chile, nuclear breeder reactors, and the B-1 bomber.

Explaining the delicate balancing act required of a Senator that has to make tough decisions on such issues as military spending, Culver told interviewer Elizabeth Drew: "I have to decide...how to pick my shots, how to remain credible, not be irrelevant. It's hard enough to make these fights and still stay viable.

CUMMINS

The fights are very emotional; strong interests are involved. I try to approach it in a constructively critical way to fight for a cost-effective defense. So I challenge where I don't think the military is doing enough to provide us with the proper readiness, and I challenge on excessive expenditures." Culver a strong advocate of "arms control by mutual agreement," was a vocal supporter of the ratification of the Strategic Arms Limitation Treaty (SALT), believing emphatically that nuclear war is not a viable solution on any level.

While a Senator, Culver has served on the Environment and Public Works Committee, the Armed Services Committee, the Judiciary Committee, and the Small Business Committee, as well as several subcommittees.

Culver ran for, and lost, his 1980 Senate seat, and after becoming a private citizen once again, eventually taught a number of courses at the University of Massachusetts, and Harvard University. Culver is married to Ann Cooper, and the couple have four children.

CUMMINS, ALBERT BAIRD, (1850-1926) — eighteenth governor of Iowa (1902-08), and United States Senator, was born on February 15, 1850 near Carmichaels, Pennsylvania to Thomas Layton and Sarah Baird (Flenniken) Cummins. He attended Waynesburg College in Pennsylvania, graduating in 1869. After moving to Iowa, he got a clerical position with the Clayton County recorder's office in the town of Elkader. He also worked a short time for the Milwaukee & St. Paul Railway as an express messenger.

Cummins got into engineering by accident when he was asked by a friend to take the position of assistant surveyor for Indiana's Allen County. Cummins did such an impressive job while working on the construction of the Cincinnati, Richmond & Ft. Wayne Railroad that he was promoted to the position of assistant to the chief engineer. His next and final engineering job was for the Northern Central Michigan Railroad.

Deciding to pursue a law career, he got his education working for, and studying at, the Chicago law firm of McClelland & Hodges. After passing the Illinois bar in 1875, he went into law practice at the firm of McClelland & Cummins. Three years later, he moved back to Iowa and became a partner with his brother James in their own law office. After James retired from practicing law, Albert became a partner at the law firm of Wright, Cummins & Wright, a prominent firm known throughout Iowa. In later years, he was a partner in the firms of Cummins & Wright, and Cummins, Hewitt & Wright.

Interested in politics for a number of years, he was a supporter of the Republican Party, attending, and serving in various posts, at a number of state and national conventions. From 1888 to 1890 he served as a member of the Iowa general assembly. He twice ran, unsuccessfully, for the United States Senate, in 1894, and in 1900. In 1901 Cummins ran for the Iowa governorship, and was elected into office. The Republican Party was broken up into two factions during that time, and while the progressives aligned themselves with him, he often had to struggle with the conservatives. However, he was a popular governor, and was reelected in 1903, and 1905.

Cummins resigned from the governorship and became a member of the U.S. Senate in November of 1908, to fill the unfinished term of the incumbent, William B. Allison. He was reelected for the three subsequent terms, but was defeated in the 1926 primary. While chairing the Senate Committee on Interstate Commerce, he helped draft the Esch-Cummins Act, initially called the Transportation Act of 1920, which was to take the control of the nation's railroads out of the hands of the Federal Government. Although the Congress did not agree with the main issue, the measure offered financial help in the refurbishing of the nation's railroad system.

One source described Cummins thusly: "Although his career was a stormy one, he himself was even-tempered, conscientious, deliberate in judgment, and, while tenacious in his views, always courteous and tolerant."

Cummins was married to Ida Lucetta Gallery, and the couple had one daughter. He died on July 30, 1926, in Des Moines, Iowa.

CUNNINGHAM, PAUL HARVEY, (1890-1961) — a U.S. Representative from Iowa; born on a farm in Indiana County, near Kent, Pa., June 15, 1890; attended the public schools; was graduated from State Teachers College, Indiana, Pa., in 1911, from the literary department of the University of Michigan at Ann Arbor in 1914, and from its law department in 1915; was admitted to the bar in 1915 and commenced practice in Grand Rapids, Mich.; during the First World War served as a first lieutenant of Infantry 1917-1919; moved to Des Moines, Iowa, in 1919 and continued the practice of law; member of the Iowa National Guard 1920-1923; member of the State house of representatives 1933- 1937; elected as a Republican to the Seventy-seventh and to the eight succeeding Congresses (January 3, 1941-January 3, 1959); unsuccessful candidate for reelection in 1958 to the Eighty-sixth Congress; resumed the practice of law; died at his summer home on Gull Lake, Brainerd, Minn., July 16, 1961; interment in Masonic Cemetery, Des Moines, Iowa.

D

DAMON, CATHRYN, (1931-1987) — was an actress best known for her work on the quirky comedy television series *Soap*.

Born in Seattle, Washington on September 11, 1931, Damon originally yearned to become a dancer, which she did at the age of sixteen when she moved to New York and studied with the Ballet Repertory Company. She later became a part of the Metropolitan Opera Ballet, dancing as a soloist, then eventually made her way to the Broadway stage. She appeared in such Off-Broadway shows as the revival of *The Boys from Syracuse* and *The Secret Life of Walter Mitty.* Her Broadway work included *The Prisoner of Second Avenue, The Last of the Red-Hot Lovers,* and *Flora, The Red Menace,* among others. Damon also did national tours of shows including *The Dining Room, Sweet Bird of Youth,* and *The Effect of Gamma Rays on Man-in-the-Moon Marigolds,* along with performances in plays by Chekhov and Shakespeare.

In 1977, Damon began playing the part she would become best know for, that of Mary Campbell, the long-suffering wife of the flaky Burt Campbell, and relative to an even larger group of nuts. Damon gained a lot of loyal viewers with her sympathetic portrayal of a woman who was always trying to hold it together in the face of never-ending chaos, and received an Emmy Award in 1980 as best actress in a comedy series.

The actress guest starred on other television shows including *Matlock; Murder, She Wrote; Webster; The Love Boat;* and *Mike Hammer.* She also appeared in feature films such as *How to Beat the High Cost of Living, The Walls Came Tumbling Down,* and *She's Having a Baby.*

Cathryn Damon died from cancer on May 4, 1987, at the age of 56.

DAWSON, ALBERT FOSTER, (1872-1949) — a U.S. Representative from Iowa; born in Spragueville, Iowa, January 26, 1872; attended the public schools and the University of Wisconsin at Madison; engaged in newspaper work at Preston, Iowa, in 1891 and 1892 and at Clinton, Iowa, from 1892 to 1894; secretary to Representative George M. Curtis and Senator William B. Allison of Iowa 1895-1905; studied finance at George Washington University, Washington, D.C.; elected as a Republican to the Fifty-ninth, Sixtieth, and Sixty-first Congresses (March 4, 1905-March 3, 1911); declined the candidacy for renomination in 1910 and also an appointment as private secretary to President William H. Taft tendered in 1910; president of the First National Bank of Davenport, Iowa, 1911-1929; executive secretary of the Republican National Senatorial Committee in 1930; public utility executive 1941-1945; retired from business activities and resided in Highland Park, Ill., until his death March 9, 1949, on a train as it neared Cincinnati, Ohio; interment in Preston Cemetery, Preston, Iowa.

DE FOREST, LEE, (1873-1961) — was an inventor and research engneer who is considered "the father of radio."

Born on August 26, 1873 in Council Bluffs, Iowa, he received hs Ph.B. from Yale University in 1896 and his Ph.D. in 1899. Even as a child, De Forest was interested in inventing. He spent his childhood trying to build locomotives; constructing his own electric motor; and claiming to discover the secret of perpetual motion. At Yale, focused his talents on studying, reading about electricity and designing an underground trolley.

After graduating from Yale, De Forest went to Chicago to seek employment. He worked as a laborer in the factory of the Western Electric Company; eventually being promoted to the telephone laboratory. While employed there, he spent every spare moment working on a device for detecting wireless signals and early in his research discovered that he could use a telephone receiver as an indicating device in receiving such signals.

De Forest was the holder of more than 300 invention patents, including those for the audion vacuum tube which led to the development of the radio, motion pictures and television.

De Forest was married three times: to Nora Stanton Blatch in 1908; to Mary Mayo in 1912; and to Marie Mosquini in 1930. He died on June 30, 1961.

DENNIS, EUGENE, (1905-1961) — was the general secretary of the Communist Party of the United States.

Dennis was born Francis Xavier Waldron, Jr. on August 10, 1905 in Seattle, Washington. He attended the University of Washington for one semester, but due to his father's illness, had to quit in order to help support his family. Due to the hard times he and his family had to endure, he was drawn to the principles of the Communist Party, joining in 1926. The party paid him a weekly salary of fifteen dollars to teach economics at a Woodland, Washington Communist camp.

Dennis (who took the name Eugene Dennis in 1935) began to get arrested quite often, usually on such charges as unlawful assembly, refusal to disperse, or speaking within one hundred feet of a hotel. On March 6, 1930 there was a nationwide demonstration backed by the Communist Party against unemployment, and Dennis was once again taken into custody in Los Angeles, disagreeing vigorously with his charge of incitement to riot, claiming: "All the charge consists of is that I helped to organize and lead an unemployment demonstration. What we demonstrated for has now become the recognized law of the land." Receiving a 180-day jail sentence and a fine of five hundred dollars, Dennis "jumped bail" before he could serve his time, and went underground, eventually making his way to the former Soviet Union.

Dennis returned to the United States in 1935 and was chosen to the post of state secretary of the Wisconsin Democratic Party. In 1937 he was the U.S. Communist Party's representative to the Comintern, and upon his return to America the following year, was asked to serve as the party's national secretary for political and legislative affairs. In 1941 he once again became the party's Comintern representative, but his tenure was interrupted by the German invasion of Russia in June of that year, and he returned to the United States.

In 1945 Communist Party leader Earl Browder was thrown out of office, and Dennis was appointed as the party's general secretary to serve under the new leader, William Z. Foster. Dennis wasted no time in inspiring party members throughout the country to get ready for their area's municipal elections. Due to his efforts, four Communist-backed candidates were elected to Oakland, California's city council.

Two months before, however, in March of 1947, Dennis was once again embroiled in controversy, a situation that would further convince Americans that Communism was not a viable system of belief. On March 26, 1947 Eugene Dennis appeared before the House Committee on Un-American Activities, intending to read a prepared statement. However, he was not allowed to do so, and instead, faced a number of questions concerning the conduct of his life. When he refused to answer his accusers, he was subpoenaed to appear once again on April 9, but sent his lawyer instead, a decision that garnered him a one-year prison sentence for contempt of Congress.

Dennis's problems were compounded by another indictment on July 20, 1948, in which he was included with several other Communist Party leaders for conspiracy in supporting the forcible overthrow of the United States government (known as the Smith Act). The trial took from January 1949 until October of that year, and Dennis made the decision to defend himself in the proceedings. Although he tried to show that his party was only out to improve the lot of society, the judge made several unsympathetic rulings, and when Dennis vehemently challenged them, the judge held him in contempt. The final judgement was a guilty verdict, and a fine of $10,000. Dennis lost on his two appeal attempts, with the verdict being upheld by both the U.S. Court of Appeals and the U.S. Supreme Court.

During his appeal process, Dennis had already begun doing his jail time for his earlier Congressional contempt charge. A few months after his release, he was intending to go underground to avoid serving his Smith Act conspiracy sentence. However, due to his missing the connection with his contact, he ended up serving his time, from July 1951 to March 1955.

During 1956-57, the party tried to regain the momentum it had lost, but due to various world events, coupled with internal divisions, the organization eventually fell apart. By the time Dennis had become the national chairman of the party, there was nothing left to lead.

Dennis had a long-term relationship with Peggy Schneiderman, and the couple had two sons. He died on January 31, 1961. In 1977, Schneiderman published Dennis's memoirs, entitled *The Autobiography of an American Communist.*

DILLON, JOHN FORREST, (1831-) — jurist and legal author, was born in Northampton, N. Y., Dec. 25. His parents moved to Davenport, Ia., in 1838 and his home was there until his move to New York City in 1879. At seventeen he took up the study of medicine, and at the age of twenty he was admitted to practice; but he soon abandoned that profession for one more suited to his tastes.

He was admitted to the bar in 1852, was elected state prosecuting attorney the same year, and six years later, judge of the seventh judicial district of Iowa. His administration of his public duties gave such general satisfaction that he was requested by the bar of the district to continue in office, and he was nominated and reelected without opposition. He was elected one of the judges of the supreme court in 1863, and reelected in 1869. He was then chief justice of the court, but before he had qualified for a second term, he was nominated by President Grant to be circuit judge for the eight circuit, embracing the states of Minnesota, Iowa, Nebraska, Missouri, Kansas and Arkansas, and afterward Colorado. The duties of the circuit involved an annual travel of many thousands of miles.

In 1879 he accepted the position of professor of real estate and equity jurisprudence in the Columbia College Law School, New York City, and on May 26th of that year he resigned as circuit judge of the United States. The position of general counsel of the Union Pacific Railroad Co., was offered to him at the same time. Judge Dillon felt that he should accept these places, and in September he moved to New York City. Judge Dillon held the professorship of Columbia Law School for three years, when, feeling unable to give adequate attention both to the duties of that position and to the pressing demands of large professional engagements, he resigned, and gave his entire attention to the practice of his profession.

Judge Dillon was the author of legal works. The study he gave to the reported decisions of the supreme court of Iowa, as a judge in the court of that state, resulted in the publication of his first legal work, a "Digest of Iowa Reports." He also found time to establish, and to edit for a year, "The Central Law Journal," the only law periodical then published in the Mississippi Valley-as well as to edit and publish five volumes of circuit court reports (1871-80), and to deliver each winter a course of lectures on medical jurisprudence in the Iowa State University. In may, 1875, Judge Dillon made a tour through Europe, visiting many countries, and attending as a member the third annual conference of the Association for the Reform and Condification of the Law of Nations, which met at The Hague. In 1883 and 1889 he made other visits to Europe, and in 1884 was elected a member of l'Institut de Droit International. He delivered numerous addresses before the bar associations of the country on such subjects as "The Inns of Court and Westminster Hall," "American Institutions and Laws," "Uncertainty in our Laws," and "Bentham and his school of Jurisprudence."

In 1853 Judge Dillon married the daughter of Hiram Price, of Iowa, by whom he had two sons and two daughters.

DOLLIVER, JAMES ISAAC, (1894-1978) —
(nephew of Jonathan Prentiss Dolliver), a U.S. Representative from Iowa; born in Park Ridge, Cook County, Ill., August 31, 1894; attended the public schools in Hot Springs, S.Dak.; was graduated from Morningside College, Sioux City, Iowa, in 1915; taught school at Alta and Humboldt, Iowa, 1915-1917; during the First World War served in the United States Army as a private in the Third Service Company of the Signal Corps; was graduated from the University of Chicago Law School in 1921; was admitted to the bar the same year and commenced practice in Chicago; moved to Fort Dodge, Webster County, Iowa, in 1922; prosecuting attorney of Webster County, 1924-1929; member of the school board of Fort Dodge Independent School District 1938-1945; elected as a Republican to the Seventy-ninth and to the five succeeding Congresses (January 3, 1945-January 3, 1957); unsuccessful candidate for reelection in 1956 to the Eighty-fifth Congress; served as a regional legal counsel for International Cooperation Administration in the Middle East, 1957-

1959; retired in 1959 resided in Spirit Lake, Iowa; died in Rolla, Mo., December 10, 1978; interment in Oakland Cemetery, Fort Dodge, Iowa.

DOWELL, CASSIUS CLAY, (1864-1940) — a U.S. Representative from Iowa; born on a farm near Summerset, Warren County, Iowa, February 29, 1864; attended the public schools, Baptist College at Des Moines, Iowa, and Simpson College, Indianola, Iowa; was graduated from the liberal arts department of Drake University, Des Moines, Iowa, in 1886 and from its law department in 1887; was admitted to the bar in 1888 and commenced practice in Des Moines; member of the State house of representatives 1894-1898; served in the State senate 1902-1912; elected as a Republican to the Sixty-fourth and to the nine succeeding Congresses (March 4, 1915-January 3, 1935); chairman, Committee on Elections No. 3 (Sixty-sixth and Sixty- seventh Congresses), Committee on Roads (Sixty-eighth through Seventy- first Congresses); unsuccessful candidate for reelection in 1934 to the Seventy-fourth Congress; resumed the practice of law in Des Moines; elected to the Seventy-fifth and Seventy-sixth Congresses and served from January 3, 1937, until his death in Washington, D.C., February 4, 1940; interment in Woodland Cemetery, Des Moines, Iowa.

DRAKE, FRANCIS MARION, (1830-1903) — sixteenth governor of Iowa (1896-98), was born in Rushville, Illinois on December 30, 1830, son of John Adams and Harriet Jane (O'Neal) Drake. His parents moved to Davis County, Iowa in 1846, and founded the village of Drakeville, where Francis attended school until he was sixteen years old. Becoming a clerk in his father's general merchandise store, he assisted in carrying on the business until 1852. At the age of twenty-two, he led a train across the plains to California, fighting and defeating on the way a party of 300 Pawnee Indians, although his own force numbered but twenty men. Encouraged by the success of this venture, he again crossed the plains in 1854, reaching Sacramento, California, with ninety-seven cows, five oxen and five horses, having lost on the way only three cows, a result which made the trip one of the most notable ever undertaken. Returning by sea, he was devastated when the steamer *Yankee Blade* went down with a loss of several hundred lives. Drake then entered into partnership with his father and brother in a general mercantile business, the connection continuing until 1858, when he withdrew to engage in business for himself at Unionville, Iowa.

At the outbreak of the Civil War, he raised a company among his townsmen, and on the governor's order, he joined the independent regiment of Iowa volunteers commanded by Colonel Edwards. He was commissioned as major and commanded the Federal troops which defended the city of St. Joseph, Missouri, against the Confederate General Price. In 1862, Major Drake became lieutenant-colonel of the 36th Iowa Infantry, with which he served for several years. At the battle of Elkin's Ford, Arkansas, in April, 1864, he defeated General Marmaduke and his forces, gaining from his brigade commander the commendation, "Too much praise cannot be given Colonel Drake for his distinguished gallantry and determined courage in this contest." A few weeks later, having been assigned to the command of the 3rd brigade of Solomon's division, he set out with a large train to gather supplies for the forces of General Steele; the expedition was attacked by Confederate cavalry, and Colonel Drake was wounded and taken prisoner, only to be at once released, the nature of his injury being such that recovery was thought to be impossible. He was away from his command but six months, returning to camp and active duty while still on crutches. He was now brevetted brigadier-general and served until the end of the war.

When he returned to Centervile, Iowa, he began the practice of law in partnership with Judge Amos Harris. Later he gave up law to engage in the development of railroads, supplying capital for five companies in his own state, among them the Albia and Centerville, of which he was president, and the Indiana, Illinois and Iowa. He was also president of the Centerville National Bank and the First National Bank of Albia. In 1895 he was elected governor of his state, and served one term. Drake University at Des Moines, Iowa, an institution under the patronage of the Disciples of Christ, was so named from his large gifts to it and Iowa College at Grinnell, and the Wesleyan College at Mt. Pleasant, Iowa, also enjoyed his beneficence.

Drake was married to Mary Jane Lord of Bloomfield, Iowa, and the couple had two sons and four daughters. He died on November 20, 1903.

E

EICLLER, EDWARD CLAYTON, (1878-1944) — a U.S. Representative from Iowa; born on a farm near Noble, Washington County, Iowa, December 16, 1878; attended the public schools, Washington (Iowa) Academy, and Morgan Park (Ill.) Academy; was graduated from the University of Chicago, in 1904; studied law;

EISENHOWER

was admitted to the bar in 1906 and commenced practice in Washington, Iowa; served as assistant registrar of the University of Chicago 1907-1909; moved to Burlington, Iowa, in 1909 and served as assistant attorney for a railroad company 1909-1918; returned to Washington, Iowa, in 1918 and continued the practice of law; delegate to the Democratic National Convention in 1932; elected as a Democrat to the Seventy-third, Seventy-fourth, and Seventy-fifth Congresses and served from March 4, 1933, to December 2, 1938, when he resigned to accept a Presidential appointment; was renominated in 1938 but later withdrew and was not a candidate for reelection; appointed by President Franklin D. Roosevelt on December 2, 1938, as a commissioner of the Securities and Exchange Commission in Washington, D.C., and served until February 2, 1942, being chairman of the Commission at the time; appointed chief justice of the District Court of the United States for the District of Columbia on February 2, 1942, in which capacity he served until his death in Alexandria, Va., on November 29, 1944; interment in Woodlawn Cemetery, Washington, Iowa.

EISENHOWER, MRS. DWIGHT, (1896-1979) — wife of President Dwight D. Eisenhower, she was also known as "Mamie," and was born in Boone, Iowa on November 14, 1896. She was one of four daughters of John Sheldon and Elivera Mathilda (Carlson) Doud. Two of her sisters died while they were yet teenagers. Mamie's father did extremely well in the meat packing business and was able to retire at the age of thirty-six. He then moved the family to Denver, Colorado where Mamie completed her schooling.

Miss Doud met Lt. Dwight D. Eisenhower while on vacation with her family in San Antonio, Texas. Lt. Eisenhower was stationed at Fort Sam Houston. On Valentine's Day in 1916, he gave Miss Doud an engagement ring and on the first of July, 1916, the couple was married in the Doud home in Denver. After a ten-day honeymoon, the couple established their first of many homes in a two-room officers' quarters at Fort Sam Houston. In 1917, their first child, Doud Dwight was born but died at the age of three from scarlet fever. In 1922, their second son, John Sheldon Doud, was born.

Because of Lt. Eisenhower's occupation, the young family moved often, some twenty different times in thirty years. They lived in different cities and countries all over the world such as Paris, the Panama Canal Zone, the Philippines, and all throughout the United States. Mamie Eisenhower's duties as a military man's wife were many and varied. During World War II, while her husband was Supreme Commander of the Alllied forces, Mrs. Eisenhower contributed to the war effort by serving as a hostess for the Stage Door Canteen and as a waitress at the Soldiers, Sailors, and Marines Club. At other times, it was her duty to throw formal dinners and parties for military leaders, government officials, and royalty. In 1952, when her husband was running for the presidency, Mamie was required to travel with him on his nation-wide tour which took them almost 50,000 miles in the Eisenhower train, to make appearances at several large political rallies. When she became first lady, she was required to entertain as many as 2,000 people and give many receptions and official dinners at which many important people would be in attendance.

ELTHON

Eisenhower had a great respect for his wife and seemed to treasure her greatly. It was he who gave her the nickname "Mamie," and on his political tour before the presidency, he would introduce her by saying, "And now I want you to meet my Mamie." Mrs. Eisenhower was an enthusiastic and friendly person who has been described as "completely non-political." She had many personal interests of which reading mystery novels and visiting with her grand-children ranked the highest.

The former first lady was named honorary president of Girl Scouts of America and decorated with the Order of Malta in 1952, among several other honors.

Mamie Eisenhower died at the Walter Reed Army Medical Center in Washington, D.C. on November 1, 1979.

ELTHON, LES, (1898-1967) — served as Governor of Iowa for only a month following the death of Governor William Beardsley.

Born in Fertile, Iowa on June 9, 1898, he attended Augsburg Seminary, then went on to Iowa State Teacher's College and Hamilton's University of Business. He worked at three careers after his schooling; as a high school teacher (and later principal), farmer, and overseer of a quarry.

In 1932, Elthon, a Republican, won a seat in the Iowa State Senate where he served until 1953, becoming Lieutenant Governor that same year. After the death of his superior, Governor William Beardsley, Elthon served as governor for a little over a month, then returned to his former position as lieutenant governor after the election of a new governor. After leaving office in 1957, he returned to his hometown of Fertile, where he was elected Mayor. He served in that postion until 1963 when he was reelected as a Senator for the state of Iowa. Due to failing health, he resigned in 1965.

Elthon died on April 16, 1967, and was survived by his wife Synneva Hjemebud and their six children.

ELWAY, JOHN, (1960-) — is a football player with the Denver Broncos.

Born in Port Angeles, Washington on June 28, 1960, his father Jack was a college football coach. A star football player in high school, one of Elway's biggest talents on the field was that, according to his football coach, "...he could see everything on the court...(and) had great ability to see the whole field and not focus only on a primary receiver."

Elway enrolled at Stanford and was named that school's starting quarterback in his sophomore year. His star began to rise almost immediately when, in a game with the formidable Oklahoma, he led his team to an upset victory. In that game he completed twenty of thirty-four passes, and for the entire season, Elway completed 248 of 379 passes. He was also the first Stanford sophomore in 18 years to have been chosen to the first team all-America lists for the position of quarterback. In 1981, his junior year, he had trouble with his game due to an injured ankle. However, during that season, he managed to be the school's star right fielder for their baseball team. He was so good that New York Yankees owner George Steinbrenner signed the student to a $140,000 contract to play with a Class-A Yankee farm team in upstate New York.

Elway had another solid year of football playing in his senior year of college, and his statistics for the entire four years at Stanford were 774 completions in 1,246 trys and 77 touchdown passes.

ELWAY

1983, the year that Elway was first drafted into the National Football League, was called by observers "the year of the quarterback," as six members of that position were chosen, the very first being Elway. He caused some controversy when he balked at playing for the team who had chosen him--the Baltimore Colts, because the club was "a franchise in disarray, with a coach, Frank Kush, whose reputation for being a brutal disciplinarian made him anathema to both Jack and John Elway." Elway had the luxury of choice because he had also been offered a multimillion-dollar baseball contract by George Steinbrenner. Although he was dubbed a "spoiled brat" by some, he held his ground and asked that the Colts trade him to a West Coast team, immediately accepting the new home chosen for him, the Denver Broncos.

With his reputation preceding him, the Denver fans couldn't wait to see their new quarterback in action, and head coach Dan Reeves decided that Elway should begin the season, replacing the team's veteran quarterback, Steve DeBerg. However Elway found himself on the bench after seven games and two wins; he was back on the field only after DeBerg suffered an injury that sidelined him for the rest of the season. After the team lost in the first round of the playoffs, it was obvious to some observers that Elway had been expected to be the person who would almost singlehandedly carry the team to great heights, but he was still needing time to adjust to the faster pace of professional football versus college.

Understandably depressed about his first pro season, Elway remembered feeling as though it was "me against the world," and almost quit the game. However, several years later he explained to an interviewer his reasons for persevering: "One of my strengths is my competitiveness. I wouldn't trade that for anything--the will to win and never give up. I can say that, to this day, I've given 110 percent on every play. I always want to win, no matter what it takes." By the 1984 season, Elway was feeling more secure in his game, and although the team once again lost in the playoffs, Elway completed more than half of his 380 passes for 2,598 yards, and during the 1985 season he was first in NFL total offense statistics, completing 54 percent of 605 passes. In trying to explain what his weaknesses were on the field, he explained to one reporter that he was sometimes "forcing the football instead of trying to put the football someplace where it shouldn't go...trying to make the great plays all the time instead of being smart and taking what the defense gives you."

It was Elway's handiwork that secured the AFC championship in 1986, when in the last 5 minutes of the game, after a series of plays, he finally threw the touchdown pass that put the contest into overtime. In the final minutes he threw two long passes that led to the team's winning field goal. The team's opponents in Super Bowl XXI were the New York Giants, and although the Broncos were ahead 10-9 in the first half, they eventually lost the game 39-20.

In 1987 Elway had what was considered his best season ever, completing 224 of 410 passes, and suffering only twelve interceptions against nineteen touchdowns. The Broncos secured the AFC championship once again, and this time Elway was acknowledged as having been the main reason. Former San Diego Chargers coach Al Saunders told a New York *Daily News* reporter: "There's absolutely no way in the world that Denver would be here if John wasn't their quarterback. A one-man team? Yes, I couldn't agree more." Unfortunately Elway and his teammates got swept away by a huge loss in Super Bowl XXII against the Washington Redskins when the latter trounced them 42- 10.

Elway continued to fluctuate in his time on the football field, struggling in 1988 and the beginning of the 1989 season, but coming back strong in the second half of the latter, going on to help his team win the AFC championship over the Cleveland Browns 37-21. When the team went into Super Bowl XXIV, however, they faced both the San Francisco 49ers, and their talented quarterback, Joe Montana, who not only helped his team run roughshod over Denver 55-10, but also garnered the most-valuable-player award.

Although his playing abilities can fluctuate from year to year, as do those of most athletes, he's still number one with Denver Broncos' owner Pat Bowlen, who told an interviewer: "There's a perception that Superman can't fly anymore. That's nonsense. We wouldn't trade John Elway for any quarterback in football."

Elway is married to Janet Buchan and the couple have two children.

ENGLE, PAUL, (1908-1991) — poet, author and teacher, was born in Cedar Rapids, Iowa to Thomas Allen and Evelyn Reinheimer Engle. His father was a horse trainer and dealer and as a young boy, Engle would help his father care for the horses. His school's librarian encouraged him in his interest of poetry and he began writing his first verses in high school. After graduating from high school, Engle attended Coe College and earned his B.A. in 1931. He considered going into the ministry (his family was Methodist) but after trying to preach at the Stumptown church decided that he had "heard no call" and gave up on the idea. While he was at Coe, he had his first sonnet, "The Second Coming," published. In 1931, he entered the University of Iowa and earned his M.A. the following year. His thesis entitled "One Slim Feather," was a collection of poems that won the Yale Series of younger Poets Prize and was published as *Worn Earth,* by the Yale University Press in 1932. It was the first University of Iowa poetry thesis to be published as a book. Engle had also broken away from the norm by writing a creative work as his thesis, which he believed was the first one of its kind in the history of that school. From 1932 to 1933, Engle was at Columbia University doing graduate work in literature and anthropology and in 1933 became a Rhodes Scholar, studying at Merton College, Oxford until 1936 when he received his A.B. degree. While he was at Oxford, Engle published two more volumes of his poetry, *American Song,* and *Break the Heart's Anger.*

In 1937, Engle returned to America and became employed as part of the University of Iowa's faculty. In 1942, he became acting director of the Iowa Writers' Workshop and in 1943, director. In the 1940's and 1950's instead of spending all of his time writing, he devoted more time to developing the Writer's Workshop program which proved extremely successful. In the workshop, Engle taught such soon-to-be-successful writers as Kurt Vonnegut, Gwendolyn Brooks, Flannery O'Connor and others. He devoted a great deal of time in helping others to become successful writers.

Engle wrote and edited more than twenty books including poetry, essays, fiction and literary criticism. Those works include: *Corn, New Englanders, West of Midnight, American Child: A Sonnet Sequence, Book and Child: Three Sonnets, Poems in Praise, Christmas Poems, A Woman Unashamed and Other*

Poems, and several others. His most notable work, however, remains that which he did in helping others to write better. In 1966, he and his soon to be second wife, Hua-ling founded the International Writing Program in Iowa City, the only writing program of its kind in the world at that time. The program drew writers from all over the world to meet together and critique each others' work as well as learn each others' language. This work earned Engle and his wife a nomination for the Nobel Peace Prize in 1976. In that same year, Engle retired from the directorship of the International Writing Program and became a consultant. He continued to work on his own writing until his death in 1991.

In 1936 Engle had married Mary Nissen, with whom he had two daughters, Mary and Sara. Unfortunately, the marriage ended in divorce and in 1971, he married Hua-ling Nieh.

Paul Engle died on March 22, 1991 in Chicago, Illinois.

ERBE, NORMAN A., (1919-) — was Governor of Iowa from 1961 to 1963.

Born in Boone, Iowa on October 25, 1919, he went into the United States Army at the beginning of World War II, and was an infantry company commander during 1941-42. He then transferred to the United States Air Force, serving as a pilot between 1943 and 1945. After the war, he attended the University of Iowa, earning a Bachelor of Arts degree in 1946, and a law degree the following year, after which, he went into a private law practice.

His career in politics began in 1952 when he became the County Attorney General for the Iowa Highway Commission. He held that post until 1955, and was elected as Attorney General for the state in

1956, serving until 1961. He ran for Governor of Iowa on the Republican ticket in 1960 and won, taking office the following year. While in office, he increased funding to educational programs and formed a commission to study the problem of alcoholism. He also got involved in the study of prisoners, going as far as having the State Board of Control create a diagnostic clinic in order to get an idea of the viability of rehabilitation. Under his term, the Iowan people became participants in the Kerr-Mills medical program, and were able to utilize the federal low rental housing program as well.

Erbe ran for a second term, but was defeated by Harold Hughes. After leaving office, Erbe began working as an assistant to the president of Diamond Laboratories. He later became the executive director of the National Paraplegia Foundation, and also worked as regional representative of the Secretary of the United States Department of Transportation.

He is married to Jacqueline Doran and the couple have three children.

ESTES, SIMON LAMONT, (1938-) — bass-baritone, was born in Centerville, Iowa. His father had never received an education beyond the third grade, and one of his ancestors had been sold as a slave for $500 just before the signing of the emancipation proclamation. The family was deeply religious and Simon had been recruited to sing as a boy soprano in the choir of the Second Baptist Church. Estes was outstanding in sports in high school, but because his parents urged him to get an education, Estes passed up opportunities to play sports and chose instead to go to college. He entered the University of Iowa on an athletic scholarship, but changed his focus to pre-med by his second year. In his senior year, he switched from pre-med to Theology and then to social psychology.

In 1960, Estes found his singing voice again and decided that he would rather sing that do anything else. He auditioned unsuccessfully for the University of Iowa's 300 voice choir and then joined the Old Gold Singers, a campus group that sang pop songs of which he was the first black singer. When Charles Kellis, a voice teacher at the university, heard Estes sing, he asked him if he would like to sing opera. When Estes conceded that he would, Kellis began to work with him without charge and was largely responsible for getting Estes the audition that won him a Rockefeller grant and a full scholarship at the Julliard School of Music in New York City.

After a year and a half at Julliard, Estes went to Germany. He landed a contract with the Deutsche Oper in West Berlin and made his debut as Ramfis in an April 1965 production of Verdi's *Aoda*. In 1966, he entered the first international Tchaikovsky music competition and went to Moscow. By the time he got there he had learned only one Russian song, but he so impressed the judges during his performance that he won the silver medal. When Estes returned to America, he received quite a reception including an invitation to the White House by President Lyndon B. Johnson.

Because Estes is black, he met with much prejudice on the road to his success as an operatic singer. Many times he was turned down because companies were afraid they would lose their backing if they hired a black singer. He found that he had to work harder and be better than his white competitors and has made it a lifelong habit of always giving "110 percent."

The most important performance of Estes career came when he was cast in the title role of the 1978 Bayreuth production of the *Flying Dutchman*. His success in this part brought him to a place in his career where he had reached a solid maturity level and could no longer be considered just an aspiring singer. Estes made his debut at New York's Metropolitan Opera House in Wagner's Tannhalser in 1982. In 1985, he sang the role of Porgy in Gershwin's *Porgy and Bess* at the Met where he also sang Wotan for the first time in 1986. In 1984, he had signed a four year recording contract with Philips that required him to put out a minimum of four releases a year. Other operas he has appeared in include the Boston Opera, Chicago Lyric Opera, Vienna Staatsoper, Paris Opera, and numerous others. Roles he has appeared in include that of Figaro in *The Barber of Seville,* Banquo in *Macbeth,* Oroveso in *Norma,* Amonasro in *Aida,* Amonsaro in *Aida,* Gremin in *Eugene Onegin,* and many others.

In 1980, Simon Estes married Yvonne Baer whom he had met in Zurich while singing there in 1977. The couple has two daughters, Jennifer Barbara and Lynne Ashley. Along with his music interests, Estes gives talks to kids in schools about drugs and social problems and has established scholarships in his name in general studies and in music at three universities.

EVANS, HIRAM KINSMAN, (1863-1941) — a U.S. Representative from Iowa; born in Walnut Township, Wayne County, Iowa, March 17, 1863; attended the country schools and Seymour and Allerton (Iowa) High Schools; was graduated from the law department of the University of Iowa at Iowa City in 1886; was admitted to the bar in 1886 and commenced practice in Holdrege, Nebr.; moved to Seymour, Iowa, in 1887, and to Corydon, Iowa, in 1889 and continued the practice of law; prosecuting attorney for Wayne County 1891-1895; member of the State house of representatives in 1896 and 1897; member of the board of regents of the University of Iowa 1897-1904; mayor of Corydon 1901-1903; judge of the third judicial district of Iowa from 1904 until 1923, when he resigned; elected as a Republican to the Sixty-eighth Congress to fill the vacancy caused by the resignation of Horace M. Towner and served from June 4, 1923, to March 3, 1925; declined to be a candidate for renomination in 1924; resumed the practice of law in Corydon, Iowa; appointed by the Governor of Iowa as a member of the State board of parole on July 1, 1927, and served to July 1, 1933; died in Corydon, Iowa, July 9, 1941; interment in Corydon Cemetery.

F

FELLER, ROBERT, (1918 -) — baseball pitcher, was born in Van Meter, Iowa, the son of William A. Feller, a farmer, and Lena (Forret) Feller. His father supported his love of baseball by helping him to organize neighborhood teams and by playing catch with him behind the barn. In high school, young Bob Feller began playing semi-professional baseball and was making up to $50 per Sunday. He knew at that time that baseball would become his career and had decided that he liked playing baseball better than anything else.

At sixteen years of age, Feller was signed by the Cleveland Indians because they had heard of his reputation of striking out players. He had to get permission from Adel High School to stay with the Indians until their last game on September 27 before he had to return to high school and finish his senior year.

During 1937 and 1938, Bob Feller's pitches were more often based on luck than control. He hadn't yet learned to gain control of all the energy that he put into throwing the ball and sometimes he completely missed the mark. Once in awhile, he even threw it into the stands. He struck out a lot of players but he walked a bunch as well. He pitched his first no-hitter on April 16, 1940 in a game against Chicago. In 1946, he struck out 348 batters. Some statisticians argue about whether he had the most strike-outs or whether the record belonged to Rube Waddell, whom some claim struck out 348 batters in 1904. In any case, either record was broken in 1965, when Sandy Koufax struck out 382 batters. Records that Bob Feller does hold include pitching three no-hitters, twelve one-hitters, and 208 bases on balls in 1938. Overall, he pitched 570 major league games, won 266 and lost 162, allowed 3,271 hits, 1,384 earned runs, fanned 258, and walked 1,764. In 1962, he was inducted into baseball's Hall of Fame.

Feller was mostly known for his incredible fast ball which was clocked at 107.9 miles per hour during a promotion at Griffith Stadium. Because of this he received the nickname "Rapid Robert." During a game he would pitch between 115 and 130 times and lose up to four pounds on a hot day. He did so well financially during those early years that he bought a home for his parents and financed their annual trek to Florida for the winter months. In his peak years with the Indians, he earned over $80,000 per year.

FICKE

In his later years after retiring from playing baseball, Feller and his wife Ann have traveled the countryside speaking to kids, signing autographs and throwing a few pitches.

FICKE, ARTHUR DAVISON, (1883-1945) — poet and author, was born in Davenport, Iowa on November 10, 1883 to Frances Davison Ficke and Charles August Ficke. His father was a lawyer and to please him, Arthur obtained a law degree and worked in his practice for ten years. As a child, he attended Davenport schools and afterward, Harvard. He took his law degree at the University of Iowa while teaching English. Never losing his first love which was for writing, he wrote two studies of Japanese art, a play and eight volumes of poetry while practicing law.

Ficke wrote fifteen volumes of poetry during his career and as well had many of his poems published in several periodicals. Those volumes include: *From the Isles: A Series of Songs out of Greece, The Happy Princess and Other Poems, The Earth Passion, Boundary, and Other Poems, The Breaking of Bonds: A Drama of the Social Unrest, Mr. Faust, Sonnets of a Portrait-Painter, The Man on the Hilltop and Other Poems, An April Elegy,* and several others. Although *Sonnets of a Portrait-Painter* was his most notable work, he unfortunately never left a huge impression as a poet, for after his death, the only one of his publications that still existed was his *Chats on Japanese Prints.*

Ficke once took part in a hoax that was almost completely out of character for him. It was dubbed the Spectra Hoax and involved a volume of poems that he and a friend put together under the pseudonyms of Anne Knish (Ficke) and Emanuel Morgan

(Ficke's friend Witter Bynner.) The poems, although published in book form and in magazines, were completely a joke and finally, in April 1918, Bynner admitted to that fact.

Ficke married Evelyn Blunt on October 1, 1907 and had one son, Stanhope Blunt. His marriage to Evelyn failed in 1922 and he married Gladys Brown, whom he had met while in France in the early 1920's. This took place after a short affair he had with Edna St. Vincent during a stay in New York City. He had been corresponding with Miss St. Vincent for some time and had in effect mentored her in poetry writing. The pair parted company, however, when they discovered that they would not be compatible as life partners. After marrying Gladys Brown on December 8, 1923, Ficke left his law practice and took up writing full time.

Arthur Davison Ficke died on November 30, 1945.

FULTON, ROBERT D., (1929-) — was Governor of Iowa for a very short time during 1969.

Born in Waterloo, Iowa on May 13, 1929, he studied at Iowa State Teachers College from 1947 to 1949. He went on to State University of Iowa, earning a Bachelor of Arts degree in 1952 and a law degree in 1958, after which he went into private law practice. His education was interrupted for two years, between 1953 and 1955 while he served in the United States Air Force.

Three years after his discharge, he was elected to the Iowa House of U.S. Representatives, serving in that post until 1961. He went on to the State Senate the following year, serving until 1965. In 1964, he had also been elected Lieutenant Governor, under

FUNSTON

Democratic Governor, Harold Hughes, serving in that capacity for five years.

After Governor Hughes resigned to serve in the Senate, Fulton served as governor for fifteen days in January of 1969 until the newly-elected governor, Robert Ray took office. Having made the decision to quit as lieutenant governor even before the election, Fulton returned to private practice after the transition was made. He later ran against Ray in the 1970 contest, but was defeated.

Fulton is married to Rachel Marie Breanlt and the couple have four children.

FUNSTON, GEORGE KEITH, (1910-1992) business manager and president of the New York Stock Exchange, was born in Waterloo, Iowa to George E. and Genevieve (Keith) Funston. Growing up in Sioux Falls, South Dakota, Funston graduated from high school in 1927. He then enrolled in Trinity College in Hartford, Connecticut and graduated with a B.A. in economics and history in 1932. While at Trinity, he also taught Sunday School and was chief of the student library assistants. After graduating from Trinity, Funston went to graduate school at Harvard University's School of Business Administration. He earned his M.B.A. in 1934 and became research assistant in accounting at the School of Business Administration the following year.

In 1935, Funston landed a job with the American Radiator Company in New York City, as assistant to the sales vice- president and later as assistant to the treasurer. In 1940, he went to work for the Sylvania Electric Products Company in New York and just before World War II, took a leave of absence from his job and went to work with the War Production Board first as assistant to the deputy chairman and later to the Chairman. In June 1944, he accepted the position as president of Trinity College, his alma mater, and served there until 1951 when he accepted the position of president of the New York Stock Exchange.

At Trinity, Funston was mostly noted for his successful fund raising. While he was there, enrollment also double. He made many changes including those made to the accounting system, admissions, and student guidance. He established a new placement service and put in place several new administrative policies. While he was at Trinity, he was also involved in directorships of seven corporations: Hartford Steam Boiler Inspection and Insurance Company, B.F. Goodrich Company, General Foods Corporation, Aetna Insurance Company, Connecticut General Life Insurance Company, Owens-Corning Fiberglas Corporation and the Hartford National Bank and Trust Company. At the same time, he served as member of the Connecticut State Highway Commission, the Connecticut State Commission on Government Organization, the air force committee on ROTC affairs, and of the Army advisory council of Hartford. He was a trustee of the Lenox School, of the Taft School, of the Watkinson Library, and of the Church Society for College Work. He was also the director of the First National Bank in Hartford, the first president of the Connecticut Council of Higher Education, and member of the executive committee of the New England Association of Colleges and Secondary Schools.

Funston's acceptance of the presidency of the New York Stock Exchange made him the third salaried president of that institution since its inception in 1792. He succeeded president William McChesney Martin and Emil Schram and signed a contract for a salary of $100,000 per year over a three year period of time. While at the NYSE, Funston introduced a plan which enabled small investors to buy stock for as little as $40 per month. He also convinced companies to release more extensive financial information to investors, helped to obtain voting power for owners of very few shares of stock and invested in computers to enable stock transactions to be processed more quickly. He realized that computers would play a major role in the future of the industry and anticipated the use someday of automated teller machines and direct deposit.

Funston was awarded several honorary degrees including a D.H.L. from Wesleyan University; and LL.D. degrees from the University of Pennsylvania and Resellaer Polytechnic Institute.

Keith Funston married Elizabeth Kennedy of Pittsburgh in 1939 and had three children: Marguerite Scott, Elizabeth Gail, and G. Keith Jr.

Funston died on May 15, 1992 in Greenwich, Connecticut.

G

GALLUP, GEORGE HORACE, (1901-1984) — public opinion statistician, was born in Jefferson, Iowa on November 18, 1901. His father, George Henry, was a speculator in farm and ranch lands. Because of family financial problems, young George was forced to pay his own way through college. He attended the State University of Iowa and became editor of the college newspaper, the *Daily Iowan*. He graduated in 1923 and stayed on as an instructor in journalism while he earned his M.A. degree in psychology which he finished in 1925. He later earned a Ph.D. in journalism in 1928. His doctoral thesis was a good indication of what his future occupation would be: A *New Technique for Objective Methods for Measuring Reader Interest in Newspapers*.

After earning his Ph.D., Gallup headed up the department of journalism at Drake University for two years, 1929-1931, and then took a position with Northwestern University as professor of journalism and advertising for one year. In 1932, he landed a job with the advertising agency of Young and Rubicam in New York, as director of research, where he stayed until 1947. From 1935- 1937, he was also visiting professor at the Pulitzer School of Journalism at Columbia University.

While at Young and Rubicam, Gallup worked out a system of measuring the public's opinion of the firm's products. At the same time, in 1935, he founded the American Institute of Public Opinion, where the poll questions were originated, answers gathered and the results organized. In 1939, he founded the Audience Research Institute, Inc. whose primary purpose it was to evaluate the public reaction to elements of motion pictures.

Gallup based his polls on 3,000 samples of a cross-section of the population of the country. The questioning was done by 1,200 part-time interviewers. The first successful prediction made by the AIPO, whose stated purpose was "impartially to measure and report public opinion on political and social issues of the day, without regard to the rightness or wisdom of the views expressed," was that Franklin D. Roosevelt would win the presidential election in 1936. The first incorrect prediction the AIPO made was that Thomas Dewey would win the 1948 presidential election, but Harry Truman was the winner instead. George Gallup attributed this mistake to having closed the polls too early and thus not getting an accurate reading of the public opinion.

George Gallup also authored several articles and books including *The Business Department of School Publications, Public Opinion in a Democracy, A Guide to Public Opinion Polls,* and *Gallup Poll Almanacs.*

He received several honorary Doctorate degrees from Northwestern University, Drake University, Boston University, Tufts College and Colgate University. He received an award from Syracuse University for distinguished achievement and the University of Missouri gave him the Missouri Honor Award.

In 1925, Gallup married Ophelia Smith Miller and had three children: Alec Miller, George Horace, Jr., and Julia.

George Gallup died on July 26, 1984 in Tschingel, Switzerland.

GARST, WARREN, (1850-1924) — nineteenth governor of Iowa (1908-09), was born on December 4, 1850, in Dayton, Ohio, the son of Michael and Maria Louisa (Morrison) Garst. After attending public schools, Garst got a position as a brakeman for the Chicago & Northwestern Railroad Co. in Boone, Iowa. He later moved to Coon Rapids where he became involved in the family mercantile business with his father and brother. He then got into banking when he became one of the founders of the Bank of Coon Rapids.

Politics was his next inclination, and he was elected to the Iowa State Senate on the Republican ticket in 1893, as well as for two subsequent terms. From 1894 to 1906, the state was going through a major growth period, and state policy was being revised at a rapid rate in such areas as railroads, taxation, public utilities, education, and highways, and Garst was a big part of those changes as chairman of the Appropriations Committee. In 1906, Garst was nominated for, and won, the post of lieutenant- governor. When his superior, Governor Cummins, left office to take a vacant seat in the United States Senate, Garst took over the governorship in November of 1908.

Garst retired from public office for a time, pursuing business interests, then reentered that arena after Governor Clarke named him as the state's first industrial commissioner, a post in which he was overseer of the new Workmen's Compensation Law; after the law was firmly established, he retired for good.

Garst was married twice: to Lizzie P. Johnson (who died in 1881), and Clara Clark. He had three children. Garst died on October 5, 1924 in Des Moines.

GARTNER, MICHAEL GAY, (1938-) — journalist and broadcasting executive, was born in Des Moines, Iowa to Mary Marguerite (Gay) Gartner and Carl David Gartner, a newspaper man. Michael Gartner's first newspaper job was answering telephones for the sports department of the *Des Moines register.* He has worked in many positions of the newspaper business, starting with copy boy and eventually becoming a part owner later in life. In 1960, he received his B.A. from Carleton College in Minnesota and landed a job with the *Wall Street Journal.* Starting out as a reporter, he eventually moved into the enviable position of page-one editor. In 1969, he earned his law degree from New York University, but never went in to that field of work.

In 1974 Gartner left the *Wall Street Journal* and moved back to Iowa, becoming the executive editor of the *Des Moines Register.* In 1975, he became vice-president, in 1977, executive vice-president, and in 1978, president and chief operating officer of the Des Moines Register and Tribune Company. In 1979, he made a decision to shut down the newspaper's afternoon edition of the Des Moines *Tribune,* a decision which put a lot of people out of work. (His name would later become synonymous with personnel and budget cuts and Gartner would not be a very well liked man among employees.) In 1984, he attempted to buy the Des Moines *Register,* a move which cost him his job. The newspaper went up for sale again, in 1986, and Gannett bought it and the Tribune Company in for $260 million. Ironically, Gartner became a millionaire from that sale because of the several thousand shares of stock that he owned in the private company. In 1985, he co-founded Midway Newspapers that included the Iowa *Daily Tribune,* five weekly papers, and ten shoppers' guides. Gannet then approached Gartner to manage its newest addi-tion, the Louisville *Courier-Journal.* Here again, Gartner felt it necessary to trim the staff and get rid of the afternoon edition, the Louisville *Times.*

In 1988, NBC News announced that Michael Gartner would succeed Lawrence Grossman as its president. Because NBC was in a financial hole at the time, Gartner again sharpened his scissors and went about cutting the budget and the staff to relieve some of the financial pressure. The unhappy employ-ees of NBC began to call him things like "cold-hearted" and "a newsman that thinks like an accountant." Gartner was not moved and dismissed it with the reasoning that it was what he had to do in order to run the newstation efficiently. To his credit, Gartner was a key player in the 1988, $10 million acquisition of 38 percent of Visnews, an international video news service, and NBC was almost back in the black by 1990.

Michael Gartner married Barbara McCoy on May 25, 1968 and had three children, Melissa, Christopher, and Michael. The family resides in Des Moines, Iowa and Michael Gartner also keeps an apartment in New York City where he resides on the weekends.

GEAR, JOHN HENRY, (1825-1900) — a U.S. Representative and a U.S. Senator from Iowa; born in Ithaca, Tompkins County, N.Y., April 7, 1825; attended the common schools; moved to Galena, Ill., in 1836, to Fort Snelling, Iowa, in 1838, and to Burlington in 1843, where he engaged in mercantile pursuits; mayor of Burlington 1863; member, State house of representatives 1871-1873, serving as speaker two terms; Governor of Iowa 1878- 1881; elected as a Republican to the Fiftieth and Fifty-first Congresses (March 4, 1887-March 3, 1891); unsuccessful candidate for reelection in 1890; appointed by President Benjamin Harrison as Assistant Secretary of the Treasury 1892-1893; elected to the Fifty-third Congress (March 4, 1893-March 3, 1895); elected as a Republican to the United States Senate in 1894; reelected in 1900 and served from March 4, 1895, until his death on July 14, 1900, before the start of his second term; chairman, Committee on Pacific Railroads (Fifty-fourth through Fifty-Sixth Congresses); died in Washington, D.C.; interment in Aspen Grove Cemetery, Burlington, Iowa.

GILCHRIST

GILCHRIST, FRED CRAMER, (1868-1950) — a U.S. Representative from Iowa; born in California, Washington County, Pa., June 2, 1868; moved with his parents to Cedar Falls, Iowa, in 1871; attended the public schools; was graduated from State Teachers' College, Cedar Falls, Iowa, in 1886; teacher and superintendent of schools in Laurens and Rolfe, Iowa, 1886-1890; superintendent of schools of Pocahontas County, Iowa, 1890-1892; was graduated from the law department of the State University of Iowa at Iowa City in 1893; was admitted to the bar in 1893 and commenced practice in Laurens, Iowa; member of the State house of representatives 1902- 1904; president of the board of education of Laurens, Iowa, 1905-1928; served in the State senate 1923- 1931; elected as a Republican to the Seventy-second and to the six succeeding Congresses (March 4, 1931-January 3, 1945); unsuccessful candidate for renomination in 1944; resumed the practice of law; died in Laurens, Iowa, March 10, 1950; interment in Laurens Cemetery.

GLASPELL, SUSAN KEATING, (1882-1948) — journalist, novelist and playwright, was born in Davenport, Iowa to Elmer S. Glaspell and Alice Keating Glaspell. In spite of the fact that she was expected to be a teacher, Susan had her heart set early on becoming a writer. After graduating from high school, she took a job as a reporter for $3 per week in her hometown. Later, she attended Drake University in Des Moines, Iowa and worked as a college correspondent for a local newspaper. In 1899, she graduated with a Ph.B. degree and took a job with the *Des Moines Daily News.*

After less than two years with the *Daily News,* she quit and moved back to Davenport to write freelance. She had already sold several short stories by the time she made her decision and in 1909, published her first novel, *The Glory of the Conquered*. In 1911, she published her second novel and in 1912, her first collection of short stories entitled *Lifted Masks*. In 1913, she married George Cram Cook, whom she had met during a year abroad.

Up to the time when she met George Cook, most of Susan Glaspell's stories were idealistic, romantic type stories set in the midwestern town of "Freeport" (the pseudonym for Davenport which she used in her stories). When Mr. Cook read her work, he decided that her writing was too romantic needed to contain more realism. Consequently, by her second novel, her writing had become different, more purposeful, even with a hint of political overtones. She also began to write plays for the theatre that her husband helped to found in 1915. Between 1915 and 1930, she wrote fourteen plays, the best being *Inheritors,* and *The Verge*. Others she wrote include: *Suppressed Desires; Trifles; The People; The Outsider; Woman's Honor; Tickless Time; Bernice; Chains of Dew; The Comic Artist; Alison's House* and two others.

Glaspell and Cook moved to Greece in 1922 but Mr. Cook died unexpectedly in 1924. Grieved at her husband's passing, Glaspell returned to Cape Cod and continued to write. Her most notable work around that time was a biography of her husband which she titled *The Road to the Temple*. Altogether during her career, she wrote fourteen plays, nine novels, forty-three short stories, a children's tale, some essays and one biography. Her novels include: *The Visioning, Fidelity, The Morning is Near Us, Norma Ashe, Judge Rankin's Daughter,* and others. Her short stories include: "Finality in Freeport," "The Hearing Ear,"

GOOD

"Jury of Her Peers," "Government Goat," "The Busy Duck," "Pollen," "The Escape," and others.

Glaspell re-married to Norman Matson and lived in Provincetown, continuing to write until her death in 1948 of viral pneumonia.

GOOD, JAMES WILLIAM, (1866-1929) — a U.S. Representative from Iowa; born near Cedar Rapids, Linn County, Iowa, September 24, 1866; attended the common schools, and was graduated from Coe College, Cedar Rapids, Iowa, in 1892 and from the law department of the University of Michigan at Ann Arbor in 1893; was admitted to the bar in 1893 and commenced practice in Indianapolis, Ind., the same year; moved to Cedar Rapids, Iowa, in 1896 and continued the practice of law; served as city attorney 1906-1908; elected as a Republican to the Sixty-first and to the six succeeding Congresses and served from March 4, 1909, until his resignation on June 15, 1921; chairman, Committee on Appropriations (Sixty-sixth and Sixty-seventh Congresses); moved to Evanston, Ill., in 1921 and engaged in the practice of law in Chicago, Ill.; appointed Secretary of War in the Cabinet of President Hoover and served from March 5, 1929, until his death in Washington, D.C., November 18, 1929; interment in Oak Hill Cemetery, Cedar Rapids, Iowa.

GOODWIN, ROBERT KINGMAN, (1905-1983) — a U.S. Representative from Iowa; born in Des Moines, Iowa, May 23, 1905; attended the public schools; was graduated from Drabe University, Des Moines, Iowa, in 1928 and later attended the law school of George Washington University, Washington, D.C.; moved to Redfield, Dallas County, Iowa, in 1929 and engaged in the brick and tile manufacturing business and

116

farming 1934-1949; mayor of Redfield, Iowa, 1938-1940; delegate to the Republican State conventions in 1936 and 1938; vice president of the Dallas County Farm Bureau in 1939 and 1940; elected as a Republican to the Seventy-sixth Congress to fill the vacancy caused by the death of Cassius C. Dowell and served from March 5, 1940, to January 3, 1941; was not a candidate for renomination in 1940; director of the Central National Bank & Trust Co., 1941- 1965; commissioned a lieutenant in the United States Naval Reserve in June 1942 and served until November 2, 1945; delegate to the Republican National Convention in 1952; member of the Republican National Committee 1952-1956; civilian aide to the Secretary of the Army 1952-1956; trustee and vice president of Herbert Hoover Foundation, Inc.; resumed his manufacturing business; was a resident of Des Moines, Iowa, until his death in Rochester, Minn., February 21, 1983; interment in Resthaven, Des Moines, Iowa.

GOULD, BEATRICE BLACKMAR, (1998-1989) — author, co- editor of Ladies' Home Journal, was born in Emmetsburg, Iowa to Harry E. and Mary Kathleen (Fluke) Blackmar. Her father was a superintendent of public schools and was among the first to have milk and hot lunches served to children at school. Beatrice attended elementary and high school in Iowa City and Ottumwa and later went to the University of Iowa. After graduation, she worked as a reporter for the Ottumwa *Courier,* the Des Moines *Capital,* and the Des Moines *Evening Tribune.* She later received a Lydia Roberts Fellowship and entered the School of Journalism of Columbia University receiving her B.S. degree in journalism in 1923. Beatrice Blackmar married Bruce Gould on October 4 of that same year.

GOULD

In 1926, Beatrice Blackmar Gould went to work as a writer and woman's editor on the New York *Sunday World.* In 1927, she and her husband co-wrote the play *Man's Estate,* two others they eventually wrote together are: *The Terrible Turk,* and *First Gentlemen of Her Time.* They also co-wrote a screenplay entitled, *Reunion.* For awhile the Goulds turned to free-lance writing and contributed to such magazines as the *Saturday Evening Post, Cosmopolitan, Liberty, Vanity Fair,* the *North American Review,* the *American Mercury, Pictorial Review,* and the *New Republic.* Mrs. Gould also contributed regularly to *Collier's, Cosmopolitan,* and the *Ladies' Home Journal.* In 1935, she and her husband went to work for the *Journal* as co-editors. Under their direction, the *Journal* tripled it circulation, to 7.5 million subscribers and the quality of the articles and stories it carried improved. In addition to her duties with the *Journal,* Mrs. Gould was the director of General Foods from 1959 to 1962 and she co-wrote with her husband the autobiographical book, *American Story.* The Goulds retired from the *Journal* in 1967.

During World War II, the Goulds had travelled to Europe to study military and social conditions in the combat areas. In 1945, Mrs. Gould visited the liberated areas to study the toll the war had taken on the families of Europe. Mrs. Gould, who was an advocate of aid to Great Britain during the war, had taken in two foster children who had to be evacuated from England during that time.

In 1946, Mrs. Gould was honored with an award from the Association of Women Directors of the National Association of Broadcasters and in 1947 was honored with an achievement award by the Women's National Press Club. In 1946, Mr. and Mrs. Gould together were recipients of an annual award for distinguished service to journalism by the University of Missouri.

Mrs. Gould was a strong advocate of being a mother to her children and making her home a priority. As a result of that belief, she limited her work week to three days in order to spend time with her daughter and to take care of her home.

Beatrice Gould died in Hopewell, New Jersey on January 30, 1989.

GOULD, (CHARLES) BRUCE, (1898-1989) — editor, was born in Luana, Iowa to Wilbur Samuel and Edna Earle (Davidson) Gould. He was a descendant of the Goulds who had come from Ipswich, England and founded Ipswich, Massachusetts in 1638. Bruce Gould grew up in Des Moines and graduated from East Des Moines High School in 1916. Even at a young age he was interested in writing and editing, for in high school he was actively involved with editing the school newsletter and the school yearbook. He also acted in several school plays which sparked a desire in him to be a playwright. After high school, he attended Grinnell College for one year before joining the United States Naval Reserve Flying Corps during World War I.

After his tour of duty was over, Gould attended the University of Iowa and majored in English. While there, he and two friends founded an undergraduate magazine which they called *Frivol.* He was also, during that time, a member of the staff of the *Daily Iowan* where he met Beatrice Blackmar, a co-worker.

On October 4, 1923, Bruce Gould married Beatrice Blackmar while he was a graduate student at Columbia. His desire to be a playwright became a determination and so from 1923 to 1924, he studied play writing under Hatcher Hughes while he worked as a reporter at the New York *Sun.* In 1924, he went to work for the New York *Evening Post,* first as a reporter, then as its literary editor, and finally as editor. A few years later, he became editor of the *Saturday Evening Post.* During this time, he was contributing articles to *Collier's, Cosmopolitan,* and the *Ladies' Home Journal,* the latter of which appointed Gould and his wife as its co-editors in 1935.

During their twenty-seven year career with the *Journal,* the Goulds implemented many positive changes that resulted in steady growth in readership and prestige for the magazine. In 1943, the net paid circulation for the *Journal* was 4,375,000, the highest in the world. In 1946, those figures rose to 4,682,191, the highest in its history to that date. During their tenure, the magazine reached its peak circulation of more than 4.5 million copies.

Aside from writing several articles, Gould collaborated with aviator Anthony Fokker on two books: *Sky Larking: The Romantic Adventure of Flying,* and *The Flying Dutchman.* Gould and his wife collaborated on several plays together including, "Man's Estate," "The Terrible Turk," and "Reunion" and in the 1960's, they wrote an autobiography entitled, *American Story.*

Bruce Gould died at his home in Hopewell, New Jersey of congestive heart failure. The date was August 27, 1989.

GRANDY, FREDERICK LAWRENCE, (1948-   ) — a U.S. Representative from Iowa; born in Sioux City, Iowa, June 29, 1948; attended public schools; graduated from Phillips Exeter Academy, 1966; graduated from Harvard University, 1970; aide to U.S. Representative Wiley Mayne, 1970-1971; professional actor, 1971-1985; elected as a Republican to the One Hundredth Congress (January 3, 1987-January 3, 1989); is a resident of Sioux City, Iowa.

GRANT, CAREY, (1904-1986) actor, was born Alexander Archibald Leach in Bristol, England. His father was a presser in a clothing firm. His mother was sent to a mental institution when he was twelve, because of a nervous breakdown and Cary went to live with his paternal grandmother. He did not see his mother again for twenty years; after he had made his break into acting. Grant did not take much to education after he realized that his dreams of going to college were impossible ones. At the age of thirteen, he ran off to join the Bob Pender Troupe as an acrobat and comedian, but his father pulled him back and made him go to school. When he was fifteen, he ran off for good, rejoined the Troupe and went with them to New York in 1920 for an engagement at the Hippodrome and a tour of vaudeville. When the Troupe went back home to England, Grant stayed and tried to make a go of it alone in New York. He was not able to find acting jobs, however, and instead had to take all kinds of odd jobs to earn his way. Finally, he went back to England and there met Arthur Hammerstein who help him land a position as understudy for Paul Gregory in the musical, *Golden Dawn*. It meant traveling back New York City. The year was 1927. By 1932, Grant had played in several musicals and twelve operettas.

In 1932, Grant decided to take a drive out to California. Once in Hollywood, he took a screen test with the wife of a friend at Paramount, and was immediately offered a contract. It was at that time that he changed his name to Cary Grant because his real name, Archie Leach, lacked any kind of flair.

GRANT

He made his debut into motion pictures with *This is the Night,* with Lili Damita and Charles Ruggles and he was on his way to a lucrative career. Other films he made with Paramount that year include: *Hot Saturday, Merrily We Go to Hell, Madame Butterfly,* and *Blonde Venus.* In 1937, he became a free-lance performer when his contract with Paramount ended and made such films as *Topper, The Awful Truth, Bringing Up Baby,* and several others. After making the film *The Philadelphia Story* with Katherine Hepburn in 1940, Grant donated the $125,000 he made to the British War Relief. In 1942, he helped to entertain the armed forces after the start of World War II, and in that same year, became a naturalized citizen of the United States.

In a career that spanned thirty-four years, Grant made 72 films and didn't take a salary for any after 1958. Instead, he asked for 75 percent of the profits or ten percent of the gross income of each film, whichever was greater, and after seven years, he owned each film outright.

Cary Grant was married five times. His first wife was Virginia Cherrill; the second, Barbara Hutton; then Betsy Drake; Dyan Cannon, with whom he had a daughter in 1966; and lastly, Barbara Harris. At one point he underwent psychotherapy and was treated with LSD to help him with what he considered inadequacies. Fortunately, these shortcomings did not lessen his popularity any. The handsome features, complete with the cleft chin that was his trademark, the suave good-naturedness and the sophistication never left Grant. In 1964 he was the number one favorite of teenagers and in 1965, he was their second choice.

Grant never won an Oscar in spite of being nominated twice, but many other people in his films did. Finally, in 1970, the Academy of Motion Picture Arts honored him with a special award for "his unique mastery of the art of screen acting."

Grant died in Davenport, Iowa on November 29, 1986 at the age of eighty-one.

GRASSLEY, CHARLES EMEST, (1933-   ) — a U.S. Representative and a U.S. Senator from Iowa; born in New Hartford, Butler County, Iowa, September 17, 1933; attended the public schools; graduated, University of Northern Iowa, Cedar Falls, 1955; received a graduate degree from the same university in 1956; pursued graduate work, University of Iowa, Iowa City, 1957-1958; engaged in agriculture; part-time university instructor; member, Iowa house of representatives 1959-1974; elected in 1974 as a Republican to the Ninety-fourth Congress; reelected to the Ninety-fifth and Ninety-sixth Congresses (January 3, 1975-January 3, 1981); was not a candidate in 1980 for reelection to the House of Representatives but was elected to the United States Senate for the term commencing January 3, 1981; reelected in 1986 for the term ending January 3, 1993.

GREEN, WILLIAM RAYMOND, (1856-1947) — a U.S. Representative from Iowa; born in Colchester, New London County, Conn., November 7, 1856; attended the public schools in Malden, Ill. and Princeton (Ill.) High School; was graduated from Oberlin College at Oberlin, Ohio, in 1879; studied law; was admitted to the bar in 1882 and commenced practice in Dow City, Iowa; moved his office to Audubon, Iowa, in 1884; judge of the district court in the fifteenth judicial district of Iowa from 1894 until 1911, when he resigned; elected as a Republican to the Sixty-second Congress to fill the vacancy caused by the resignation of Walter I. Smith; reelected to the Sixty-third and to the seven succeeding Congresses and served from June 5, 1911, until March 31, 1928, when he resigned; chairman, Committee on Ways and Means (Sixty-eighth through Seventieth Congresses); appointed a judge of the Court of Claims of the United States and served from April 1, 1928, until May 29, 1940, when he resigned, but was recalled and continued to serve until June 1942; retired from active pursuits and resided at Bellport, N.Y., until his death there on June 11, 1947; interment in Rock Creek Cemetery, Washington, D.C.

GREIGG, STANLEY LLOYD, (1931-   ) — a U.S. Representative from Iowa; born in Ireton, Sioux County, Iowa, May 7, 1931; moved with his parents to Hawarden, Iowa, in 1938 and to Sioux City in 1941; attended the public schools; graduated from Morningside College, B.A., 1954; M.A., Syracuse University, Maxwell Graduate School, 1956; served in the United States Navy, 1957-1959; returned to Morningside College in 1959 and was named Dean of Men; elected to the city council of Sioux City in 1961 and was selected to be mayor by council members in January 1964; elected as a Democrat to the Eighty-ninth Congress (January 3, 1965-January 3, 1967); unsuccessful candidate for reelection in 1966 to the Ninetieth Congress; director, Post Office Department's Office of Regional Administration, 1967-1969; deputy chairman, Democratic National Committee, 1970-1972; director, Lawrence F. O'Brien Center, Dag Hammarskjold College, 1972; director, Office of Intergovernmental Relations, Congressional Budget Office, 1975 to present; is a resident of Bethesda, Md.

GRIMES, JAMES WILSON, (1816-1872) — third governor of Iowa (1854-58), was born in Deering, Hillsboro County, New Hampshire on October 20, 1816, son of John and Elizabeth (Wilson) Grimes. His ancestors were Scotch-Irish emigrants from the north of Ireland, who settled at Londonderry, New Hampshire in 1719. His father was a thrifty farmer of sterling integrity and worth. The son received his classical education at Hampton Academy and Dartmouth College. He studied law under James Walker, at Peterboro, New Hampshire, and in May 1836, began a practice at Burlington, Iowa, which was then a part of the Black Hawk purchase in Wisconsin Territory. He was highly successful as a lawyer, and from 1841 to 1853, practiced in partnerhship with Henry W. Starr.

His first public service was as secretary of the Indian Commission at Rock Island, on September 27, 1836, where the Sacs and Foxes relinquished to the United States their lands along the Missouri River. During 1837-38, he was assistant-librarian in the Wisconsin library, and after the formation of Iowa Territory, represented Des Moines County in its legislature in 1838 and 1843, serving in the general assembly of the state in 1852. In August, 1854, he was elected by both Whig and Free-Soil Democratic parties as governor of Iowa. Though reared among Whig principles, his whole career was marked by freedom from party bias. During his administration he opposed the Missouri Compromise and did much to foster Free-Soil sentiment throughout Iowa.

In 1856, the capital of the state was changed from Iowa City to Des Moines. Grimes served as a commissioner for the founding of the Insane Hospital at Mt. Pleasant, giving careful attention to the trust. In July, 1856, he convened a special session of the general assembly to act on land grants received from Congress for the construction of railroads. In August of the same year, he addressed a remonstrance to President Pierce against the treatment of Iowa settlers in Kansas. He relinquished the position of governor in January, 1858, and in the same year was elected to the U.S. Senate for a term of six years. He was reelected and served from March 4, 1859 until December 6, 1869, when he resigned on account of ill-health.

Grimes was one of the founders of the Republican Party, which he represented in the Senate. Though seldom making a set speech, he was always a ready and vigorous debater. He was a prominent worker on the pensions, naval affairs, District of Columbia and other committees, and on July 4, 1861, he obtained an order from the secretary of war setting free the escaped slaves confined in a Washington jail, thus inaugurating the first official act of emancipation. He urged the building of iron-clads, and on March 13, 1862, spoke on the achievements of the western naval flotilla, becoming a recognized authority in all matters pertaining to the navy. Among the works due largely to his advocacy were the return of the Naval Academy from Newport to Annapolis, the establishment of a national armory at Rock Island, and of a navy yard at League Island. Politically he was remarkable for independence of character, and, though a Republican, opposed a high protective tariff and President Lincoln's enlargement of the regular army.

During the impeachment trial of President Johnson, he considered himself in the light of a judge rather than a representative, and although his physical condition required severe fortitude to do so, he entered the Senate and cast his vote for acquittal. Later he said: "Neither the honors nor the wealth of the world could have induced me to act otherwise than I did; and I have never for a moment regretted that I voted as I did. I shall always thank God that He gave me courage to stand firm in the midst of the clamor, and by my vote, not only save the Republican Party, but prevent such a precedent being established as would in the end have converted ours into a sort of South American republic, in which there would be a revolution whenever there happened to be an adverse majority in Congress to the President for the time being." Though then greatly censured by his party, the New York *Times* said years afterward: "No braver or more faithful man ever sat in the Senate than Mr. Grimes, who, almost alone, saved his party from an incalculable blunder..."

Grimes founded a free library in Burlington, a professorship in Iowa College (Grinnell), and scholarships both at that college and Dartmouth. The degree of LL.D. was conferred upon him by both Dartmouth and Iowa colleges in 1865.

He was married to Elizabeth Sarah Nealley. After living in Europe for two years, with temporary intervals of improved health, he died suddenly in Burlington, Iowa on February 7, 1872.

GUTHRIE, JANET, (1938 -) — race car driver and first woman ever to compete in the Indianapolis 500. She was born in Iowa City, Iowa, the eldest of William Lain Guthrie's five children. Mr. Guthrie was an airline pilot and Janet learned to fly at a young age. She was thirteen when she started learning and seventeen when she earned her pilot's license. At the age of twenty, she had her instructor's license. Her family moved to Florida where she attended prep school and later, she attended the University of

GUTHRIE

Michigan, majoring in physics. She completed her B.S. degree in 1960.

After college, Miss Guthrie worked as an aerospace research and development engineer at the Republic Aviation Corporation in Farmingdale, Long Island. While there, she tested for NASA's scientist astronaut program -- one of only four women to do so -- but was later eliminated because she did not have a Ph.D.

In 1961, Miss Guthrie started to pursue an interest in race car driving. After purchasing a used Jaguar XK 120 and joining local sports car clubs, she began entering gymkhana competitions. In 1962, she became the women's gymkhana champion of Long Island. Later, she enrolled in race car driving classes, bought a used Jaguar XK 140 and rebuilt the engine. She then began driving in races and endurance competitions.

Guthrie was able to quit her job in 1967 and do some free lance technical editing while devoting more time to racing. Between 1964 and 1975, she had raced in approximately 100 races, including the Daytona twenty-four hour endurance race, and had a record of nine straight finishes in the country's top endurance events.

In 1975, Guthrie went to work as a "consumer information specialist" for Toyota. A few months later, she received a call from Rolla-Vollstedt, an Oregon lumber executive, requesting her to drive one of two race cars he was planning on entering in the Indy 500 that year. Guthrie accepted Vollstedt's offer and announced her intention in March of 1976, to race in the Indy. At Indianapolis in May of that year, Guthrie passed the rookie test but was unable to get her car up to the qualifying speed in order to race in the Indy 500.

In 1977, Guthrie had another chance at the Indy, this time with a new car which Vollstedt also provided for her. On a practice run she crashed into a wall at 191 m.p.h., but fortunately she and the car recovered in time to make the big race on May 29. Unfortunately, Guthrie met with disappointment again when her car had engine trouble and she had to quit the race after only twenty-seven laps. As a result, she finished in twenty-ninth place. Fortunately, she had yet another chance at the Indy the following year and this time finished in ninth place.

Although Guthrie is a contender in a typically male sports event, she has not lost her femininity in the least. Inside the pits as well as outside, she is as well manicured as her environment will allow and is always a lady. She is not married, however, and considers this aspect of her life a sacrifice she has to make in order to continue racing.

Miss Guthrie has won several awards during her racing career, including the Curtis Turner award from the National Association for Stock Car Racing in 1976; she first in her class in the Sebring twelve-hour endurance race in 1970; was North Atlantic Road Racing Champion in 1973 and was name to the women's Sports Hall of Fame in 1980.

H

HALL, JAMES NORMAN, (1897-1951) — social worker, soldier and author, was born in Colfax, Iowa, son of Arthur Wright and Ella Annette (Young) Hall. Hall took an early interest in writing, his literary hero being James Whitcomb Riley. His mother also served as encouragement for his love of books by reading to him and his siblings after Saturday night baths.

After graduating from Colfax High School in 1904, Hall worked in a clothing store while trying to decide whether or not to go to college. Having decided to go, he attended Grinnell College, from where he also graduated in 1910 with a Ph.B.

After graduating from college, between the years of 1910 and 1914, Hall was a case worker at the Society for the Prevention of Cruelty to Children. Meanwhile, he continued to write and submit articles in between rejection slips.

In 1914, Hall went to England, enlisted in the British Army and fought in France as a tailgunner. In 1918, he was commissioned a captain in the Lafayette Escadrille and while flying a fighter plane, was shot down and taken prisoner.

In 1919, Hall was sent home and commissioned to write, along with Charles Nordoff, about the History of the Lafayette Flying Corps. The two writers developed an extraordinary partnership during the writing of the book and decided in 1920 to move together to Tahiti to write. They first received a commission from *Harper's* to produce a series of articles on the South Sea Islands and they were off. After writing the articles, the team parted in their writing pursuits and each man wrote solo for awhile, however, neither met with much success. It was eight years before Hall and Nordoff would write together again.

Hall and Nordoff's first published book after their reunion, was *Falcons of France,* which told the stories of their flying experiences in the Escadrille. Next, they completed their most notable work, the *Bounty* trilogy. The three novels consisted of *Mutiny on the Bounty, Men Against the Sea,* and *Pitcairn's Island.*

They tell the story of Captain William Bligh and the men that sailed with him and revolted against him on the ship *Bounty*.

Other novels they produced include *The Hurricane, The Dark River, Out of Gas, Botany Bay, Men Without Country,* and *The High Barbaree.* On his own, Hall wrote such novels as *Kitchener's Mob, High Adventure, On the Stream of Travel, Mid-Pacific, Flying With Chaucer,* and many others.

Nordoff divorced his native wife and moved back to California in 1940. Seven years later he was dead from suicide. Discouraged and depressed over his friend's death, Hall found it difficult to write. He persevered and in 1951, managed to publish *The Far Lands* which was well received and established him as a solo author. He continued to write -- essays, novels and poetry -- until his death.

In 1925, Hall had married the half Tahitian girl, Sarah Winchester with whom he had two children.

In 1950, Grinnell College awarded Hall an honorary LL.D. degree at his class reunion.

James Hall died on July 6, 1951 in Papeete, Tahiti. He was buried on a hill overlooking the bay that had been so much a part of his writing.

HAMILTON, DANIEL WEBSTER, (1861-1936) — a U.S. Representative from Iowa; born near Dixon, Ogle County, Ill., December 10, 1861; moved to Miami County, Kans., with his parents in 1868 and to Prairie Township, Keokuk County, Iowa, in 1874; attended the country schools and was graduated from the law department of the University of Iowa at Iowa City in June 1884; was admitted to the bar in 1884 and commenced practice in Sigourney, Iowa; postmaster of Sigourney 1894-1898; elected as a Democrat to the Sixtieth Congress (March 4, 1907-March 3, 1909);

unsuccessful candidate for reelection in 1908 to the Sixty-first Congress; resumed the practice of law in Sigourney, Iowa; moved to Grinnell, Iowa, when elected judge of the district court of the sixth judicial district of Iowa in 1918, in which capacity he served until his death in Rochester, Minn., August 21, 1936; interment in No. 16 Cemetery, near Thornburg, in Keokuk County, Iowa.

HAMMILL, JOHN, (1875-1936) — twenty-fourth governor of Iowa (1925-31), was born on October 14, 1875, in Linden, Wisconsin, the son of George and Mary (Brewer) Hammill. He attended Iowa State University, receiving an LL.B. degree in 1897, and soon after, was practicing law in Britt, Iowa. He entered the political arena when he ran for attorney of Hancock County on the Republican ticket, serving two terms, from 1902 to 1906. Between 1908 and 1912, he served in the Iowa State Senate. From 1920 to 1924 he was lieutenant-governor of the state, and secured the governorship in 1924, serving for three terms.

One of his first decisions as governor was to convince the state legislature to pass a measure in favor of the creation of the State Banking Board, whose responsibility it was to establish banking laws. Another measure he was able to secure was one in which the responsibility of the state's primary roads was to be under the aegis of the State Highway Commission. Other decisions made during his tenure included the creation of the Child Welfare Department, whose responsibility it was to oversee the state institutions that took care of children; the inclusion of junior colleges under the public school system umbrella; and the admittance, by a constitutional amendment, of women to the state's General Assembly.

After retiring from the governorship in 1931, Hammill returned to a private law practice, and also had a large farm where he engaged in a thriving livestock business. Although no longer in politics, Hammill served on the Better Iowa Schools Commission and the National Committee of Prisons and Prison Labor. One source described him thusly: "A sincere, straightforward and unassuming man, he was one of the most popular governors in the history of Iowa and was much loved by the people of his community."

Hammill was married to Fannie Richards. He died on April 6, 1936 in Minneapolis, Minnesota.

HANSEN, JOHN ROBERT, (1901-1974) — a U.S. Representative from Iowa; born in Manning, Carroll County, Iowa, August 24, 1901; attended the Manning public schools; attended the State University of Iowa, 1919-1921; sales representative, general manager, and president of Dultmeier Manufacturing Co., Manning, Iowa, 1921-1962, and president of Dultmeier Sales, Omaha, Nebr., 1934-1957; member of the Carroll County Democratic Central committee, 1932-1944, and chairman, 1944-1952; delegate to Democratic National Convention in 1948 and 1964; district committeeman on the Democratic State central committee, 1952- 1957; Sixth District Democratic chairman, 1953- 1957; member of the Board of Control of State Institutions, 1957- 1960; member of executive council of the Governor's Alcoholism Commission and the Commission on Interstate Cooperation, 1957- 1960; Democratic nominee for Lieutenant Governor in 1960; elected as a Democrat to the Eighty-ninth Congress (January 3, 1965- January 3, 1967); unsuccessful candidate for reelection in 1966 to the Ninetieth Congress; member, Iowa State Highway Commission, from February 1967 until retirement on July 1, 1969; died in Des Moines, Iowa, September 23, 1974; interment in Manning Cemetery, Manning, Iowa.

HARDING, WILLIAM LLOYD, (1877-1934) — twenty-second governor of Iowa (1917-21), was born on October 3, 1877 in Sibley, Iowa, the son of Orlando Boardman and Emma (Moyer) Harding. He attended Morningside College in Sioux City, Iowa, then secured a law degree from the University of South Dakota in 1905. After graduating, he headed a successful law office in Sioux City.

Harding got involved in politics, and was elected to the Iowa State Legislature in 1906 on the Republican ticket, a post he was reelected to twice more. Creating an impressive record there, he was elected lieutenant-governor in 1912, and again in 1914, then secured the governorship in 1916, serving two terms. Due to the fact that he was governor during World War I, he had to deal with a lot of added issues concerning the war effort. As per the needs of Iowa, he supported education for children, both in the cities and rural areas, established state parks, and tried to create a foreign trade corporation that would oversee the buying and exporting of American agricultural products to other countries.

When Harding left the governorship, he returned to the practice of law as a private citizen in the Des Moines firm of Oliver, Harding & Oliver. He also spent a great deal of his time lecturing. Harding was married to Carrie May Lamoreaux, and the couple had one daughter. He died on December 17, 1934, in Des Moines, Iowa.

HARKIN, THOMAS RICHARD, (1939-   ) — a U.S. Representative and U.S. Senator from Iowa; born in Cumming, Warren County, Iowa, November 19, 1939; attended the public schools; graduated, Iowa State University, Ames, 1962; graduated, Catholic University of America Law School, Washington, D.C., 1972; admitted to the Iowa bar in 1972 and commenced practice in Des Moines; served in United States Navy 1962-1967; attorney for Polk County, Iowa, Legal Aid Society 1973; member, board of directors, Iowa Consumers League; elected in 1974 as a Democrat to the Ninety-fourth Congress; reelected to the four succeeding Congresses (January 3, 1975-January 3, 1985); was not a candidate for reelection in 1984 to the House of Representatives but was elected to the United States Senate for the term ending January 3, 1991.

HARRINGTON, VINCENT FRANCIS, (1903-1943) — a U.S. Representative from Iowa; born in Sioux City, Woodbury County, Iowa, May 16, 1903; attended the public schools and Trinity College of his native city; was graduated from the University of Notre Dame, South Bend, Ind., in 1925; instructor in history and economics and athletic director at the University of Portland, Portland, Oreg., 1926-1927; returned to Sioux City, Iowa, in 1927 and became vice president and general manager of a mortgage company; member of the State senate 1933-1937; was nominated as a candidate for Lieutenant Governor of Iowa in 1936 but withdrew to accept a nomination for the House of Representatives; elected as a Democrat to the Seventy-fifth, Seventy-sixth, and Seventy- seventh Congresses and served from January 3, 1937, until his resignation on September 5, 1942, to accept a commission as major in the Air Corps, United

HEGGEN

States Army; died at Rutlandshire, England: on November 29, 1943, while on active duty in England interment in the United States Military Cemetery at Brookwood, thirty miles southwest of London, England.

HEGGEN, THOMAS ORLO, (1919-1949) — was an author and playwrigh. His most noted work was the popular novel and play, "Mister Roberts."

Born in Fort Dodge, Iowa on December 23, 1919, he atended Oklahoma City University, Oklahoma State College and the University of Minnesota. He received a B.A. degree from the University of Minnesota. Heggen worked briefly in the editorial department of *Reader's Digest* magazine. He served in the U.S. Navy, participating in campaigns in Guam, Peleliu, Iwo Jima and Okinawa. He was released from active duty in 1946 with the rank of lieutenant.

Heggen's novel, "Mister Roberts," was published in 1946 by Houghton Mifflin Co. The book was written in part while Heggen was serving as communications officer aboard an attack cargo ship in the Pacific Ocean. Heggen wrote a play based on the novel in collaboration with Joshua Logan. The play was produced by Leland Hayward and starred Henry Fonda in the title role. The play was a huge success, remaining at the Alvin Theater in New York for three years and 1,077 performances. It was also performed on the road in cities throughout the United States, as well as in London and Paris. The novel was also adapted into a film version.

By 1949, more than 100,000 copies of "Mister Roberts" were sold, plus 6,00 play versions and 750,000 paperback copies. Eventually, one million copies of the paperback version were sold. Heggen received the Perry Award of the Americana Theater

Wing for the outstanding play of 1947-48 and the Donaldson Award as co-author of the play in that same year. A memorial library was established in his name at the University of Minnesota.

Heggen married Carol Lynn Gilmer in 1942. The couple did not have children. He died on May 19, 1949.

HEMPSTEAD, STEPHEN, (1812-1883) — second governor of Iowa (1850-54), was born in New London, Connecticut on October 1, 1812, the son of Joseph and Celinda (Hutchinson) Hempstead. Stephen Hempstead moved with his parents to St. Louis, Missouri in 1828, and the family eventually settled on a farm near Bellefontaine. Soon after, he began working as a clerk in Galena, Illinois. During the Black Hawk War in 1832 he served as an officer of an artillery company organized to protect the town from the Sac and Fox Indians, who, under their leader, Black Hawk, were threatening the area near Rock River. After the defeat of this renowned chieftain, Hempstead studied for two years at Illinois College, later reading law with his uncle, Judge Charles S. Hempstead, a prominent lawyer of Galena. In 1836, he was admitted to practice in all courts of Wisconsin (to which territory the Iowa district belonged), and settled in Dubuque, Iowa, where he made his permanent home.

Upon the organization of the territorial government of Iowa in July, 1838, Hempstead was elected to represent Dubuque and the adjoining counties in the legislative council, which assembled at Burlington in November of that year. He was a born leader, and always held a foremost position in that body. At the next session, he was elected president of the council, filling the position most acceptably, and in 1845, was reelected at the session held in Iowa City, then the capital of the territory. In 1848, he was appointed with Judge Mason, of Burlington, and Judge Woodward, of Muscatine, to the codifying commission which compiled "The Code of Iowa" of 1851. He was elected governor of Iowa in 1850, a position which he honorably filled for four years (the term as per the constitution of 1846, under which Iowa became a state). His oratory was forcible and eloquent, and his administration of affairs, highly commendable.

In 1855, he was elected a county judge of Dubuque County, and held the office for a period of fourteen years. Upon the abolishment of the office in 1869, he was at once elected auditor of Dubuque County, serving by reelection until 1873; when his health became impaired, he retired from public life. He was induced about a year before his death, however, to accept the office of justice of the peace. His decisions were considered equitable and just.

Governor Hempstead was married to Lavinia Moore, and the couple had three sons and three daughters. He died on February 16, 1883.

HERBST, JOSEPHINE, (1897-1969) — author, was born in Sioux City, Iowa to William Benton and Mary (Frey) Herbst. She attended Morningside College, the University of Iowa, and the University of California at Berkley where she completed her A.B. degree in 1918.

During the 1920's and 1930's, Miss Herbst held a variety of jobs including that of editorial reader for H.C. Mencken and George Jean Nathan on *Smart Set.* She also wrote for Scribner's and for Mencken on the *American Mercury.*

In 1935, she was a correspondent for the *New York Post* in Germany and managed to speak to members of the underground opposition to Hitler's regime. In that same year she was in Cuba during the general strike and in Spain in 1937, during that country's civil war -- she was one of the few women correspondents allowed to visit the front lines. She also spent some time in Paris where she became friends with Ernest Hemingway, Nathan Asch, and John Herrmann, the latter whom she married in 1926. After Pearl Harbor, Herbst volunteered to work in the Office of the Coordinator of Information in Washington where she put together anti-Nazi propaganda for broadcast overseas. However, shortly after she began, she was dismissed from this position because of her left wing political views. After her dismissal she never again became involved in political or social activism.

In the late 1920's, Miss Herbst had begun to get her own works published. Her first book, *Nothing is Sacred,* was published in 1928, and tells the story of a midwestern family who face a series of crises involving debt, alcohol and adultery. Both of the novels she wrote during that decade tended to deal with the decay of traditional values in society. During the 1930's, her greatest literary achievement was the Trexler-Wendel trilogy: *Pity is Not Enough, The Executioner waits,* and *Rope of Gold.* These three books follow the development of the American society from the Civil War to the Depression and shows how capitalism overpowered generations of people and caused them to lose their sense of integrity before the social and economic crises of the 1930's promoted the expansion of radical views and the working class began to question the efficacy of the system itself.

Other books she went on to write include *Satan's Sergeants, Somewhere the Tempest Fell,* and *New Green World.* For her work, Miss Herbst was awarded a Guggenheim fellowship in fiction in 1936; a Longview Foundation award in 1960; a Rockefeller Foundation grant in 1965; and a National Institute of Arts and Letters grant in 1966.

Josephine Herbst died on January 28, 1969, in New York City. Miss Herbst held to the belief that "The artist seeks to tell us what the world is or isn't; what it should be or even what it cannot be outside the realm of some transcendent dream."

HERRING, CLYDE LAVERNE, (1879-1945) — twenty-sixth governor of Iowa (1933-37), and United States Senator (1937-43), was born on May 3, 1879 in Jackson, Michigan, the son of James Gwynn and Stella Mae (Addison) Herring. After receiving his education in public schools, Herring secured a job in Detroit as a jewelry store clerk, and after that, moved to Colorado where he worked as a rancher; it was there that he received the appointment of postmaster from President Theodore Roosevelt. Herring returned to Iowa in 1906, settling in Massena, and running a farm. His next business venture was in the automobile industry, where in Atlantic, Iowa, he sold cars for Henry Ford, whom he had met earlier in Detroit. He did the same work for the Ford Automobile Co. in Des Moines, then in 1912, he established the Herring Motor Co., which manufactured and sold not only cars, but car supplies, tractors, and even Curtis airplanes. By 1926 he had founded, and was overseer of, the Herring Wissler Co. which distributed wholesale automobile parts.

Herring's interest in politics was sparked by his post as U.S. fuel administrator for Polk County during World War I. After the war, he ran for, unsuccessfully, governor of Iowa, and the U.S. Senate, both on the Democratic ticket. In 1932, he again ran for the governorship, this time successfully, becoming the second Democrat in Iowa to win that office. His first decision as governor, in the midst of the Great Depression, was a ban on any foreclosures on farms and homes, and soon after, he helped push through the Farm and Home Mortgage Moratorium Law. Initially there was some resistance to the measure, but eventuallly, the U.S. Circuit Court of Appeals upheld the decision, and the law ended up being used as an example for other states to follow.

Another somewhat courageous decision Herring made was to close the Iowa banks for a time in order to protect both the stockholders and the depositors. He went one step further by creating legislation in which the banks would be reorganized and rehabilitated. The law, known as "Senate File 111" was impressive enough to be used as a model by the U.S. Government, specifically by President Franklin D. Roosevelt, who proclaimed a holiday for national banks, which according to one source, "brought about nationwide conservation and rehabilitation of the entire banking system." Other decisions by Herring included: the establishment of a financial control system, under which the state government could only spend the exact amount of whatever revenues were available at any given time; a state monopoly liquor system; and the issuance of old-age assistance legislation.

Herring served in the United States Senate from 1937 to 1943. His subsequent appointment was as Senior Deputy Administrator for the Office of Price Administration, a post he served in for less than a year, after which, he left public life and returned to his business interests. Herring was married to Emma Pearl Spinney, and the couple had three sons. He died in Washington, D.C. on September 15, 1945.

HICKENLOOPER, BOURKE BLAKEMORE,
(1896-1971) — twenty- ninth governor of Iowa (1943-45), and United States Senator, was born on July 21, 1896 in Blockton, Iowa. He attended Iowa State College, earning a B.S. degree in 1920, and continued his education at the University of Iowa where he received a law degree in 1922, passing the Iowa bar soon after. His first law position was for the firm of Johnson, Donnelly, and Lynch. In 1935 he teamed up with another attorney and established the law firm of Hickenlooper and Mitvalsky, a company name which one reporter wryly noted, made for a "tricky shingle."

1935 was also the year that Hickenlooper entered the political arena when he was elected to the Iowa House of Representatives on the Republican ticket. During 1939-43, he served as lieutenant-governor, then in the latter year, was elected to the governorship where he served one term. During his tenure, the most impressive feat by Hickenlooper was his helping to increase the state's income by $9,000,000, which gave the budget a surplus of $54,000,000. After leaving the governorship, Hickenlooper served in the United States Senate from 1945 to 1969, during which time he was appointed to two powerful committees: the Senate's Special Committee on Atomic Energy, and the Joint Congressional Committee on Atomic Energy.

Hickenlooper was married to Verna Eilene Bensch and the couple had two children. He died on September 4, 1971.

HOEGH, LEO A., (1908-) — was Governor of Iowa from 1954 to 1957.

Born in Audubon City, Iowa on March 30, 1908, he attended the University of Iowa, receiving a Bachelor of Arts degree in 1929, and a law degree in 1932. In 1937 he began serving in the Iowa House of Representatives, a position he held until 1942. During 1941, he was the City Attorney for Charton, and during 1953-55, he served as Attorney General of Iowa.

In 1954, he was the victor in the governor's race against Democratic candidate, Clyde E. Herring, taking office in January of 1955. His accomplishments during his term included escalation of the highway construction program, modernizing the school system, which included the increase of state funds to education, and the upgrading of Iowa's agricultural research facilities. He was able to implement these improvements after raising the sales tax on such things as alcohol, cigarettes and gasoline, as well as increasing corporate income tax.

However, his decision to raise these taxes contributed to his defeat in the subsequent election, which he lost to Herschel Loveless. His post-governor jobs included serving as a civil defense administrator (1957-58); director of the Office of Civil and Defense Mobilization; and director and general counsel of the Soypro International.

Elthon is married to Mary Louise Foster and the couple have two daughters.

HOEVEN, CHARLES BERNARD, (1895-1980) — a U.S. Representative from Iowa; born in Hospers, Sioux County, Iowa, March 30, 1895; at tended the public schools and Alton (Iowa) High school State University of Iowa at Iowa City, B.A., in 1920 and' from its law department, LL.B., 1922; was admitted to the bar in 1922 and commenced practice in Alton, Iowa; during the First World War served as a sergeant, Company Three Hundred and Fiftieth Infantry, Eighty-eighth Division, and with the Intelligence Service, First Battalion, in England and France; county attorney of Sioux County, Iowa, 1925-1937; member of the State senate 1937-1941, serving as president pro-tempore 1939-1941; temporary and permanent chairman of Iowa Republican State Judicial convention in 1942; delegate to each Iowa State Republican convention from 1925 to 1970 and chairman in 1940; delegate to Republican National Convention, 1964; elected as a Republican to the Seventy-eighth and to the ten succeeding Congresses (January 3, 1943-January 3, 1965); chairman, Republican Conference (Eighty-ninth Congress); was not a candidate for renomination in 1964 to the Eighty-ninth Congress; vice president of savings bank; resided in Orange City, Iowa, where he died November 9, 1980; interment in Nassau Township Cemetery, Alton, Iowa.

HOOVER, HERBERT CLARK, (1874-1964) — began his professional life as a very successful mining engineer and was eventually elected as the thirty-first President of the United States.

Born on August 10, 1874 in West Branch, Iowa, Hoover's father died of a heart attack when the boy was six. His mother turned to the Quaker religion and often traveled to attend revival meetings. After she died, when Herbert was ten years old, he went to live with relatives in Oregon where he attended his uncle's school. He later enrolled at Stanford University, choosing geology as his major, and secured summer work withthe U.S. Geological Survey.

While in college, Hoover became known for his business acumen. In 1895, he graduated from Stanford and went to work in the mines of California, receiving several promotions within a short period of time. It was the beginning of an impressive career in the mining industry. He was hired by a company in London who sent him to Australia where he found gold in one of the mines, which brought wealth to the company and him. He continued his successful mining endeavors in China as chief engineer for the Chinese Engineering and Mining Company where he discovered a vast amount of coal. His reputation in the mining industry grew rapidly due to his knowledge concerning all aspects of the business, plus his ability to continually find various metals such as lead, zinc, copper and silver. He was often brought in as a troubleshooter and his ability to get several companies back on their feet financially garnered him the description "doctor of sick mines." By 1913, Hoover had made himself a small fortune of almost $4 million.

During most of this time, Hoover resided in London, and began writing several articles concerning the financial and technical aspects on mining, and also published the 1909 book *Principles of Mining* which was used for many years as a training manual in mining schools. He was a supporter of various reforms such as the eight-hour day, and mining safety. He also served as president of the American Institute of Mining and Metallurgical Engineers, and was also the publisher of *Mining Magazine.*

By the time Hoover was forty, he was a rich man, and was in search of a new challenge. After the start of World War I, He was appointed as overseer of the Commission for Relief. The first country to be the recipient of the much-needed food was Belgium, a country which had been pillaged by the German army. Due to his hard-headed stubbornness and his ability to persuade people to give contributions, he was able to get the warring factions to co-exist while helping to feed the almost 9 million people in need. He also did the same for 2 million people in France. His methods and results did not go unnoticed by President Woodrow Wilson who gave Hoover the position of food administrator in 1917, nor by many other Americans who gave him the name, the Great Engineer.

While the war was still raging, he was faced with the dilemma of what to do with surplus food and other products if the war should end suddenly. He came up with the idea of sending the extra food to war-torn Europe. Hoover was then named as chairman of the Inter-Allied Food Council. Other posts he held during that time include: director general of the American Relief Administration; economic director of the Supreme Economic Council; and chairman of the European Coal Council. He also served as personal advisor to President Wilson at the Versailles Peace Conference.

Hoover, more than likely due to his Quaker upbringing, believed in social change brought about by equal opportunity, hard work, service to the community, and a basic simplicity of life. Many of these ideas were often expounded upon in magazine articles penned by him, as well as in his book *American Individualism* (1922). Disagreeing with those alarmists who insisted that all of America's troubles were caused by the "Reds," he called on those who might be "pioneers" to examine "continents of human welfare of which we have penetrated only the coastal plain."

When Woodrow Wilson named Hoover as vice-chairman of the Second Industrial Conference, which took place in December of 1919, the latter offered up several proposals such as a more equitable profit distribution between capital and labor, equal pay for men and women, strict child labor laws, a minimum wage law, and better housing.

In 1920, his supporters tried to convince Hoover to announce his candidacy for the Republican Presidential nomination, but he declined. After Warren G. Harding became President, Hoover was appointed to the post of secretary of commerce. During that time, he was mainly involved with farming and labor concerns, and with the President's help, was able to force the steel industry to relinquish the twelve-hour work day. One of Hoover's other accomplishments was the Boulder Canyon Project Act of 1928, which helped build the Boulder Dam. In 1947, it was renamed the Hoover Dam in his honor.

After Hoover's handling of the relief efforts concerning the Mississippi flood in 1927, he was being touted for political office. When Calvin Coolidge made the decision not to run for another term, Hoover accepted his party's nomination this time, which was confirmed easily at the Republican National Convention in Kansas City. The two major issues in the contest between Hoover and his opponent, Governor Alfred E. Smith, was prohibition and Smith's Catholicism, the second of which was a major issue, especially in the South. However, Hoover's main platform dealt with the issue of prosperity for the country that would hopefully come from heightened productivity in such areas as agriculture and the building of new highways.

Hoover won the election by over six million votes. The progressive stance that Hoover had been associated with even as a young man, was still apparent during his Presidency. He believed passionately in reforms, and immediately went to work to improve such social problems as conservation, civil rights, prison reform, child welfare, and the plight of the Native American. Another issue he supported was farm cooperatives, and as such, he passed the Agricultural Marketing Act of June 1929. The bill ended up being a big help after the Great Depression hit later that year. As Hoover wrote in his autobiography, *Memoirs,* he was able to turn the Federal Farm Board "into a depression remedy."

Hoover, whose financial instincts were often correct, sensed long before he was elected President that things could get out of control with the heavy proliferation of stock market speculation. By the time he was in office, it was too late to take any action that wouldn't eventually make things worse. As such, Hoover was not necessarily surprised when the stock market crashed in October of 1929. However, immediately afterward, he wasted no time in trying to remedy what he could and formed the Conference for Continued Industrial Progress, a group of leaders from different types of industry, including agricultural, financial and labor.

The one glaring weakness in Hoover's plan for the country was his apparent inability to offer direct federal relief to individuals, while he mostly concentrated on helping banking and industrial institutions that had failed. His attitude was that the bureaucracy of federal programs would not be as effective as voluntary relief from individuals, believing that in times of need, the true giving nature of people would show itself. In addition, Hoover was worried that such a huge outlay of funds would exhaust the government treasury, and that people would be less inclined to want to work, an ethic he was adamant about. However, he was finally forced to accept the inevitable and come up with programs to help alleviate the problem, such as the Reconstruction Finance Corporation, which provided funds to both business and individuals, as well as the President's Emergency Committee on Employment, and the President's Organization on Unemployment Relief. While Hoover's obvious disdain of welfare contributed to his eventual downfall, another incident finalized it when a large group of out-of-work war veterans and their families converged on Washington, D.C. in 1932, hoping to convince the President to give them an advance on a bonus they weren't supposed to receive until 1945. When their main camp was broken up by General Douglas MacArthur, who had overridden Hoover's original orders, the President's silence was deafening, as the veterans were now homeless and Hoover was seen as the villain.

In the 1932 race for the Presidency against Franklin D. Roosevelt, Hoover's popularity was at an all time low, and he lost the election by more than seven million votes. The situation got worse as Hoover and the President-elect argued about various things while the economy continued to plummet. The situation got so bad that it spawned the Twentieth Amendment, which changed the taking of office by an incoming President from March to January. According to the Dictionary of American Biography, Hoover "left the White House a lonely and bitter figure, shunned by many former friends."

After returning to private life, Hoover wrote several books, the first being *The Challenge to Liberty* in 1934. He followed that with a series of eight volumes (beginning in 1936 and ending in 1961), entitled *Addresses Upon the American Road*. He continued to be vocal about various issues and offered advice to Presidents Truman and Eisenhower.

HOOVER

Favoring isolationism, he told Truman that he had "no patience with people who formulated politics in respect to other nations 'short of war.' They always lead to war." Hoover felt that the responsibility of the United States "should be to persuade, hold up our banner of what we thought was right and let it go at that."

At President Truman's request, Hoover was overseer of the food supplies that were shipped from the United States to thirty- eight countries in 1946. In addition, during both the Truman and Eisenhower administrations (1947-49 and 1953-55), he organized the Hoover Commissions to help streamline governmental bureaucracy. Due to his advisory position within the government, his reputation improved greatly from the dark days after his Presidency and he came to be considered an elder statesman.

Hoover remained active until his death, publishing a biography on Woodrow Wilson in 1958, and a four-volume set of books concerning American relief, entitled *An American Epic* (1959-1964). Other books written by Hoover were: *American Ideals Versus the New Deal*, 1936; *America's First Crusade*, 1942; *The Problems of Lasting Peace*, 1942; *The Basis of Lasting Peace*, 1945; and a three-volume set of his autobiography entitled *The Memoirs of Herbert Hoover*, 1951-52.

In addition, several books were written about him, including: *Herbert Hoover: A Reminiscent Biography*, by Will Irwin, 1928; *The Truth About Hoover*, by Herbert Corey, 1932; *Our Unknown Ex-President*, by Eugene Lyons, 1948 (revised as *Herbert Hoover: A Biography*), 1964; *Herbert Hoover: Public Servant and Leader of the Loyal Opposition*, by Harold Wolfe, 1956; *Herbert Hoover: A Challenge for Today*, by Carol Green Wilson, 1968; *Herbert Hoover:*

Forgotten Progressive, by Joan Hoff Wilson, 1975; and *Herbert Hoover: A Public Life,* by David Burner, 1979.

Hoover was married to Lou Henry and the couple had two sons. He died on October 20, 1964.

HOPE, CLIFFORD RAGSDALE, (1893-1970) — congressman, was born in Birmingham, Iowa, to Harry M. Hope, a storekeeper and farmer, and Armitta Ragsdale. When Hope was young, the family moved to a ranch outside of Garden City, Kansas where he attended high school. After graduation, he attended Nebraska Wesleyan University for a year and then transferred to Washburn University in Topeka, Kansas where he studied law, completing his LL.B. degree in 1917.

For two years after graduation, Hope served with the Thirty- fifth and Eighty-fifth Infantry Divisions in the United States and France. When discharged in 1919, he went back to Garden City and began practicing law. In 1920, 22 and 24, he was elected to the Kansas House of Representatives from Finney County and in 1925, he was elected speaker of the house. In 1926, Hope ran for Congress as a Republican and was successful in securing a position in the Seventh District of western Kansas. In 1927, he was elected to the United States House of Representatives and sought appointment to the Committee on Agriculture. He ended up serving thirty consecutive years on that committee.

Clifford Hope's greatest contribution was in his advocacy of the American family farm. In his own words, he called it "one of our fundamental social institutions." Perhaps it was because he came from a farm family that he had such deep convictions about its value. Nevertheless, he did a great deal to write

HOPE

and help pass legislation as well as set up programs to assist farmers. In 1932, he and Senator Peter Norbeck sponsored the voluntary Domestic Allotment Plot which became the foundation of the Agricultural Act of 1933 and Hope was responsible for the Soil Conservation and Domestic Allotment Act of 1935.

In 1946, Hope coauthored the Research and Marketing Act, which promoted a scientific approach to production, utilization and distribution of food. In 1948, he coauthored the Hope-Aiken price-support law, which endorsed high fixed price subsistence for farmers and less federal control over production of agriculture. In 1953, he initiated the Farm Credit Act which increased the farmers' control over the federal farm credit system and in the same year, he coauthored the Hope-Aiken Watershed Act which made available federal aid to landowners for the conservation of water and topsoil. In 1954, Hope helped to get passed the Agricultural Trade Development and Assistance Act which allowed for overseas sale of farm surplus and charitable distribution of surplus to needy areas in the United States as well as foreign countries.

In 1956, Hope returned to Garden City and founded the Great Plains Wheat Company. He also helped to build a junior college in that city. In 1968, he was elected president of the Kansas State Historical Society.

Hope was a member of the United States Delegation at the first meeting of the Food and Agricultural Organization in Quebec in 1945; in Copenhagen in 1946; in Washington in 1949; and in Rome in 1951. He was the Congressional Advisor to the United States Delegation to the Inter-American Conservation Conference in 1948; to the International Wheat conferences in 1948, 1949 and 1952; and he was appointed by President Truman in 1952 as a member of the Missouri Basin Survey Commission.

Clifford Hope married Pauline Sanders and had three children: Edward, Clifford and Martha.

Hope died in Garden City on May 16, 1970.

HOPKINS, HARRY LLOYD, (1890-1946) — was a relief administrator,commerce secretary, and a close adviser to President Franklin D. Roosevelt.

Born in Sioux City, Iowa on August 17, 1890, he gaduated *cum laude* from Grinnell College, earning a B.A. degree in 1912. After deciding to forego a career in newspaper work, he went to New York City where he was hired by Christodora House, a social settlement, to act as a counselor for its summer camp for poor children at Bound Brook, New Jersey. This appointment, the opening step in a distinguished career in social service work, led to a connection with the Association for Improving the Condition of the Poor in New York City as an investigator and later as supervisor of case work. During 1913-17, he was executive secretary of the Board of Child Welfare of the city of New York, in which capacity he helped to inaugurate and administer the widows' pension system.

On January 1, 1918, after having been rejected from military service in the First World War due to poor eyesight, he was appointed secretary to the general manager of the American Red Cross at the national headquarters in Washington, D.C., and moved up the ranks to manager of the Southern division in Atlanta. In 1922, he returned to New York City and was made assistant director of the Association for Improving the Condition of the Poor. Two years later, he became director of the New York Tuberculosis (later the New York Tuberculosis and Health)

Association and during the following nine years, was engaged in developing its programs of public health service and research in preventive medicine.

In 1931, Franklin D. Roosevelt, then governor of New York State, appointed him executive director of New York State's temporary relief administration, which had been created to combat the privation and suffering growing out of the business depression. He was later made chairman of the administration, succeeding Jesse Isador Straus, but continued to serve as director of the New York Tuberculosis and Health Association.

In 1933, President Roosevelt appointed him administrator of the Federal Emergency Relief Administration, better known as the FERA, which Congress had established to cope with the problem of public relief. At that time, there were approximately 14,000,000 unemployed persons in the United States and state and local relief funds were approaching exhaustion. An appropriation of $500,000,000 had been created by Congress to be expended in making direct grants to the states to aid the needy. Hopkins thus assumed command of the greatest public relief program in the world's history. The creation of FERA was the beginning of a partnership arrangement between the federal government, the states and localities in handling the relief problem. The initial appropriation of $500,000,000 was later supplemented by additional amounts, with FERA contributing a total of $2,900,000,000 of more than the $4,000,000,000 required to carry the public relief load from May of 1933 through December of 1935, when the final loans were determined. At the peak of this program, five and a half million cases, representing twenty and a half million people, were receiving relief either in the form of direct relief or work relief, or through one of the special FERA programs, such as emergency education, college student aid and rural rehabilitation.

Among the tangible results of the work relief activities during this period were the construction or improvement of over 200,000 miles of highways, roads and streets; 14,000 bridges, 5,000 parks; 11,000 playgrounds and recreation fields, and 62,000 buildings. Under the rural rehabilitation program, 200,000 farm families were assisted in supporting themselves instead of being carried on direct relief.

From November of 1933 to March of 1934, the work activities of the FERA were largely replaced by the works program of the civil works administration, also directed by Hopkins, which gave employment to 4,500,000 persons. FERA also administered the Federal Surplus Relief Corp., of which he was president. As federal emergency relief administrator, Hopkins also served on the national emergency council, headed by the President. In April of 1935, he was appointed administrator of the Works Progress Administration, better known as the WPA (later changed to Works Projects Administration). WPA was a newly created agency that gradually superseded FERA as the government's work relief organization. During the next three years, the WPA furnished employment to 7,000,000 different persons taken from the relief rolls. The WPA executed a wide ranging program of public works construction (highways, bridges, parks, water and sewer systems, airports); it operated sewing rooms for unemployed women; supervised the canning of meat, fruits and vegetables for distribution by relief organizations, and carried on a wide variety of research and statistical surveys; library, museum and clinical work; educational and research programs, and a federal arts project. One of the agency's divisions, organized during Hopkins' administration, was the national youth administration which inaugurated a wide-spread program to give employment to college students.

In December of 1938, Hopkins resigned as WPA administrator and entered President Roosevelt's cabinet as Secretary of Commerce, a post he filled until September 1940. During these years he graduated into the small, inner circle of the President's most intimate friends and advisers and became one of the country's foremost political figures. After the outbreak of the Second World War, he lived at the White House, performing various important confidential missions and services for the President. He was in command of the Roosevelt board of strategy at the Democratic National Convention in Chicago in 1940 when the President was renominated for a third term, and early in 1941, he went to England as Roosevelt's personal envoy to confer with Prime Minister Churchill and other officials of the British government. Later he was designated special assistant to the President in charge of all defense aid by the United States to the Nations resisting military aggression in the war.

In July of 1941 he made a second trip to England, extending his journey to Moscow to consult Joseph Stalin, the premier of Russia. On the return trip he traveled from a Scottish port with Prime Minister Churchill to the latter's historic conference with President Roosevelt at sea. In 1942, he was chairman of the Munition Assignments Board, which was the distribution center for American produced military material among the various battle fronts.

Hopkins was married twice: to Ethel Gross by whom he had four children, and Barbara MacPherson

Duncan, by whom he had a daughter. He died on January 29, 1946.

HOUGH, EMERSON, (1857-1923) — journalist and author, was born in Newton, Iowa to Joseph and Elizabeth Hough (pronounced "Huff"). His father determined that he should be a lawyer and so he attended the State University of Iowa, graduating with a law degree in 1880.

Intrigued by frontier life, Hough set up his law practice in small mining town in New Mexico. The problem was that he wasn't the least bit interested in law and was soon drawn away by all the interesting distractions around him. He began to draw sketches and write stories about life on the frontier and submitted articles to publications such as the *Golden Era* and *Field and Stream*. He also worked for newspapers in Hutchinson, Kansas; Des Moines, Iowa; and Sandusky, Ohio in order to earn money (his writing career didn't become lucrative until the end.) In 1889, he took a job managing the Chicago office of *Field and Stream* where he earned $15.00 per week.

Hough's first published work was *The Singing Mouse,* a book of children's stories which came out in 1895. His first non-fiction, *The Story of the Cowboy,* was published in 1917 and became a personal favorite of Teddy Roosevelt. Next, he wrote his first novel, *The Girl at the Halfway House,* which was published in 1900. Two years later, his popular success, *The Mississippi Bubble* was published. This book he had written between the hours of 10 p.m. and 4 a.m. while working four jobs. Life was not easy for Hough, for he generally worked twenty hour days in order to make enough money to live on and still write. In between books, Hough submitted articles on a regular basis to different magazines including *Outing, Century, Everybody's Collier's, Reader's, McClure's,* the *Saturday Evening Post,* and *Atlantic Monthly.* Other books he wrote during his career include: *The Way to the West, The Law of the Land, The Story of the Outlaw, 54-40 or Fight!, The Sowing, John Rawn, The Lady and the Pirate, The Passing of the Frontier,* and several others.

Hough also carried a burden for the conservation and preservation of wildlife and as a result, wrote hundreds of articles on behalf of the national park system. He once toured Yellowstone National Park on skis and was instrumental in convincing Congress to pass an act protecting the park's buffalo. But it was his books on the American west for which Hough was best known.

Hough received a nice break in his not so lucrative writing career when his novel, *The Covered Wagon,* published in 1922, was made into an epic motion picture the following year. The irony of it is that Hough also died in that same year.

Emerson Hugh married Charlotte Amelia Cheseboro in 1897. He died April 30, 1923.

Those who have written about Emerson Hough have also disagreed about his temperament and personality. Some say that he was a difficult man; racist, and quarrelsome and obsessive. Others say that he was genial and patriotic. Perhaps he was both.

HUGHES, HAROLD, (1922-) — was Governor of Iowa from 1963 to 1969.

Born in Ida Grove, Iowa on February 10, 1922, he studied at the State University of Iowa during 1941-42. In the latter year he entered the United States Army, serving until 1945. The following year, he began working in the field of transportation and commerce, at one point, creating his own rate and tariff service, the Iowa Better Trucking Bureau, which was eventually responsible for equitable truck rates in at least thirty counties. Due to his impressive work in that area, he was elected to the Iowa Commission of Commerce in 1958, a position he ran for because of what he felt was a lack of responsibility by those already in the commission. Toward the end of his term in that post he noted: "I believe we have restored dignity to the commission and people again have a feeling of confidence and fair play."

While with the commission, Hughes made a bid for the governor's office in 1960, on the Democratic ticket, not making it past the primary. However, in his second try, two years later, he was successful, due to his no-nonsense approach in campaigning, which, according to was free of the glad-handing, back-slapping, and baby-kissing that sometimes mark political campaigns."

Elected in November of 1962, some of his decisions as Governor included the revoking of the death penalty, the formation of a State Civil Rights Commission, the creation of a radio-television system for education, and an upgrading of the laws concerning unemployment compensation and workmen's compensation.

As Governor, Hughes made his first address to the Iowa Legislature in January of 1963, saying: "It is sometimes said that the knack of skillful government is to hang back, do as little as possible, and make no mistakes. I hope there is another way--for between you and me, this prospect does not invite my soul. Frankly, I expect to experiment and make some mistakes-- whether it be in installing new programs in departments or hiring a band. But I can assure

you that this new administration will not stop mov-
ing--towards the goals to which we have pledged
ourselves with the people of Iowa...The time has
come to set aside old prejudices, face our problems
squarely, and work together to fulfill our state's
immeasurable potential."

Hughes moved on from the governor's office to
the United States Senate, serving from 1969 to 1975.
He is married to Eva Mae Mercer and the couple have
three children.

HUNSAKER, JEROME CLARKE, (1886-1984) —
aeronautical engineer and professor emeritus, was in
Creston, Iowa, the son of Walter J. and Alma (Clarke)
Hunsaker.

Hunsaker was an officer in the Navy's construction corps from 1909 to 1926. He received his
Master of Science degree from the Massachusetts
Institute of Technology in 1912, and became an
instructor there in the same year. In 1913, he went
to Europe to study the dynamical stability of airplanes. Returning to M.I.T. in 1914 he helped to
construct a wind tunnel there which he had learned
about while in Europe. In the same year, he established the first college course devoted to aerodynam-
ics and airplane design. In 1916, he completed his
D.Sc. degree and left M.I.T.

During the first World War, Hunsaker was responsible for the design, construction and acquisition of
Naval aircraft. During this time, he designed the
NC4 which made its transatlantic flight in 1919. In
1923, Hunsaker took a position as assistant Naval
attachi at London. In 1926, he returned to the United
States and retired from the Navy. From 1926 to
1928, he worked for Bell Telephone Laboratories as
assistant vice-president and from 1928 to 1933, he

was vice-president of the Goodyear-Zeppelin Corporation. In 1933, Hunsaker returned to M.I.T. and became head of the Department of Mechanical Engineering and head of the Department of Aeronautical Engineering. In 1941, he became chairman of the National Advisory Committee for Aeronautics (NACA - later known as NASA) where he stayed until 1956. Also in 1941, he resigned as general coordinator for Navy research and returned to M.I.T. where he was professor of mechanical engineering until his retirement in 1952. He continued to lecture at M.I.T. for five more years after retiring and later became a private consultant.

Honors and awards bestowed on Hunsaker during his career include the Navy Cross and Medal for Merit, the French Legion of Honor, the Daniel Guggenheim Medal, the Franklin Medal, the Wright Brothers Medal, the Godfrey L. Cabot Trophy, the Langley Medal, the Gold Medal of Royal Aeronautical Society and the Navy Award for distinguished public service.

Jerome Hunsaker married Alice Porter in 1911 and had four children: two sons and two daughters.

Hunsaker's lifetime spanned the entire history of aviation. He left behind quite a legacy, for he had indeed helped to lay the foundation of modern aeronautics. Hunsaker died on September 10, 1984 at the age of 98.

I

IRWIN, ROBERT BENJAMIN, (1883-1951) — official of organization for the blind and educator, was born in Rockford, Iowa, to Robert Payne Irwin and

IRWIN

Hattie Edith Chappell Irwin. Young Irwin became blind after a bout with inflammatory rheumatism at the age of five, infected his eyes. During those days, there was no readily available medical help nothing could be done to save his eyes from blindness. At the age of seven, Irwin was sent to a school for the blind where he had to live apart from his family except during summer vacations. He graduated in 1901 and went on to attend the University of Washington the following fall. He and his brother, during the previous summer, sold stereopticon views throughout the area where they lived near Puget Sound, in order to earn money for Irwin's college education. In 1906, he earned his B.A. from the University of Washington and in 1907, an M.A. degree from Harvard University Graduate School.

In 1909, Irwin received an appointment as superintendent of classes for the blind in Cleveland area public schools which were experimenting with educating blind children while they continued to live at home. This was a project especially close to Irwin's heart since he had been forced to leave home at such a young age in order to receive an education. Irwin organized Braille reading classes, established the first sight-saving classes in the United States; and helped get books printed in 24 point type for those who were seeing impaired but not completely blind. He also established the Clear Type Publishing Committee which would print the large type books at cost.

In 1923, Irwin became director and later executive director of the American Foundation for the Blind, Inc. which was a non- profit agency supported by endowments and private contributions. He helped to increase the literature available to the blind by developing different methods with which to educate and train them and he also drafted most of the legislation enacted for their benefit.

Irwin founded the Howe Publishing Company which developed the system of Braille interpointing and published and distributed books in Braille until 1931. He was also largely responsible for the government taking over this job in the same year. He was chairman of the American Uniform Type Committee and as such, helped to establish a standard Braille system for use throughout the English-speaking world. He helped to develop "Talking Books" which were made in the studio of the American Foundation for the Blind and was influential in the passage of the Pratt-Smoot Act which appropriated $100,000 per year for the Library of Congress to produce books in Braille and Talking Books. He participated in drafting many other Federal laws to benefit the blind including a provision for financial relief to the blind as an inclusion in the Social Security Act.

In 1938, Irwin received an appointment as executive vice president of the National Industries for the Blind which acts as a liaison between Federal and other purchasing agents and the different workshops for the blind, and assists in expanding employment possibilities for them. He was also responsible for organizing the first world conference on work for the blind which was held in 1931 in New York City. In 1946, he became executive director of the American Foundation for Overseas Blind which assisted the blind in all parts of the world.

Other activities Irwin has been involved with which assist the blind include sponsoring special programs and legislation for blind war veterans; acting as chairman on the subcommittee on visually handicapped for the White House Conference on

Child Health and Protection; and many other activities. He was also a member of the American Association of Social Workers, the National Conference of Social Work, the American Public Welfare Association, the New Jersey State Commission for the Blind and the National Education Association.

In 1917, Robert Irwin married Mary Blanchard who later became secretary to the Cleartype Publishing Committee.

Irwin's own published writings include, *Blind Relief Laws, Their Theory and Practice,* and *Sight-Saving Classes in the Public Schools.* He revised *Blind Relief Laws* and *A Comparative Study of Braille Grade One and a Half and Braille Grade Two.* His autobiography, *As I Saw It,* was published after his death.

Robert Irwin died on December 12, 1951.

J

JACKSON, FRANK DARR, (1854-1938) — fifteenth governor of Iowa (1894-96), was born in Arcade, Wyoming County, New York on January 26, 1854. Both his father and mother entered the service of the Union during the Civil War, the former holding the rank of first lieutenant of the 78th regiment, New York volunteers, and the latter being at the front for fourteen months as a hospital nurse. At the end of the war, his family moved to Jesup, Buchanan County, Iowa, and in 1870 he entered the Iowa Agricultural College in Ames. Three years later, he took up the study of law at the State University in Iowa City, where he graduated in 1874. He was admitted to the bar in 1875, and at once began the practice of law in Independence, Iowa. In 1880 he moved to Greene, Iowa, where he was highly successful as a lawyer and politician.

He became secretary of the senate of the 19th general assembly, and was reelected to that office in 1884. He was soon recognized as the leader of the young Republican element of the state, and in 1884, was elected secretary of state by a large majority, being reelected in 1886 and 1888. At the close of his third term, he, with others, formed the Royal Union Life Insurance Co. (of which he was made president), with headquarters in Des Moines. In 1893, he was nominated for governor, and carried the state by a 33,000 plurality. He was inaugurated on January 11, 1894.

In all emergencies, Governor Jackson acted with a firmness and energy which showed that he sympathized with the laboring people of the state; still, however, he would exhaust every resource if necessary to maintain law and order. In December, 1894, he declined to be a candidate for reelection and retired from public life at the end of his administration, to devote all his energies to his insurance company.

Governor Jackson was married to Anne F. Brock, and the couple had four sons. He died on November 16, 1938.

JACOBSEN, WILLIAM SEBASTIAN, (1887-1955) — (son of Bernhard Martin Jacobsen), a U.S. Representative from Iowa; born in Clinton, Clinton County, Iowa, January 15, 1887; attended the public schools and the Normal College of American Gymnastics Union, Indianapolis, Ind.; director of physical education of the Turner Society and Y.M.C.A., Clinton, Iowa, 1910-1915; manager and part owner of a mercantile store in Clinton, Iowa, 1915-1927; secretary, treasurer, manager, and organizer of Clinton Thrift Co., 1927- 1937; also manager of business property and farm interests; delegate to Democratic State conventions 1932-1944; delegate to the Democratic National Conventions in 1936 and 1944; elected as a Democrat to the Seventy-fifth, Seventy-sixth, and Seventy- seventh Congresses (January 3, 1937-January 3, 1943); unsuccessful candidate for reelection in 1942 to the Seventy- eighth Congress; liaison officer, War Assets Administration, Washington, D.C., July 1945 to January 1947; acting postmaster, Clinton, Iowa, August 1, 1951, to January 1954; died in Dubuque, Iowa, April 10, 1955; interment in Springdale Cemetery, Clinton, Iowa.

JAMIESON, WILLIAM DARIUS, (1873-1925) — (great- grandson of James R. Gillis), a U.S. Representative from Iowa; born near Wapello, Louisa County, Iowa, November 9, 1873; attended the common schools and the University of Iowa at Iowa City; studied law at the National University Law School, Washington, D.C.; edited and published the Ida Grove Pioneer in 1893 and 1894, the Columbus Junction Gazette 1899- 1901, the Shenandoah World 1901-1916, and was also editor of the Hamburg Democrat; member of the State senate from January 1, 1907, until March 3, 1909, when he resigned to enter Congress; elected as a Democrat to the Sixty-first Congress (March 4, 1909- March 3, 1911); declined to be a candidate for renomination in 1910; resumed newspaper activities in Shenandoah, Iowa; postmaster of Shenandoah from May 29, 1915, until September 1, 1916, when he resigned; assistant treasurer of the Democratic National Committee in 1916 and its director of finance 1917-1920; delegate at large to the Democratic National Convention in 1920; engaged in the practice of law in Washington, D.C.; editor of the Window Seat, a weekly syndicate letter for country newspapers, from 1925 until his death in Washington, D.C., November 18, 1949; interment in Fort Lincoln Cemetery.

JENSEN, BENTON FRANKLIN, (1892-1970) — a U.S. Representative from Iowa; born in Marion, Linn County, Iowa, December 16, 1892; attended the rural and high schools; employed by a lumber company as yardman and assistant auditor 1914-1917; during the First World War served as a second lieutenant in 1919; manager of a lumber company 1919-1938; elected as a Republican to the Seventy-sixth and to the twelve succeeding Congresses (January 3, 1939-January 3, 1965); unsuccessful candidate for reelection in 1964 to the Eighty-ninth Congress; returned to Exira, Iowa; died in Washington, D.C., February 5, 1970; interment in Exira Cemetery, Exira, Iowa.

JENSEN, VIRGINIA ALLEN, (1927-) — writer, born in Des Moines, Iowa to Byron Gilchrist and Elsa (Erickson) Allen. Virginia Allen attended Bennington College where she received her B.A. in 1950, and later did graduate work at the University of Minnesota. On March 21, 1953, she married Flemming Jakob Jensen and had three children, Merete, Annette, and Kirsten.

In 1960, Virginia Jensen became the director of the International Children's Book Service in Gentofte, Denmark. She has also served on the board of directors of the Danish section of the International Board on Books for Young People. She has authored several books for young people including, *Lars Pe-*

ter's Birthday, Hop Hans, Lars Peters Bicycle, and *Sara and the Door.* As well, she has translated several children's books from the Danish including, *The Marsh Crone's Brew, Play with Paper, The Boy in the Moon, Droll, Danish, and Delicious,* and several others.

Awards and honors Jensen has received for her books include, honorable mention from the Finnish Author's Union, a Nordic Cultural Fund grant, runner-up for the Margaret Batchelder Award, a research grant from the Danish Ministry of Cultural Affairs and others.

One of her books, *What's That?,*is illustrated in special raised print so that sight-handicapped as well as sighted children can follow the story in pictures. The book has also been published in ten countries.

JOHNSON, NICHOLAS, (1934-) — United States government official and lawyer, was born in Iowa City, Iowa to Wendell A.L., a speech educator, and Edna (Bockwoldt) Johnson. When he was a young boy, Johnson built his own crystal receivers and wired his unsuspecting neighborhood for telegraph. After graduating from University High School in Iowa City, he attended the University of Texas in Austin, and obtained his B.A. degree in 1956. He then attended the University of Texas Law School and earned his LL.B. degree in 1958.

After being admitted to the Texas bar in 1948, Johnson became a law clerk for Judge John R. Brown of the United States Court of Appeals for the Fifth Circuit, and later for the Supreme Court Justice Hugo L. Black. In 1960, he became a part of the faculty at the University of California Law School, as associate professor.

In February of 1963, Johnson joined the Washington law firm of Covington and Burling where he practiced law related to government administrative agencies. The following year, on March 2, 1964, he became the head of the Maritime Administration, a unit within the Department of Commerce. He was the youngest man ever to be appointed Maritime Administrator. In his new position, Johnson quickly gained a reputation for stirring things up. He criticized MARAD's $600 million program of ship construction and operating subsidies, complaining that half the money was spent on seamen's wages which were higher than those of foreign seamen. He also suggested that subsidies should be discontinued for passenger ships. In 1965, he announced new proposals for granting subsidies which had a number of considerations to be put into effect. Among those considerations would be carrying capacity of ships, number of ships proposed, speed of the ships, estimated cost of construction and operating costs as well as manning schedules, nature of cargo gear and cargo transfer methods. He also encourage the construction of larger and different kinds of ships such as atomic-powered ships, hovercraft and hydrofoil vessels. He called for allowing subsidized ship lines to build ships abroad to save labor costs among other considerations such as smaller crews to fit the newer automated ships. Because of all the changes Johnson insisted upon, he was not very popular among shipowners, shipbuilders and union men and none of them were unhappy to see him go in 1966.

On June 18, 1966, President Johnson appointed Nicholas Johnson a member of the Federal Communications Commission, where before long he received the nickname of "Mr. Clean." Johnson proved he was not out for popularity when he accused the commissioners of the FCC of lack of organization and long-range planning. He also criticized them for allowing the commission's time to be taken up mostly with broadcast licensing. He advocated a "single national clearinghouse of communications research" to handle problems of technological and institutional change and questions about service, funding, wiretapping and other issues. He created further stirs when he voted against a merger acquisition of the American Broadcasting Corporation by the Telephone and Telegraph Corporation - his opposition did a great deal to stop the merger.

Other positions that Johnson has held include adjutant professor of law at Georgetown University from 1971-1973; visiting professor at the University of Illinois in 1976, the University of Oklahoma in 1978, Illinois State University in 1979, the University of Wisconsin in 1980, the Newhouse School of Syracuse University in 1980, the University of Iowa College of Law in 1981; visiting professor in the department of communications studies at the University of Iowa from 1982-1985; visiting professor in Western Behavioral Sciences Institute at the University of California in San Diego from 1986-1991; visiting professor at California State University in Los Angeles in 1986; co-director at the University of Iowa Institute for Health, Behavior and Environmental Policy from 1990-1993; chairman and director of the National Citizens Communications Lobby in 1975- ; and many others.

Johnson has been the recipient of numerous awards and honors including being named one of 10 outstanding young men in the United States by the U.S. Jaycees; recipient of the New Republic Public Defender award; Civil Liberties award; Dewitt Carter Riddick award from the University of Texas; the

George Stoney award from the National Federation of Local Cable Programmers and many others.

Nicholas Johnson married Karen Mary Chapman of Iowa City in 1952. The couple have three children, Julie, Sherman and Gregory.

K

KANTOR, MACKINLAY, (1904-1977) — novelist, was born in Webster City, Iowa, son of John Martin and Effie Rachel (McKinlay) Kantor. His mother was a journalist and strongly urged young MacKinlay to pursue writing. His father abandoned the family when Kantor was young and he was raised by his mother, helping her with her work at the local newspaper. In 1922, Kantor won a short story contest and was encouraged all the more to become a writer. Afterward he began to write with a fervor, one short story after another, and sent them out to publishers. Unfortunately, he found out that getting published was a different story and would not be an easy one.

In 1925, Kantor left Iowa for Chicago and ended up working on a city surveying crew after trying unsuccessfully to find a newspaper job. It was around this time that he met and married Irene Layne. In 1928, after a hard three years, Kantor succeeded in getting his first novel, *Diversey,* published. The novel received good reviews by critics but not by Senator Coleman Blease of South Carolina who was displeased with the novel's description of the gang warfare that was so prevalent in Chicago at that time.

Kantor and his wife returned to Iowa and after he landed a job as a columnist, he published two more novels. In 1933, the couple went to Westfield, New Jersey where he wrote his first historical novel, *Long Remember.* The novel was hailed by critics as a notable historical piece of work. Kantor's career at that point turned a corner and he went from aspiring writer, to seasoned novelist. Although he would dabble in other areas, he would become best known as an important contributor in the area of historical novel writing.

Another notable novel Kantor turned out a short while later was *The Voice of Bugle Ann.* This novel, like *Long Remember* received exceptional critical acclaim. The next novel to leave a mark on Kantor's career is perhaps the one he is best remembered for, *Andersonville.* This work not only received critical acclaim, but won for Kantor the 1965 Pulitzer Prize for fiction.

The last novel that Kantor wrote before his death was another historical work, *Valley Forge.* Other notable novels that he produced during his lengthy career include *Irene, I Love You,* and *Glory for Me,* the latter of which was adapted into an Oscar winning film entitled, *The Best Years of Our Life.* In between, he wrote a whole slew of other novels including, *El Goes South, The Jaybird, Turkey in the Straw, Arouse and Beware, The Romance of Rosy Ridge, The Noise of Their Wings, Here Lies Holly Springs, Valedictory, Cuba Libre, Gentle Annie, Angleworms on Toast,* and many, many more. Other honors and awards he received aside from the Pulitzer include the O. Henry Award; the Medal of Freedom; honorary D. Litt. degrees from Grinnell College, Drake University, Lincoln College, and Ripon College; and an honorary LL.D. degree from Iowa Weslayan College.

MacKinlay Kantor died in Sarasota, Florida of a heart attack on October 11, 1977.

KELLEMS, VIVIEN, (1896-1975) — industrialist, was born in Des Moines, Iowa to the Reverend David Clinton Kellems and Louisa (Flint) Kellems. The family moved to Eugene, Oregon where Vivien received her education up through high school. Later, she attended the University of Oregon with her mother as one of her classmates. Both earned their degrees at the same time, Vivien's being a B.A. in economics.

After graduation in 1918, Miss Kellems worked as a booker for the West Coast Chatauqua circuit and then for the Florida circuit. In 1920, she went back to the University of Oregon to complete graduate work in economics and obtain her Master's degree. Afterwards she went to Columbia University to work on a Ph.D. but discontinued after a year in order to pursue a business venture.

A short while later, Miss Kellems' brother, Edgar, invented a woven grip that could be used for pulling cables and wires through conduits. Seeing the potential for making a great deal of money, Miss Kellems' invested some of her own money, hired a few employees, rented a loft and began filling orders for several New York electrical companies.

The woven grip was found to be useful for a number of other areas besides cable pulling. Its was also used for holding elevator ropes, for temporary splices in heavy construction equipment, for architectural and engineering purposes, and even for traction splints in surgery. During World War II, Kellems' younger brother even designed an over-sized grip to be used for lifting 2,700-pound shells. Between 1941 and 1945, the entire output of the Kellems plant was devoted to war materials.

In 1944, Miss Kellems became known as the lady who refused to pay her taxes. She publicly voiced her intention to not pay the last quarterly installment of taxes for 1943 and attempted to persuade other business owners to do likewise. In 1947, Miss Kellems and one hundred women sympathizers challenged a Connecticut state law that prohibited women in industry from working between the hours of 10 p.m. and 6 a.m. The law was repealed. It was her only success in challenging the law. In 1948, Miss Kellems again tangled with the Federal government when she refused to withhold taxes from the wages of her employees, contesting that if she was to do so the government should pay her to be an Internal Revenue Service Agent and give her a badge as well. This again was to no avail, for the government simply took the money out of her bank account with the help of her bankers. Not an easy person to defeat, Miss Kellems again refused to pay her quarterly taxes and demanded to be indicted. Again, it came to naught and the taxes were paid. In 1944, she was forced to move her plant elsewhere because it was discovered that she had established her business in a residentially zoned area. After fussing about it a bit, Miss Kellems moved.

In 1942, Miss Kellems ran for the Republican nomination to Congress from the Fourth Connecticut District and was soundly defeated. In 1950 and again in 1956, she sought the Republican nomination for the United States Senate but failed to receive it. In the latter year, she decided to run as an independent but was thrown off the petitions. In 1954, she decided to run for governor, but was again unsuccessful. In 1962, Miss Kellems again tried unsuccessfully for the Senate and in 1965, she staged a nine-hour sit-down in a polling booth to protest against the use of party levers in voting machines which made ticket- splitting illegal.

In 1962, Miss Kellems decided to sell the company and in January of 1975, at the age of seventy-eight, she breathed her last.

Miss Kellems claimed that she had never been married, although rumors existed to the opposite. It was a fact, however, that she had been engaged to a young Naval doctor who was killed when his ship was torpedoed, the same year that Miss Kellems graduated from college, 1918.

KENDALL, NATHAN EDWARD, (1868-1946) — a U.S. Representative from Iowa; born on a farm near Greenville, Lucas County, Iowa, March 17, 1868; attended the rural schools; studied law; was admitted to the bar in 1887 and commenced practice in Albia, Monroe County, Iowa, in 1889; city attorney 1890-1892; prosecuting attorney of Monroe County, Iowa, 1893-1897; member of the State house of representatives 1899-1909 and served as speaker in 1909; elected as a Republican to the Sixty-first and Sixty-second Congresses (March 4, 1909-March 3, 1913); was not a candidate for renomination in 1912 to the Sixty-third Congress; resumed the practice of law in Albia, Iowa; moved to Des Moines, Iowa, in 1921; Governor of Iowa 1921-1925; resided in Des Moines, Iowa, until his death on November 5, 1946; remains were cremated and the ashes interred on the lawn of "Kendall Place," his former home in Albia, Iowa.

KENDALL, NATHAN EDWARD, (1868-1936) — twenty-third governor of Iowa (1921-25), was born on March 17, 1868 in Greenville, Iowa, the son of Elijah L. and Lucinda (Stephens) Kendall. After studying law at a private law firm, he passed the Iowa bar in 1889, and was soon practicing in Albia, Iowa. Between 1890 and 1892, Kendall was the city attorney for Albia, and from 1893 to 1897, he served as prosecuting attorney of Monroe County.

Kendall got into politics in 1898 when, on the Republican ticket, he was elected to the state legislature, where he served for ten years. Then in 1908, Kendall ran for, and won, a seat in the United States Congress from Iowa's Sixth District, serving two terms. He secured the governorship in 1920, also serving two terms in that post. During his tenure, he implemented a major reorganization of state government, expanding the park system and the state highway program, making physical education mandatory in the state's public schools, creating a state soldiers' bonus law, making sure that abused, forgotten, or troubled children were taken care of under the state system, and offering vocational rehabilitation skills for disabled citizens.

One source described Kendall thusly: "He was a man of clear vision, moral courage, integrity and broad sympathies, was quick of wit and was celebrated for his gift of repartee." Kendall was married twice: to Belle Wooden (who died in 1926), and Mabel Mildred (Fry) Bonnell. He died on November 4, 1936 in Des Moines.

KENNEDY, CHARLES AUGUSTUS, (1869-1951) — a U.S. Representative from Iowa; born in Montrose, Lee County, Iowa, March 24, 1869; completed preparatory studies; interested in horticultural pursuits and later engaged in business as a nurseryman; mayor of Montrose 1890-1895; member of the State house of 1331 ordained to the ministry in 1894 and served in Orfordville, Wis., from 1894 to 1917, and in Benson, Swift County, Minn., from 1917 until elected to Congress; unsuccessful candidate as an Independent Republican for election in 1920 to the Sixty-seventh Congress; elected as a Farmer-Labor candidate to the Sixty-eighth through Seventy-first Congresses and served from March 4, 1923, until his death near Otter Tail Lake, Minn., on September 11, 1929; interment in Benson Cemetery, Benson, Minn.

KENT, CORITA, (1918-1986) — artist, was born in Fort Dodge, Iowa on November 20, 1918, daughter of Robert Vincent and Edith (Sanders) Kent. At the age of eighteen, she joined the Institute of the Most Holy and Immaculate Heart of the Blessed Virgin Mary, a Roman Catholic Community of teaching nuns. She did not want to be teacher at the time, only a nun, but she learned to teach nonetheless. She attended Immaculate Heart College and completed her B.A. degree in 1941. She was then assigned to teach at the order's elementary school for Indians in British Columbia, Canada and after five years, she returned to Los Angeles and became a part of the faculty of the Immaculate Heart College. At the same time, she began to study art at the University of Southern California, and earned her M.A. degree in 1951. In 1950, she had begun to make her first screen prints which were religious in nature with an impressionistic and somewhat avant-garde style.

In 1954, Sister Kent began to incorporate words into her pictures. The first of her pieces to include words in it was the print, "Christ and Mary" which which contained Gothic script. In the early 1960's, the words in Sister Kent's serigraphs became more pronounced, almost dominating the picture. In them, she quoted from sources such as St. Bernard, Albert Sweitzer and the Beatles. She used commercial quotes, tailored to her theme, such as, "He cared enough to send the very best" which she had printed in her Christmas cards.

KENT

Sister Kent went to Boston, Massachusetts in 1968 for two months on a leave of absence and then announced her formal resignation from the Sisters of the Immaculate Heart of Mary, however, she still remained on the faculty of the Immaculate Heart College.

Corita Kent's work is on display in permanent collections in the Victoria and Albert Museum in London, the Art Institute of Chicago, the Cincinnati Art Museum, the Library of Congress, the Metropolitan Museum of Art, the Museum of Modern Art, the Boston Museum of Fine Arts, the National Gallery of Art, the New York Public Library, the Philadelphia Museum of Art, the Virginia Museum of Fine Arts, the Bibliothique Nationale in Paris, and the Los Angeles County Museum of Art as well as many others.

Corita Kent is most well remembered for her silk-screen posters and the "Love" stamp which she designed for the United States Post Office. Her work included many book covers, greeting cards and anti-war posters.

Miss Corita Kent had never married and died of cancer in her home in Boston in September of 1986. She was sixty-seven years old.

KENT, JOHN WELLINGTON, (1920-1985) — author and illustrator of children's books, was born in Burlington, Iowa to Ralph Arthur and Marguerite (Bruhl) Kent. As a young teenager, Kent began drawing professionally to assist with the family's income during the Depression. He sold mostly advertising pieces for local agencies; his first national sale was a cartoon for *Collier's*. Kent had no formal instruction in illustrating, but on his own studied the work of others such as George Herriman, the creator of "Krazy Kat."

For the first part of his career, Kent made his living by doing free-lance illustration and writing. Then he came up with his own idea for a comic character and "King Aroo" was born. The strip was syndicated and the "King" and his animal friends achieved international distribution, being translated into as many as fifteen languages.

All of Kent's books are humorous in nature. He felt that most children's books don't have enough humor in them but that children have a very good sense of what's funny. He felt that too many children's books have a very definite message that they're trying to get across, but not enough humor. His main purpose in writing his books was to encourage young readers to go further in their reading by making it fun and enjoyable.

Along with the work he did on his own books, Kent has illustrated several children's books that other people have written. These he would receive unsolicited from an editor which was a testimony as to how well known and well respected his illustrating capabilities were. Kent described his motivation for doing children's books as basically a desire to make a living doing what he enjoyed most. Some of the books he has authored or illustrated, or both include, *Just Only John, Fly Away Home, The Blah, The Scribble Monster, Joey,* and *Joey Runs Away* as well as many, many others.

For his excellent work in illustrating and writing children's books, John Kent received the Chicago Graphics Association award, the Chicago Book Clinic award and the Texas Institute of Letters award. His *Happy-Ever-After Book* was named an "outstanding picture book of the year" in 1976 by the *New York*

KEYHOE

Times. He was a member of the National Cartoonists Society, the American Institute of Graphics Arts, Authors Guild and the Authors League of America.

Kent married June Kilstofte on June 9, 1954 and had one child, John Wellington.

Kent's other interests and hobbies included art and architecture - he designed his own house; languages; travel; music and dance; and nature.

John Kent died of leukemia on October 18, 1985 in San Antonio, Texas.

KEYHOE, DONALD E., (1897-1988) — author and former United States Marine Corps officer, most well known for his belief in and writings on UFO's. He was born in Ottumwa, Iowa, son of Calvin Grant Keyhoe and May (Cherry) Keyhoe. Young Donald attended high school in Iowa and then went to the Naval Academy Preparatory School at Annapolis, MD. He received his B.S. degree in 1919 and became a lieutenant in the U.S. Marine Corps.

Keyhoe was in a plane crash in 1922 which seriously injured his right arm and caused him to retire in 1923. While he was in the hospital recovering from the injury, he began to write. In 1924 until 1926, he was the editor of the Coast and Geodetic Survey and from 1926 to 1928, he was chief of information in the civil aeronautics branch of the U.S. Department of Commerce.

In 1926, Keyhoe was manager of the tour of the "Josephine Ford" plane which Floyd Bennett and Richard E. Byrd used to make the first flight over the North Pole on May 9, 1926. In 1927, he assisted Charles Lindbergh in his nationwide tour of the United States after he accomplished his famous solo flight to Paris.

During 1928 and 1929, Keyhoe wrote articles for the *Saturday Evening Post* such as "Flying With Lindbergh," "Lindbergh Four Years After," "Is Air Travel Safe?," and "Flying Blind." In 1939 and 1940, he was a contributor of articles to *Reader's Digest,* and *American Magazine.* He also wrote the book, *If War Comes, What Your Government Plans for You.*

In 1950, Keyhoe wrote his first article on unidentified flying objects which was printed in *True* magazine. His book, *The Flying Saucers are Real,* expounded upon what he had written in his article. The book was very successful and sold over 500,000 copies. In 1953, he continued writing on the subject of UFO's with his book *Flying Saucers from Outer Space.* In his book of 1955, *The Flying Saucer Conspiracy,* Keyhoe claimed that a conspiracy was going on within the U.S. Air Force to hide discoveries of UFO's. He claimed further that planes and pilots have "vanished" after so called "collisions" with these UFO's. The Air Force countered Keyhoe's claims by publishing a 316-page report called "Project Blue Book." In this report, the Air Force explained that only three percent of sightings of UFO's between 1947 and 1955 were unexplained phenomena and that ninety- seven percent were balloons, shooting stars, planets, etc. In 1955, Air Secretary Donald A. Quarles announced that the Air Force was planning on sending up radical new aircraft that could be mistaken as flying saucers because of their dish shapes. The last two books Keyhoe wrote were, *Flying Saucers: Top Secret,* and *Aliens From Space.* Keyhoe was also director of the National Committee on Aerial Phenomena, which tried to convince the Air Force that they should investigate U.F.O. sightings -- the group later disbanded.

KIRBY

Donald E. Keyhoe married Helen Wood Gardner on August 18, 1930. The couple had three children: two daughters, Kathleen and Caroline; and one son, Joseph.

Donald Keyhoe died on November 29, 1988 of pneumonia and cardiac arrest. He was ninety-one years old.

KIRBY, ROBERT (EMORY), (1918-) — corporation executive, was born in Ames, Iowa to Robert Stearns and Ora (Walker) Kirby. When he was only nine, Robert Kirby began earning his own spending money by selling flowers and bags of peanuts on the campus of Penn State where his father was a professor. A good student, he entered college at Penn State a year early because he was able to skip a grade in high school.

Kirby had an intense interest in jazz music and organized a successful band during his college years. He decided not to pursue music as a career, however, and instead went to work for the West Virginia Pulp and Paper Company after completing his B.S. degree in chemical engineering. Within a year, he had been promoted to assistant superintendent.
In 1956, he completed his M.B.A. degree at Harvard Business School, with distinction as a Baker Scholar.

In 1946, Kirby read an article on high frequency heating, written by the head of Westinghouse Electric's electronics research department. Impressed by the article, he visited Westinghouse's Pittsburgh headquarters and was offered a position with the company's research laboratories. He turned that offer down and instead, accepted a position with the staff of its industrial electronics division in Baltimore. By

1952, he was manager of industrial electronics engineering.

In 1956, Kirby became manager of Westinghouse's ordnance department and by 1958, had progressed to the position of general manager of its electronics division. In the latter position, Kirby became known for his "people-oriented" management style. He has stated, "I used to go out and walk through the shop every day so people would have a chance to see me, talk with me, register a complaint if they had one on their mind. There's a tendency to get too far away from the people in your organization. The good manager makes sure this doesn't happen."

In 1963, Kirby was offered the position of vice-president of engineering which he accepted. A year later, he became industrial group vice-president, and two years after that was promoted to executive vice-president, one of only two in the entire company. In this new position, he became responsible for about half of the company's lines, including construction, industrial, and consumer products.

When Westinghouse restructured into four major units in 1969, Kirby became president of the Industry and Defense company, the largest and most diversified of the four. In 1975, he became chairman and chief executive officer of Westinghouse.

In his new position as head of the company, Kirby played a major role in the reduction and reorganization of Westinghouse. He eliminated as much debt as possible and centralized divisional supervision as well as cut down on spending. He also cut down on the number of divisions, taking the total from 144 to only thirty-seven. As a result of these business strategies, Westinghouse's profits increased dramatically. Kirby held the position of chairman and C.E.O. of Westinghouse until 1983.

Robert Kirby married Barbara Anne McClintock on July 11, 1942. The couple had two daughters, Mary Linda, and Donna Susan, who is now deceased.

Kirby's leisure-time interests include crossword puzzles, magic, playing jazz music, and golf. He currently resides in Pittsburgh, Pennsylvania.

KIRKPATRICK, SANFORD, (1842-1932) — a U.S. Representative from Iowa; born near London, Madison County, Ohio, February 11, 1842; moved to Iowa in 1849 with his parents, who settled on a farm in Highland Township, Wapello County; attended the common schools 1854-1858; during the Civil War entered the Union Army as a private in the Second Iowa Infantry and served four years and four months and was promoted to first lieutenant; engaged in agricultural pursuits; moved to Ottumwa, Iowa, in 1876 and engaged in mercantile pursuits until 1887; deputy recorder of Wapello County 1876-1880; member of the Ottumwa City Council 1884-1887; representative of the Internal Revenue Service 1557- 1913; elected as a Democrat to the Sixty-third Congress (March 4, 1913-March 3, 1915); unsuccessful candidate for reelection in 1914 to the Sixty-fourth Congress; moved to Greensboro, N.C., in 1916 and engaged in agricultural pursuits; died in Greensboro, N.C., February 13, 1932; interment in Forest Lawn Cemetery.

KIRKWOOD, SAMUEL JORDAN, (1813-1894) — fifth and ninth governor of Iowa (1860-64; 1876-77), and Secretary of the Interior under President Garfield, was born in Harford County, Maryland on December 20, 1813. He received an academic education in

Washington D.C. At the age of fourteen he was employed as a druggist's clerk at the capital, and remained in that business for seven years. In 1835 he moved to Richland County, Ohio, where he studied law, and was admitted to the bar in 1843. For four years he was prosecuting attorney for the county, and in 1850 was a member of the judicial committee of the constitutional convention, which contributed largely to the state constitution which was adopted in 1851. In 1855 he moved to Iowa, where he engaged in farming and milling, near Iowa City.

In 1856 he was elected to the state senate, and served through the last session held in Iowa City, and the first held in Des Moines. In 1859, he was chosen governor of Iowa over the Democratic candidate, by a majority of 2,964. His administration proved so satisfactory during that critical period that he was reelected in 1861. It was said of him that he saved the state $500,000 from the $800,000 appropriated for defense bonds. He was a strong Union man, and as governor, sent about fifty regiments to the war, nearly all of them for three years, the result being that Iowa was one of the few states in which there was no draft. In 1862 President Lincoln offered Governor Kirkwood the post of U.S. Minister to Denmark, but he declined it.

In 1866 he was elected a member of the U.S. Senate, to fill out the unexpired term of James Harlan, and while there, served on the committee on public lands. In 1867, at the expiration of the term, he returned to Iowa City where he continued to pursue his private business. In July, 1875, he was nominated for governor for a third term by the Republicans and won the election. In February, 1877, he was again elected to the U.S. Senate, where he served until 1881.

KLUCKHORN

During his career in the Senate, he was distinguished for his clear and thoughtful consideration of all subjects brought before him, particularly those pertaining to the domestic affairs of the nation. It was probably his special knowledge in this particular area, and his wise treatment of the Indian question that induced President Garfield to appoint him Secretary of the Interior on March 5, 1881. He continued in that post after President Garfield's death until April 6, 1882, when he was succeeded by Henry M. Teller of Colorado, who had been appointed by President Arthur. Kirkwood ran for the United States House of Representatives in 1886, but was defeated by the Democratic candidate, Walter I. Hayes.

Kirkwood died in Iowa City on September 1, 1894.

KLUCKHORN, CLYDE (KAY MABEN), (1905-1960) — was an anthropologst who became an authority on the Navajo Indians.

Born in Le Mars, Iowa on January 11, 1905, he attended a numbe of colleges including Culver Military Academy in 1918 and Princeton University. He received his B.A. degree from the University of Wisconsin in 1928. Kluckhorn was also a Rhodes Scholar at Oxford University, studying Greek, Latin and classical archaeology. From that university he received his M.A. degree in 1932. He obtained his Ph.D. from Harvard in 1936.

Kluckhorn became interested in the Navajo Indians after he moved to New Mexico because of an illness. While there, Kluckhorn began to study the language and customs of the Native American tribe. At the age of 18, he travelled on horseback among the Indians, at one time becoming lost and then rescued by a Navajo search party. Kluckhorn described his experiences in his first book, *To the Foot of the Rainbow,* which was published in 1927. He continued his research throughout his life, publishing numerous books and articles on the subject.

Throughout his life Kluckhorn was a prestigious member of the faculties of several universities including the University of New Mexico and Harvard University, where he was also the director of the Russian Research Center. At the time, the center was considered the most extensive non-governmental research institution dealing with the U.S.S.R. in the western world. Kluckhorn published works in the physical, social and archaeological branches of anthropology and held a number of government positions in a full-time or advisory capacity. His name attracted the attention of the general public when his book, *Mirror for Man,* won a $10,000 prize as the best book on science for the layman.

Honors bestowed on Kluckhorn include the degree of L.H.D. from the University of New Mexico in 1949 and the Viking Fund Medal for General Anthropology in 1951.

Kluckhorn married Florence Rockwood in 1932. The couple had one son. Kluckhorn died on July 29, 1960.

KOPP, WILLIAM FREDERICK, (1869-1938) — a U.S. Representative from Iowa; born near Dodgeville, Des Moines County, Iowa, June 20, 1869; attended the common schools; was graduated from Iowa Wesleyan College at Mount Pleasant in 1892 and from the law department of the University of Iowa at Iowa City in 1894; was admitted to the bar in 1894 and commenced practice in Mount Pleasant, Iowa; prosecuting attorney of Henry County 1895-1899; postmaster of Mount Pleasant 1906-1914; member of the board of trustees of Iowa Wesleyan College 1908-1938; member of the State house of representatives 1915-1917; elected as a Republican to the Sixty-seventh and to the five succeeding Congresses (March 4, 1921-March 3, 1933); chairman, Committee on Expenditures in the Department of the Navy (Sixty-eighth Congress), Committee on Labor (Sixty-ninth through Seventy-first Congresses), Committee on Pensions (Seventy-first Congress); unsuccessful candidate for reelection in 1932 to the Seventy- third Congress; engaged in the practice of law at Mount Pleasant, Iowa, until his death there on August 24, 1938; interment in Forest Home Cemetery.

KRASCHEL, NELSON GEORGE, (1889-1957) — twenty-seventh governor of Iowa (1937-39), was born on October 27, 1889 in Macon, Illinois, the son of Fred K. and Nancy Jane (Poe) Kraschel. After attending public schools, Kraschel found that he enjoyed auctioneering, and made his living at that for several years, often calling auctions throughout the United States and Canada, and according to one source, selling over $50,000,000 worth of agricultural property.

Between 1933 and 1937, Kraschel was lieutenant governor of Iowa, serving under Governor Clyde L. Herring. In most instances, the number two spot is known to be somewhat of a figurehead position; however, Kraschel was often involved in state matters, sometimes acting as Herring's emissary on visits to Washington, D.C. In 1936, running on the Democratic ticket, Kraschel secured the governorship, serving during 1937-39. One of the biggest issues Kraschel had to face while governor concerned a strike at a Maytag plant in Newton, Iowa, instigated by the Congress of Industrial Organizations, during which the strikers occupied the plant. The governor immediately established a three- man board to attempt some kind of mediation, and in the meantime, called out the militia to secure calm and reopen the plant. The National Labor Relations Board then got involved in the situation, and in a further show of force, Kraschel requested an injunction to prevent the angry strikers from striking on the plant premises. Eventually a compromise was reached by both sides,and the strike was ended.

During his tenure, Kraschel helped establish the Board of Social Welfare. He ran for a second term in 1938, but was defeated by George Wilson. After leaving office, he returned to his business interests until 1942, when he made another attempt at the governorship, this time being defeated by Bourke Hickenlooper. In 1943, he was asked to serve as general agent for the Farm Credit Administration in Omaha, Nebraska, a post he held until it was phased out in 1949. Kraschel was married to Agnes Johnson, and the couple had three sons. He died on March 15, 1957 in Harlan, Iowa.

KRAUSHAAR, OTTO FREDERICK, (1901-1989) — college president, was born in Clinton, Iowa, the son of Otto Christian and Marie (Staehling) Kraushaar. The senior Kraushaar emigrated to the United States in search of religious freedom in the 1870's, and became president of Wartburg College at Clinton, Iowa, as well as an author and editor. Young Otto graduated from Wartburg Academy at Waverly, Iowa in 1920. After his graduation, he attended Iowa State University and graduated with a B.A. in philosophy in 1924. In 1927, he earned his M.A. from the same university and six years later, earned his Ph.D. from Harvard University.

KRAUSHAAR

In 1924, Kraushaar started teaching at the Burt (Iowa) High School. Two years later he returned to Iowa State University to teach and the following year went to Harvard, also to teach. After two years at Harvard, he went to Radcliffe College and was an instructor there from 1930 to 1933. He then joined the faculty at Smith College, became a full professor in 1939, and stayed at that institution until 1948.

In 1943, Kraushaar was commissioned a captain in the United States Army. While stationed in Cairo, Egypt, he organized the Middle East Branch of the United States Armed Forces Institute. He was successively advanced to lieutenant colonel, then colonel and parted with the Army in 1945. For his service, he was awarded the Legion of Merit Medal, the European-Middle East- African Medal, the American Theatre Medal, the Asiatic-Pacific Medal, the Philippine Liberation Medal and the Victory Medal.

After his war service, Kraushaar went back to Smith College and taught for another three years. In 1948, he was invited to become the interim president of Goucher College for Women and ten months later was named the college's sixth president.

Goucher college was the first college for women to establish a department of physiology and hygiene and its graduates were among the first women to be accepted by the Johns Hopkins School of Medicine. President Kraushaar once said, "If you educate a man, you educate an individual; if you educate a woman, you educate a family." While he presided there, Kraushaar made a number of positive changes to Goucher, including improvement in the school's finances and assisting in its becoming a nationally ranked women's college. Kraushaar retired from Goucher in 1967.

Otto Goucher contributed a number of articles to such periodicals as the *Philosophical Review,* the magazine *Forum,* and the *Journal of Philosophy,* the latter of which he was associate editor from 1940 to 1943. He has written on such subjects as Lotze and William James, foreign policy of the United States and on the role of the expert in government affairs. Other published works of his include: *Classic American Philosophers, American Non-public Schools: Patterns of Diversity, Private Schools: From the Puritans to the Present,* and *Schools in a Changing City: An Overview of Baltimore's Private Schools.*

Kraushaar was a member of the United World Federalists, Americans for Democratic Action, and the American Civil Liberties Committee.

Otto Kraushaar married Maxine MacDonald in November of 1927 and had one child, Joane.

Kraushaar died in Baltimore, Maryland on September 23, 1989.

KYL, JOHN HENRY, (1919-   ) — (father of Jon Llewellyn Kyl), a U.S. Representative from Iowa; born in Wisner, Cumming, County, Nebr., May 9, 1919; graduated from Wayne (Nebr.) Prep High School in 1937, Nebraska State Teachers College in 1940, and from the University of Nebraska in school administration in 1947; taught in the public schools of Nebraska and in Nebraska State Teachers College at Wayne, 1940-1950; unsuccessful candidate for election in 1958 to the Eighty- sixth Congress; elected as a Republican to the Eighty-sixth Congress, by special election, December 15, 1959, to fill the vacancy caused by the death of Steven V. Carter; reelected to the two succeeding Congresses and served from December 15, 1959, to January 3, 1965; unsuccessful candidate for reelection in 1964 to the Eighty-ninth

Congress; elected to the Ninetieth Congress; reelected to the two succeeding Congresses and served from January 3, 1967, to January 3, 1973; unsuccessful candidate for reelection in 1972 to the Ninety-third Congress; assistant secretary, congressional and legislative affairs, Department of the Interior, 1973-1977; executive vice president, Occidental International Corporation, 1977-1985; is a resident of Phoenix, Ariz.

L

LANDERS, ANN, (1918-) — advice columnist, was born Esther Pauline Friedman in Sioux City, Iowa to Abraham, a motion picture exhibitor, and Rebecca (Rushall) Friedman. She is twin sister to Pauline Ester Phillips whose pen name is Abigail Van Buren, or better known as "Dear Abby." Esther graduated from Sioux City High School in 1936 and attended Morningside College in the same town, majoring in psychology and journalism.

Miss Friedman became Mrs. Jules William Lederer on July 2, 1939. Although she was a housewife, she also volunteered at political and philanthropic agencies. In 1955, the Sun Times in Chicago, where the Lederers were living, needed a columnist to fill the vacant "Dear Ann Landers" spot in the paper. Mrs. Lederer applied and got the job, beating out twenty-eight more qualified women. Her first column was run on October 16, 1955 in twenty-six newspapers. Currently it runs in over nine- hundred newspapers across the country.

Ann Landers covers all types of subjects in her column including dating, divorce, philandering, sex, drugs, bi-racial marriages, living together, alcoholism, and much more. She gives practical, common sense advice in a straightforward, no-nonsense manner. People appreciate her directness and her wisdom. Her values may seem old-fashioned to some, as when she advised a young lady not to go on the road with her traveling salesman boyfriend or when she advised a young girl worried about her mother's drinking habits to seek help from a clergyman, but many people read and heed her advice.

Ann Landers receives nearly 1,000 letters every day from people seeking her advice. She frequently calls on outside experts to help her out with advice to some of the more difficult issues.

On the same subjects she has addressed in her column, Ann has also written several books, including *Since You Ask Me, Ann Landers Talks to Teenagers About Sex, Ann Landers Says: Truth is Stranger, The Ann Landers Encyclopedia: Improve Your Life Emotionally, Medically, Sexually, Spiritually,* and *Ann Landers Speaks Out.* Booklets that she has written include: "Straight Dope on Drugs," "Teen Sex and 10 Ways to Cool It," "High School Sex and How to Deal With It: A Guide for Teens and Their Parents," and "Bugged By Parents? How to Get More Freedom."

Ann Landers has also been the recipient of numerous awards and honors including an award from the National Family Service Association; the Adolf Meyer award from the Association of Mental Health; the President's Citation; two National awards from the National Council on Alcoholism; the Golden Stethoscope Award from the Illinois Medical Association; the Humanitarianism award from the International Lions Club; and several more including honorary degrees from Morningside College; Wilberforce College; and the University of Cincinnati.

LANE

After thirty-six years of marriage, Ann Landers and her husband split up. When readers inquired as to why, she refused to give any explanation.

LANE, JOSEPH REED, (1858-1931) — a U.S. Representative from Iowa; born in Davenport, Scott County, Iowa, May 6, 1858; attended the public schools; was graduated from Knox College, Galesburg, Ill., in 1878 and from the law department of the State University of Iowa at Iowa City in 1880; was admitted to the bar in the latter year and commenced practice in Davenport, Iowa; served as regent of the State University of Iowa; member of the city council 1884-1889; elected as a Republican to the Fifty- sixth Congress (March 4, 1899-March 3, 1901); was not a candidate for renomination in 1900; resumed the practice of law in Davenport, Iowa; delegate to the Republican National Convention in 1908; died in Davenport, Iowa, on May 1, 1931; interment in Oakdale Cemetery.

LANGDON, HARRY, (1884-1944) — comedian, was born in Council Bluffs, Iowa to William Wiley Langdon and Levina (Lookenbill) Langdon. His parents were Salvation Army officers who had five children, of which Harry was the third. The family was very poor and Harry had to go to work at a very young age in order to supplement the family's income. Then, at the age of thirteen, he left home and went with a traveling medicine-show company.

Harry Langdon spent the next twenty-five years traveling the vaudeville circuit. One act that he became famous for during the first World War was "Johnny's New Car," in which he portrayed a stranded motorist trying to start his car. On November 23, 1904, Langdon married Rose Frances Clark, a fellow vaudeville performer. Sadly, the marriage ended in divorce in 1929.

In 1923, Langdon signed a contract with Principle Pictures Corporation, who then sold it to Mack Sennett. Langdon made twenty-five two-reel films with Sennett and became one of the most popular silent movie comedians during that time.

In 1926, Langdon was offered and signed a contract with the First National Corporation to make six full length comedy films, with a salary of approximately $7,500 per week. When he took the contract, he also took with him several of Sennett's best employees, including director Harry Edwards and writer Frank Capra. With Harry and Frank working with him, Langdon's first three films, *Tramp, Tramp, Tramp, The Strong Man,* and *Long Pants,* were a smashing success. Unfortunately, Langdon got so cocky and full of himself that he thought he no longer needed Edwards and Capra. After a dispute, the team split up and Langdon started writing his own material. As a result, the next three films, *Three's a Crowd, The Chaser,* and *Heart Trouble,* were veritable flops and Langdon's contract was dropped. Not the least of Langdon's troubles with the films was the fact that he was lousy at handling money. He had the films' budgets spent before the scripts were even written. He was equally in-ept with his personal finances and was bankrupt by 1931. It has been said that Harry Langdon once turned down a three-thousand dollar a week job of writing a daily comic strip because he claimed he was too busy and too successful.

Langdon tried to make a comeback in Hollywood after spending a year and a half back in vaudeville but was unsuccessful in his attempts because he had not kept up with the changes and his material was sadly outdated. Though he made a few shorts and some feature length films, Langdon never made his coveted comeback and he died of a cerebral hemorrhage on December 22, 1944.

Langdon had married twice more after his first marriage failed. His second marriage to Helen Walton, also failed after five years, but his third marriage was in tact at the time of his death. He was survived by his wife, Mabel Watts Sheldon and their son, Harry Philmore, Jr.

LARRABEE, WILLIAM, (1832-1912) — thirteenth governor of Iowa (1886-90), was born in Ledyard, Connecticut on January 20, 1832, son of Adam and Hannah Gallup (Lester) Larrabee. His father, a graduate of West Point Military Academy, was a captain of artillery in the War of 1812, and was severely wounded in the battle of La Cole Mills, Canada. Larrabee was educated at the common schools of the neighborhood, and in 1853, moved to Iowa. During the first winter there, he taught school in Hardin, Alamakee County, and afterward, for three years, ran a farm near there. He then became engaged in milling and manufacturing. In 1872 he engaged in banking, although still continuing his manufacturing interests, and by his well known capacity, integrity and financial standing, succeeded in building up an extensive business connection, aiding various commercial enterprises in the states and accumulating a comfortable competence. Larrabee was one of the founders of the Republican Party in Iowa, and was always an active and consistent supporter of its principles.

In 1867 he was elected to the state senate, and served continuously for eighteen years, being five times renominated by acclamation, and as regularly reelected. At the commencement of his second term, he was appointed chairman of the Committee on Ways and Means, thus becoming prominent in the management of the state monies and other important trusts. He took an active part in the passage of the excellent laws regarding railroads and rapidly became a marked figure among the lawmakers. In 1885, before the expiration of his last term, he was nominated for governor and was elected for two successive terms, declining a renomination in 1890. He was appointed chairman of the State Board of Control and continued to serve in that capacity for two years, resigning the office in February, 1900. He spent about six months visiting Palestine and various countries in Europe. He was the author of *The Railroad Question* (1893), which was recognized as an authority on the subject. He was the inventor of a grain separator, for which he had obtained a patent.

Larrabee was married to Ann M. Appelman, and the couple had six children. He died on November 16, 1912.

LEACHMAN, CLORIS, (1926-) — actress, was born in Des Moines, Iowa, the oldest child in her family. Her father was a lumber company manager and the family lived on the outskirts of Des Moines in a house with no running water. Cloris learned to play the piano at five years of age, using a cardboard keyboard instead of a real piano since the family couldn't afford one. When she was a little older, her mother urged her to hitch a ride on a coal truck to Drake University in Des Moines to try out for a part in a student play. She got the part and later she appeared on radio shows, receiving a scholarship to study broadcast drama at Northwestern University in Evanston, Illionis. A Des Moines radio station later gave her her own program giving advice to homemakers. After high school, Cloris attended Northwestern University on an Edgar Bergen scholarship to major in theatre. Unfortunately, Miss Leachman was not a very good student and dropped out after only a year. Before she left Chicago, she indirectly entered the annual "Miss Chicago" competition (a friend had sent in an entry for her), and ended up in the Miss American pageant in Atlantic City, Jew Jersey in 1946. Even though she didn't win the competition, she won a $1,000 talent scholarship.

After the contest, Miss Leachman went to New York and and got her first real acting job as an extra in the movie *Carnegie Hall*. In 1948, she made her debut on a Broadway stage in a full length feature entitled, *Sundown Beach*. The play was unfortunately condemned by critics and shutdown after only seven performances. In 1950, she played Celia in a Theatre Guild production of *As You Like It* which was much better received by critics. Other Broadway plays she landed parts in include, *A Story for a Sunday Evening; Let Me Hear the Melody,* in which she beat out Ginger Rogers, Paulette Goddard and Shelley Winters for the lead role; *Lo and Behold; Dear Barbarians;* and *Sunday Breakfast,* among others.

In the mid-1950's, Miss Leachman left the Broadway stage and took to television drama where she earned the title of "the best bad girl on television." After one more stint on Broadway, she made her motion picture debut in *Kiss Me Deadly*.

Throughout the 1950's and early 1960's, Leachman appeared in small or guest parts in several television dramas, but perhaps the one she is best known for is as Mary Richards' obnoxious next door neighbor, Phyllis, on the *Mary Tyler Moore Show*. For her performance on the show, Miss Leachman received two successive Emmy awards as best supporting actress in a comedy series. Because she wasn't a weekly guest on the show, Miss Leachman was free to accept other engagements such as, *Lovers and Other Strangers; The People Next Door,* and *The Last Picture Show,* for which she won an Oscar in 1972 for best supporting actress of 1971. Other motion picture films she has had roles in include, *Charley and the Angel, Dillinger, Happy Mother's Day, Love, George, Daisy Miller, Young Frankenstein, Crazy Mama, High Anxiety, The North Avenue Irregulars, Scavenger Hunt, Herbie Goes Bananas, History of the World, Part I, Shadow Play, Walk Like a Man,* and *Hansel and Gretel.* Other made for television movies she has been in include: *A Brand New Life, Dying Room Only, Death Sentence, Thursday's Game, Someone I Touched,* and *The Haunts of the Very Rich.*

Cloris Leachman is known as an extremely versatile actress and, though she has played many roles of homely women, is actually a very beautiful woman. She was also one of the original founding members of the Actor's Guild. She has won a total of six Emmy awards for her performances.

Cloris Leachman married George H. England in the mid-1950's and had five children, Adam, Bryan, George, Morgan, and Dinah. After being separated for awhile, the couple divorced in 1979.

LEAHY, WILLIAM DANIEL, (1875-1959) — was a United States ambasador who played a large part in shaping the policies of the United States Navy.

Born in Hampton, Iowa on May 6, 1875, he ws graduated from the United States Naval Academy in 1897. He first saw military service in the Spanish War during the Philippine Insurrection. In 1912, he was chief of staff of the Nicaraguan occupation and in 1916, held the same position in the Haitian campaign.

During World War I, Leahy attained the rank of captain after being in command of the *U.S.S. Dolphin* in the Mexican Punitive Expedition of 1916. From 1927 until 1931, he was chief of the Bureau of Ordnance with the rank of rear admiral. In 1936 and 1937, he was promoted to admiral in command of the Battle Force and he was chief of Naval Operations until he retired in 1939 at the age of 65. Leahy was the only officer in naval history to have been chief of the two important bureaus of Ordnance and Navigation as well as chief of Naval Operations. President Franklin Roosevelt awarded him the D.S.M. in 1939. In that same year, Leahy was appointed governor of Puerto Rico.

In 1940, as Leahy was finishing his second term as governor, President Roosevelt selected him as ambassador to France. His appointment was unanimously confirmed by the U.S. Senate. It was generally believed that as ambassador, Leahy would strengthen Petain's hands in his negotiations with Germany by assuring him of the understanding and friendship of the United States. The French also approved of the selection, viewing Leahy's appointment as further expression of the Roosevelt Administration's interest in the problem of the West Indies.

In December 1940, Leahy sailed for France. But soon events were making it increasingly clear that his main task, the stiffening of Petain's spine against collaboration, was an impossibly difficult one. The growing demand at home for the U.S. to sever diplomatic relations with Vichy entirely and recognize De Gaulle also added to his problems.

Leahy served as chief of staff to presidents Roosevelt and Harry S. Truman during World War II.

He was also senior advisor to President Roosevelt during the Yalta meeting.

He married Louise Tennent Harrington in 1904. The couple had one son. Leahy died on July 20, 1959.

LE COMPTE, Karl Miles, (1887-1972) — a U.S. Representative from Iowa; born in Corydon, Wayne County, Iowa, May 25, 1887; attended the public schools and was graduated from the State University of Iowa at Iowa City in 1909; became owner and publisher of the Corydon Times-Republican in 1910; during the First World War served as a private in the medical detachment of United States General Hospital No. 26 in 1918; member of the State senate 1917-1921; elected as a Republican to the Seventy- sixth and to the nine succeeding Congresses (January 3, 1939- January 3, 1959); chairman, Committee on House Administration (Eightieth and Eighty-third Congresses); was not a candidate for renomination in 1958 to the Eighty-sixth Congress; returned to news-paper publishing; retired but continued as a contrib-uting editor; died in Centerville, Iowa, September 30, 1972; interment in Corydon Cemetery, Corydon, Iowa.

LEEDOM, BOYD (STEWART), (1906-1969) — chairman of the National Labor Relations Board (NLRB), was born in Alvord, Iowa to Chester Nevius Leedom, a farmer and Gertrude Emmaline Stewart. In 1907, the family moved to western South Dakota and young Leedom attended public schools and Black Hills Teachers College. Later, he earned his LL.B. degree at the University of South Dakota in 1929.

In the same year that he completed his degree at the University of South Dakota, Leedom began to practice law. During World War II, he served two years stateside in the U.S. Navy and then returned to Iowa and his law practice. Later, he served for two years in the South Dakota State Senate and in 1950, ran unsuccessfully for the Republican nomination for governor. In 1951, he received an appointment to the South Dakota Supreme Court. In 1954 and 1955, Leedom was appointed by Secretary of Labor James P. Mitchell to serve as referee on the National Railroad Adjustment Board. Secretary Mitchell was so impressed with Leedom's handling of labor disputes that he advised President Eisenhower to nominate Leedom for the chairmanship of the National Labor Relations Board (NLRB). President Eisenhower did just that in February of 1955 and then in November of that same year, appointed Leedom as chairman of the NLRB, where he served for ten years -- two consecutive terms.

Leedom was known as a moderate within the NLRB. He spent much of his time handling administrative problems and had a background of being non-controversial. He also generally avoided open political activity. However, Leedom and the NLRB were under constant attack from the Democratic politicians for alleged anti- labor bias. Because he was concerned about a large caseload and delays Leedom hired a consulting firm to come in and conduct an efficiency study of the agency. The study resulted in the McKinsey Report which exposed sluggishness in the labor and management areas and proposed greater distribution of authority to regional offices. Leedom tried to quietly and slowly put into effect what the report suggested, but word of the report was leaked to the press by a Democratic politician with a personal vendetta against Leedom. Leedom and the NLRB came under attack for the delays and alleged anti-labor bias. The attacks hurt

Leedom's position and during the Kennedy and Johnson administrations, his role within the NLRB changed dramatically. Kennedy assigned a new chairman and other new board members. Then the board, made up of mostly Kennedy appointees, reversed many key decisions that the Eisenhower board had made. Leedom disputed the reversals, but to no avail. President Johnson did not reappoint him and he became a trial examiner for the board instead.

Boyd Leedom married Irene Cecil Robertson on December 29, 1927 and the couple had three children: Chester Boyd, Linda Ann and Mary Catherine.

Leedom was a devout Methodist and Sunday School teacher. He also promoted the Billy Graham Evangelistic Crusade and served as president of International Christian Leadership.

Leedom died in Arlington, Virginia in 1969.

LEFFLER, SHEPHERD, (1811-1879) — (brother of Isaac Leffler), a U.S. Representative from Iowa; born on his grandfather's plantation, "Sylvia's Plain," Washington County, Pa., near Wheeling, Va. (now West Virginia), April 24, 1811; attended private schools and was graduated from Washington College, Washington, Pa., and from the law department of Jefferson College, Canonsburg, Pa., in 1833; was admitted to the bar and commenced practice in Wheeling; moved to Burlington, Iowa (then a part of Michigan Territory), in 1835; member of the Territorial house of representatives in 1839 and 1841; served in the Territorial council 1841-1843 and in 1845; member of the constitutional conventions in 1844 and 1846; permanent president during the first convention; upon the admission of Iowa as a State into the Union was elected as a Democrat to the Twenty- ninth Congress in 1846; reelected to the Thirtieth and

LEOPOLD

Thirty- first Congresses and served from December 28, 1846, to March 3, 1851; chairman, Committee on Invalid Pensions (Thirty-first Congress); engaged in the practice of his profession and in agricultural pursuits in Burlington; unsuccessful candidate for election in 1856 to the Thirty-fifth Congress; unsuccessful Democratic candidate for Governor of Iowa in 1875; died at his home, "Flint Hills," near Burlington, Des Moines County, Iowa, September 7, 1879; interment in Aspen Grove Cemetery.

LEOPOLD, ALDO, (1887-1948) — forester and conservationist, was born in Burlington, Iowa to Carl Leopold, an office furniture manufacturer, and Clara (Starker) Leopold. Young Aldo gained an appreciation for the environment while growing up in the Mississippi bottom lands. He attended and graduated form Lawrenceville (New Jersey) preparatory school in 1905 and entered Yale University's Sheffield Scientific School, graduating in 1908 with a B.S. degree. The following year, he received his Master of Forestry degree from the Yale School of Forestry.

After graduating from Yale, Leopold landed a job with the United States Forestry Service as a forest assistant on the Apache National Forest in Arizona. In 1911, he went to work for the Carson National Forest in New Mexico as deputy supervisor. In 1917, he received recognition for his part in the game protection movement with a medal from the Permanent Wildlife Protection Fund and an appointment to assistant director forester in charge of game, fish and recreation.

In 1918, Leopold took a break from the Forestry Service and became secretary of the Albuquerque, New Mexico Chamber of Commerce. In 1919, he returned to the Forestry Service.

In the beginning of his career with the Forestry Service, Leopold thought that in order to protect valued game species there needed to be an elimination of predators. However, his views changed when he realized that balance and long term stability of the wilderness were far better and more constructive goals. In 1921, he wrote in the *Journal of Forestry* about the need for wilderness protection in the national forests, and in 1924, the Forestry Service designated 574,000 acres in New Mexico as the Gila Wilderness area.

From 1924 to 1928, Leopold was the associate director and field consultant of the U.S. Forest Products Laboratory in Madison, Wisconsin. At the end of that four year period, he became game consultant for the Sporting Arms and Ammunition Manufacturer's Institute. In 1931, his *Report on Game Survey of the North Central States* was published and was one of the first thorough studies ever done on the game population in America. Around the same time he also developed a national game management policy for the American Game Protective Association.

In 1933, Leopold accepted a position as professor of wildlife management at the University of Wisconsin where he stayed until is death. In this position, he developed new approaches to deer management, soil conservation, and environmentally responsible agriculture. In 1935, he studied game administration in Germany and Czechoslovakia, and was concerned that America did not adopt the European method of exterminating predators in order to preserve game life. Leopold did not believe that man should try to control his environment, but rather learn to live in it as in a community.

In 1933, Leopold's *Game Management* was published and was considered to be his most important piece of writing. This piece of writing was a textbook that explained how to harvest game species in a more constructive way, leaving their reproductive capacity unimpaired. His ideas were based on the science of systems ecology and blended the most current knowledge of population dynamics, food chains, and habitat protection. In 1949, *A Sand County Almanac* was published after his death and was his best known work, becoming a sort of bible of the environmental movement between 1960 and 1970.

Between the years of 1927 and 1947, Leopold was involved with eight different conservation groups: the Society of American Foresters; the National Audubon Society; the American Forestry Association; the Wilderness Society; the Wildlife Society; the Ecological Society of America; the Special Committee on Wildlife Restoration and the Wisconsin Conservation Commission.

On October 9, 1912, Aldo Leopold married Estella Luna Bergere in Santa Fe, New Mexico and had five children, Aldo Starker, Luna Bergere, Adelina, Aldo Carl and Estella Bergere.

Aldo Leopold died of a heart attack while fighting a grass fire near his cabin on the Wisconsin River on April 21, 1948. His body was buried in Burlington, Iowa.

LEWELLING, LORENZO DOW, (1846-1900) — twelfth governor of Kansas (1893-1895) was born on December 21, 1846 in Salem, Iowa, the son of Cyrena Wilson and William Lewelling. He attended Knox College, Eastman's Business College in Poughkeepsie, New York, and Whittier College, from which he was graduated in 1867. He worked as a carpenter, a tow path boy on the Erie Canal, a railroad section hand, a teacher, and a newspaper publisher.

Between 1868 and 1880, with the exception of two years, he worked in the Iowa reformatory system, most of the time as superintendent of the Iowa Women's Reform School. From 1880 until 1882, he edited the "anti-ring" Republican paper in Des Moines. After his defeat in a race for Iowa Secretary of State and the death of his first wife, Lewelling moved to Wichita, Kansas.

In 1887, Lewelling opened a loan business, and later a commission firm handling nursery stock. Because of his knowledge of the problems of labor and management, as well as his expertise in penal reform, he was made chairman of the Sedgwick County People's Party, which had strong sentiments for fusion with the Democratic Party. As a candidate for governor in 1892, he led the entire ticket to victory and helped James Weaver, the Populist candidate for President, receive the Kansas electoral vote.

Lewelling became the twelfth Kansas governor on January 9, 1893. He claimed that his administration was the first " People's Party government on earth." A legislative war dominated his administration, and very little legislation was completed. The House of Representatives could not develop a clear majority among its Republican, Democratic, or Populist members. The issue was finally decided in favor of the Republicans by the Republican Supreme Court.

Controversy broke out with Lewelling's appointment of Mary Elizabeth Lease as superintendent of the State Board of Charities, because she did not support the fusion idea that had brought about Lewelling's election. He was also criticized for his "tramp circular," a condemnation of vagrancy laws in which he suggested that society should reconsider its traditional treatment of vagrants and the unemployed.

His support of the women's suffrage plank in the party platform of 1894 alienated the Democrats, and with a show of independence, the Populist Convention renominated the entire Lewelling slate. However, he lost to Edmund N. Morrill, the Republican candidate.

Lewelling returned to Wichita and established a dairy farm and creamery business. He later became manager of a land company and a travelling lecturer for the Modern Tontines. He was elected to a four-year term in the State Senate in 1896. He also served as a member of the State Railway Commission from 1897 until 1899. In 1900, he became a land agent for the Atchison, Topeka and Sante Fe Railroad.

Lewelling was married to Angeline Cook on April 16, 1870. He married Ida Bishop in 1886 or 1887. He was the father of four children. He died on September 3, 1990.

LEWIS, JOHN LLEWELLYN, (1880-1969) — labor leader, was born near Lucas, Iowa to Thomas H. and Anna Louisa (Watkins) Lewis, both Welsh immigrants. John Lewis' father was a coal miner who was blacklisted from working in the mines for having participated in a Knights of Labor strike. Not able to find work as a miner because of the blacklisting, Thomas Lewis had to find other sources of employment. Young John Lewis left school after the seventh grade in order to work in the mines and supplement the family income.

At the age of twenty-one, Lewis set out on his own, traveling around and working at various jobs most of which were mining. During this time he gained a valuable perspective on labor conditions which would help him in his chosen career later on.

In 1906, he returned to Lucas and became a Lucas mine delegate to the national convention of the United Mine Workers of America (UMWA). In 1908, he became legislative representative for the UMWA and in 1911 became field and legislative representative of the American Federation of Labor (AFL). From February to July 1917, he was statistician for the UMWA and was also manager for the organization's journal. From 1917-1918, he was vice- president of the UMWA, in 1919, became acting president, and from 1920 through 1960, served as its president.

In 1924, Lewis helped to plan a three-year contract between the union and the miners which called for a daily pay rate of $7.50 for all union miners. Secretary of Commerce, Hoover was thrilled with the plan and offered Lewis the position of Secretary of Labor, which he refused. Unfortunately the plan turned out to be one of the biggest mistakes of Lewis' life because the mine operators decided to hire non-union laborers and the agreement then served no purpose.

In 1935, Lewis and seven other union presidents formed a Committee of Industrial Organization (CIO) within the AFL. In 1938, after a two-year suspension, the committee was reorganized and called the Congress of Industrial Organization, with Lewis presiding. In 1936, Lewis and another member of the CIO, Sydney Hillman, founded Labor's Non-Partisan League, which at that time was in support of President Franklin D. Roosevelt's reelection. During the little steel strike of 1937, because of Roosevelt's nonsupport for labor, Lewis quit backing him and actually rallied against his run in 1940 for reelection. Lewis resigned from the CIO when Roosevelt was reelected and in 1942, pulled the Mine Workers out as well.

In 1935, Lewis had engineered the passage of the Guffey Coal Act designed to stabilize coal prices. In the 1950's, he began to cooperate with mine owners, helping them to automate and close inefficient mines. He was largely responsible for winning periodic wage increases, vacation pay, pensions, pay for underground, travel time and improved mine safety through federal inspection of mines.

John Lewis married his school teacher/mentor, Myrta Edith Bell on June 5, 1907. Myrta gave up teaching in order to help her husband with his career. The couple had two children, John L. Lewis, Jr. and Kathryn Lewis. Mrs. Lewis died in the fall of 1942. John L. Lewis died on June 11, 1969. He was considered to be the most important figure in the American labor movement in the twentieth century.

LIEURANCE, THURLOW, (1878-1963) — American Indian historian and composer famous for his use of Indian themes.

Born March 21, 1878, in Oskaloosa, Iowa, Lieurance became interested in American Indian music and customs as a child. He served as a bandmaster during the Spanish-American War, then graduated an honor student at the College of Music in Cincinnati. He earned his doctorate there in 1925. He married Edna Wooley in 1918, and they had one son.

Lieurance spent 20 years of his life researching the musical works of American Indians and recording their songs, the results of which are the most extensive collections of Indian music to date. He also composed his own music for piano and orchestra, the most famous of which was "By the Waters of the Minnetonka" (also known as Moon Deer). Other compositions include: "Nine Indian Songs," 1919, "Songs of the North American Indian," 1921, "Eight Songs From Green Timber," 1922, "Forgotten Trails," 1923 and an opera, "Drama of the Yellowstone." Lieurance was on the faculty at the University of Nebraska and in 1940 was named the dean of the department of music at Wichita University. He died in Boulder, Colorado, October 9, 1963.

LIGHTFOOT, JAMES ROSS, (1938-   ) — a U.S. Representative from Iowa; born in Sioux City, Iowa, September 27, 1938; raised on a farm near Farragut, Iowa; graduated from Farragut High School, 1956; served in the United States Army and Army Reserve, 1956-1964; managed a farm equipment plant in Corsicana, Tex., 1970-1976; served on Corsicana City Commission, 1974-1976; radio broadcaster and farm editor in Shenandoah, Iowa; elected as a Republican to the Ninety-ninth and One Hundredth Congresses (January 3, 1985-January 3, 1989); is a resident of Shenandoah, Iowa.

LOGAN, JOHN BURTON, (1923-1987) — poet and author, born in Red Oak, Iowa to James Borland, an accountant, and Agnes (Kemmas) Logan. Logan attended Coe College where he earned his B.A. degree in biology in 1943. He earned his M.A. in 1949 from the University of Iowa. He had also briefly attended Georgetown University and Notre Dame University.

Logan taught at several colleges and universities including St. John's College, Notre Dame, the University of Washington, San Francisco State University and the State University of New York. He served as poetry editor of the *Nation* and *Critic* as well as a poetry columnist for the latter. He also founded and co-edited *Choice* magazine.

Logan's work received much critical acclaim even though he is a relatively little known poet. His poetry has been compared to that of Thomas Merton and Robert Lowell. In philosophy, he has been compared to existential humanist Martin Heidegger who was a pursuer of authenticity and wholeness of human 'being'.

Logan's published works, described as being profound and visceral, include *A Cycle for Mother Cabrini,*his first book which has as its subject, the immigrant nun who contributed greatly to the city of Chicago by building schools, hospitals and orphanages; *Ghosts of the Heart; Spring of the Thief; Zig Zag Walk; Anonymous Lover; Poems in Progress;* and *The House That Jack Built,* an autobiographical novel full of the experiences of Logan's childhood.

Logan received many awards and honors for his work including Wayne State University's Miles Modern Poetry Prize in 1968, a Rockefeller Foundation grant in 1969, the National Institute of Arts and Letters Morton Dauwen Zabel Award in 1974, a State University of New York Research Foundation Fellowship in poetry in 1979, and a Guggenheim Fellowship in 1980.

John Logan married Mary Guenevere Minor, a librarian, on September 9, 1945. The couple had nine children: John, Theresa, Christina, Peter, Alice, David, Mark, Stephen and Paul. The marriage later ended in divorce.

John Logan died of heart failure and complications after gall bladder surgery in San Franciso, California on November 6, 1987.

LOVELESS, HERSCHEL C., (1911-) — was Governor of Iowa from 1957 to 1961.

Born in Hedrick, Iowa on May 5, 1911, he was an employee of the Chicago, Milwaukee, Saint Paul, and Pacific Railroad from 1927 to 1939. In the latter year he got a job working at the John Morrell Company, then in 1944, returned to his railroad position where he remained for the next three years.

From 1947 to 1949, he worked for the city of Ottumwa as superintendent of streets, then became that city's mayor in 1949. In 1953 he left that office and became owner and manager of the Municipal Equipment Company until 1956. His first bid for governor failed after he lost to the incumbent, William Beardsley, and he also failed in his bid for a Congressional seat in 1954. However, he ran against Republican Governor Leo Hoegh in the 1956 race and won due to voter anger at Hoegh's tax increases.

Loveless served two terms as governor, implementing such decisions as a small monthly stipend for teachers, a workmen's compensation and unemployment compensation increase, and the creation of a mental health fund. He also refused to extend the sales tax left by his predecessor. Loveless served as governor until January of 1961.

Later that year, he began serving on the Renegotiation Board, staying in that position until 1969 when he took the post of vice president of the Chromalloy American Corporation.

Loveless is married to Amelia R. Howard and the couple have two children.

LOWE, RALPH PHILLIPS, (1805-1883) — fourth governor of Iowa (1858-60), was born in Warren County, Ohio on November 27, 1805, son of

LOWE

Jacob Derrick and Martha (Per-Lee) Lowe. He received his early education in the schools of his hometown, and entered Miami University in 1825. He went to Asheville, Alabama before graduating, where he taught school and studied law, then formed a law partnership with his brother, Peter P. Lowe in Dayton, Ohio. In 1840 he moved to Bloomington (now Muscatine), Iowa, where he practiced his profession and engaged in farming. He was a member of the first constitutional convention, and was also a district attorney and district judge.

In 1858, Lowe was elected governor of Iowa, and served until 1860, when he was elected by the people, judge of the supreme court; before this, the election to this office had been made by the legislature. Governor Lowe was conspicuous in his connection with the so-called "Five Per Cent Claim." He held that the lands offered soldiers to enlist, in addition to a certain amount of pay per month, was "pay," and not "bounty"; that the lands were offered as cash is offered, and that they were earned; and, as between the United States and the state of Iowa, no other agreement was known than that the state should not tax lands for five years after being located, and the United States should pay the state five per cent of the sales. Accordingly, the state did not tax lands located under military warrants. If the claim were allowed, the United States would pay the state of Iowa over $800,000; Judge Lowe left the supreme bench in 1868 to prosecute the claim.

Lowe then served as U.S. District Attorney for a few years, and for ten years he lived in Washington, laboring to induce Congress to pay the claim. He had the support of William M. Evarts of New York, Allen G. Thurman, of Ohio, the late Senator McDonald, of Indiana, and Judge Shellabarger, of Washington, D.C. The court decided adversely (Miller and Field dissenting), and, knowing that Judge Lowe was fatally ill, withheld the announcement of the decision until after his death, that he might be spared the disappointment.

Lowe was married to Phoebe Carleton. He died in Washington, D.C. on December 22, 1883.

M

MAHASKAH, (ca. 1784-1834) — a Iowa chief involved in a rather humorous incident while in Washington, D.C. in 1824, was one of the most respected chiefs of the Iowa, a strong leader in war and peace, before his murder.

Born probably in an Iowa village near the mouth of the Iowa River, Mahaskah devoted his early years to avenging the death of his father, chief Wounding Arrow, who was allegedly murdered by the Sioux at a sham peace conference. Mahaskah led many war parties against the Sioux and the Osage to prove himself worthy of his heredity chieftainship, and ended his fighting career before 1824 with a daring raid deep into Osage territory at Little Osage Plains, about 250 miles north of St. Louis. During this time, Mahaskah also took several wives and was once unjustifiably imprisoned by white settlers who feared an Indian uprising.

Thomas L. McKenney describes a humorous accident which befell Mahaskah in Washington, D.C. at a treaty conference in 1824. Reluctantly having brought his seven wives with him to Washington and apparently given beyond endurance by their incessant squabbling, Mahaskah was engaged one night in chasing his wife Female Flying Pigeon around their hotel room with a chair leg when the Indian agent G.W. Kennerly burst into the room, having heard the commotion from downstairs. Embarrassed and probably drunk, Mahaskah immediately stepped out of the room through the window, forgetting he was on the second floor, and in the resulting fall broke his arm. This incident notwithstanding, when Female Flying Pigeon died in a riding accident soon after their return from Washington, D.C., Mahaskah deeply mourned her loss.

In 1833, upon the request of Gen. William Clark, Mahaskah surrendered several Iowa braves guilty of raiding the Omahas, and they were imprisoned in Fort Leavenworth. One brave escaped, vowing revenge, and in 1834 found Mahaskah in camp on the Nodaway River in northwestern Missouri and killed him.

Remembered for his honorable and, for the most part, peaceful leadership of his tribe. Mahaskah was the signer of several treaties; at Washington, Aug. 4, 1824, and at Prairie du Chien, Aug. 19, 1825 and July 15, 1830.

MAHTOIOWA, (?-1854) — also known as The Bear, was the principal chief of the Brule Teton Sioux involved in the Grattan fight near Ft. Laramie, Wyoming, about Aug. 18, 1854. Brule, Oglala, and Minneconjou Siowr had gathered at the fort to receive their annual government dispensations when an ox belonging to a Mormon immigrant was killed by a Sioux. Accounts differ: the ox was either stolen by the Sioux or near death, or had been abandoned by the Mormon. After the Mormon had complained to the fort commandant Lt. Fleming and Mahtoiowa had explained the Sioux version of the incident, a detachment of eighteen men under Lt. Grattan was sent to arrest the offending Sioux. Mahtoiowa pointed out to his tipi to the soldiers but declined to enter it himself and produce the Indian, apparently feeling this was the soldier's duty. Thereupon, Grattan, for reasons unclear, fired a howitzer into the Sioux camp and killed all but one Indian. Sioux warriors immediately surrounded and killed all but one of the Grattan detail, and in the resultant fighting around the fort, Mahtoiowa was killed.

MANFRED, FREDERICK, (1912-) — writer, was born Frederick Feikema, on a farm near Doon, Iowa. He attended public and Christian schools and then Calvin College in Grand Rapids, Michigan. His mother wanted him to enter the ministry, but he had other ideas. Although he earned a teaching certificate, he did not plan on being a teacher either. Instead, Manfred's desires leaned more in the direction of writing. During his years at Calvin, he published several poems and stories in the *Calvin College Chimes,* and *Prism.* Being that he was an extremely tall young man, 6'9," Manfred also played on the college basketball team.

After college, Manfred was not sure what to do with his life, so he wandered and worked at menial jobs for awhile until in 1936, he took his first writing job as a columnist for the New Jersey weekly newspaper, *Prospector.* In 1937, he became a sportswriter for the *Minneapolis Journal* and began writing his first novel. His life took an unfortunate downturn in 1939, when the *Journal* fired him and he came down with tuberculosis the following year, which landed him in a Sanatorium for the next two years. During his time in the Sanitorium, Manfred met his future wife, Maryanna Shorba, whom he married shortly after he left the sanitorium. After his recovery, Manfred worked for *Modern Medicine,* and became campaign manager for Hubert Humphrey's run for the mayor's office. After the election ended and Humphrey lost, Manfred took up writing again and determined to spend the rest of his life in that occupation.

Manfred's first novel, *The Golden Bowl,* which told the story of a family in South Dakota and their struggle to overcome the catastrophic effects of the Dust Bowl, was published in 1944. In that same year he received a Fellowship from the University of Minnesota and the following year, published his second book, *Boy Almighty,* an autobiographical novel. Both of his first two novels were put out by a small publishing company and did not obtain the distribution that Manfred needed to get his career off the ground. His break came when he met Sinclair Lewis who was impressed with *The Golden Bowl.* Through Lewis' contact, Doubleday agreed to publish Manfred's next novel, *This is the Year,* in 1947. Unfortunately, Doubleday dropped him in the early 1950's, after he had hastily written a trilogy of books that did not live up to his usual standard. All this time Manfred had been writing under the name of *Feike Feikema* but decided to change it to Frederick Manfred before his next novel, *Lord Grizzly* was published. That novel turned out to be one of his best and most popular.

Other novels that he has had published include, *Morning Red;*the trilogy, *The Primitive, The Brother,* and *The Giant; The Chokecherry Tree, Arrow of Love, Wanderlust,* and many others. Manfred's novels contain much intimate detail of the midwest countryside that he loves so well. He has been described as "a kind of Thomas Wolfe or Vardis Fisher of the Iowa-Minnesota-South Dakota region which he himself has entitled Siouxland." In addition to writing novels, he has contributed to periodicals such as *New Republic, Esquire, Minnesota Quarterly, American Scholar, Names, Critique, Roundup, South Dakota Review,* and several others.

In October of 1978, Manfred divorced his wife and went back to living alone near Luverne, Minnesota. He has three children, Freya, Marya, and Frederick whom he enjoys spending time with.

MARTIN, GLENN L., (1886-1955) — a pioneering aviator and airplane manufacturer.

Born in Macksburg, Iowa, on January 17, 1886, Martin's dreams of flying were inspired at an early age by his mother. His parents, Clarence Y. and Arminta (Minta) De Long Martin, moved the family to Liberal, Kansas when Martin and already manufacturing and selling kites to other children. The family moved to Salina, Kansas, in 1895 where Martin developed an interest in bicycle and auto mechanics. As a young adult he attended Kansas Wesleyan before his family moved to Santa Ana, California, in 1905.

A young entrepreneur, Martin owned and operated a Ford and Maxwell automobile agency in California, where he also did mechanical work. An avid reader, Martin learned of the Wright Brothers in 1906, then researched and built his own glider in 1907. Using an abandoned church he started his own airplane factory in 1909, building his first airplane using a Ford Model V motor. Martin taught himself to fly using this airplane and became the third American to take to the air.

To support his fledgling aircraft business Martin became a nationally known barnstormer. Known as a snappy dresser he was nicknamed "The Dude," and he traveled the United States winning prizes for his daring flights. His stunt skills landed him a role in the movie The Girl of Yesterday with Mary Pickford, where he played a villain who carried Pickford away in an airplane. Martin also continued to break world records for altitude and endurance. In 1912 he was the first person to complete a successful overwater flight, traveling from Los Angeles to Catalina Island.

In 1911 Martin moved his factory to Los Angeles, where he built training planes for the U.S. Army. In 1917 he merged his company with his former mentors, the Wright Brothers, but later in the year he pulled out of the deal and organized the Glen L. Martin Company. A factory was built in Cleveland, Ohio, which manufactured Martin Bombers (MB-2), a design which established Martin's company as one of the leading airplane manufacturers in the United States. In 1929 the company moved its operations again, this time to Middle River, Maryland, in order to be closer to Washington, D.C. Martin's designers developed a new twin- engine bomber, known as the B-10, which was twice as fast as any bomber built at that time. The Middle River plant continued building military aircraft from 1929 to 1945, including such models as the China Clipper, the Hawaiian Clipper, the Philippine Clipper, the British Maryland, the British Baltimore, the B-26 Marauder, PBM and Mars airplanes. In 1932 he received the Collier Trophy from President Roosevelt for the greatest achievement in aeronautics and in 1948 he was awarded the President's Certificate of Merit for meritorious service in aiding the United States during World War II.

Outside of aviation Martin was an avid outdoorsman and was active in conservation activities. He was a former trustee in the North American Wildlife Foundation, a former director and vice president trustee of Ducks Unlimited, member of the Maryland

State Game and Fish Protection Association and in 1943 he was honored by Sports Afield as America's Outstanding Conservationist. He was also interested in education, establishing the Minta Martin Aeronautical Endowment at the Institute of Aeronautical Sciences in New York, and donating millions to the University of Maryland's Glenn L. Martin Institute of Technology.

The Glenn Martin Company experienced hard times in the early 1950's, and during the Korean War the Navy reorganized the company. Still a multi-millionaire, Martin was only allowed to hold a position as honorary chairman of the board. He took this setback well and the company began to do better financially. However, Martin was deeply depressed by the death of his mother in 1953, and he died less than two years after her at the age of 69.

MARTIN, THOMAS ELLSWORTH, (1893-1971) — a U.S. Representative and a U.S. Senator from Iowa; born in Melrose, Monroe County, Iowa, January 18, 1893; attended the public schools; graduated from the State University of Iowa in 1916 and from its law college in 1927; graduated from Columbia University graduate school in 1928; sales analyst and accountant for a rubber company in Akron, Ohio, and Dallas, Tex., in 1916 and 1917; during the First World War served as a first lieutenant with the Thirty-fifth Infantry, United States Army 1917-1919; continued work in the rubber industry; assistant professor of military science and tactics, University of Iowa, 1921-1923; accountant; admitted to the Iowa bar in 1927 and commenced practice in Iowa City; city solicitor for Iowa City 1933-1935; mayor of Iowa City 1935-1937; elected as a Republican to the Seventy-sixth and to the seven succeeding Congresses

MAXWELL

(January 3, 1949-January 3, 1955); was not a candidate for renomination in 1954; elected as a Republican to the United States Senate in 1954, and served from January 3, 1955, to January 3, 1961; was not a candidate for renomination; retired and moved to Seattle, Wash., where he died June 27, 1971; interment in Willamette National Cemetery, Portland, Oreg.

MAXWELL, ELSA, (1883-1963) — author, actress and lecturer, was born in an opera box in Keokuk, Iowa. It seems that while her mother, was pregnant with Elsa, she attended a performance of *Mignon*and delivered the baby right there in the opera box. Elsa grew up in California, and ironically, won a medal as California's most beautiful baby (ironic, because later in life, she was not a pretty woman in the least.) She attended Miss West's private school in San Francisco and was found to have quite a talent for playing music by ear. She could play all sorts of musical instruments, however, according to Miss Maxwell, she was exploited for her gifts and never taken seriously.

Miss Maxwell started earning a living as a very young girl and did so by playing the piano in a motion-picture theatre. She eventually played for some of the greats, such as Caruso, Melba and Alda and wrote musical compositions which have been used by the likes of Kreisler, Melchior, Tibbett, Alda and others. She wrote scores for revues, musical comedies and a major symphony. She began writing songs in 1907, and some eighty of them have been published. Music was her first love but did not become her main vocation.

Although she dropped out before completing high school, Miss Maxwell later attended the University of

California and the Sorbonne in Paris. At the same time, she travelled with a Shakespeare company and played in South African Music Halls, as well as continuing to write music. It was around this time that she also began doing what she became most well known for, giving parties for the rich and famous. By the first World War, she had established quite a reputation for herself as a hostess and entertainer, doing anything for a laugh and good at inventing little games for her guests that would keep them entertained for hours. Once, at a dinner she held for a few friends in Hollywood, she put a live duckling at each lady's plate, and another time, to liven up a party she threw a banana peel on the stairway and pretended to slip on it, laughing while bouncing all the way down on her backside. But Miss Maxwell was a women of many talents for she also launched night clubs in England and America, organized the golf course at the Lido in Venice, and ran a night club on a barge in the Grand Canal, also in Venice. Once she was asked by the Prince of Monaco to spruce up Monte Carlo, so she organized and built the Monte Carlo Beach Club, the Casino Hotel and the Piscine Restaurants.

Miss Maxwell appeared in several short motion pictures including *Elsa Maxwell's Hotel for Women*, *Elsa Maxwell's Public Deb Number One*, *Riding into Society*, *Lady and the Lug*, *Stage Door Canteen*, and appeared weekly on the Jack Paar television show. She authored several books including *I Live by My Wits*, *The Life of Barbara Hutton*, and her autobiography, *My Last Fifty Years*. She had a radio program, "Elsa Maxwell's Party Line" and a gossip column which was syndicated in twenty papers with a circulation of three million.

Miss Maxwell was never married. She was quite a robust woman, weighing in at around 196 pounds. Her favorite game, which Winston Churchill taught her, was eight-pack bezique.

Miss Elsa Maxwell died in New York City on November 1, 1963.

MAYNE, WILEY, (1917-   ) — a U.S. Representative from Iowa; born in Sanborn, O'Brien County, Iowa, January 19, 1917; attended the public schools of Sanborn, Iowa; Harvard College, S.B., 1938, and attended the law school in 1938 and 1939; Iowa Law School, J.D., 1941; was a special agent to the F.B.I., 1941- 1943; served in the United States Naval Reserve as a lieutenant with destroyer escort duty in the Mediterranean, Atlantic, and Pacific, 1943- 1945; admitted to the bar in 1941 and commenced practice in Sioux City, Iowa, in 1946; president, Iowa State Bar Association, 1960-1964; chairman, Grievance Commission of Iowa Supreme Court, 1964-1966; commissioner of Uniform State Laws, 1956-1960; elected as a Republican to the Ninetieth and to the three succeeding Congresses (January 3, 1967-January 3, 1975); unsuccessful candidate for reelection in 1974 to the Ninety- fourth Congress; delegate to Food and Agricultural Organization, Rome, 1973; resumed the practice of law in Sioux City in 1975; is a resident of Sioux City, Iowa.

MAYTAG, ELMER HENRY, (1883-1940) — was a leading manufacturer and developer of household appliances, especially the washing machine.

Born in Newton, Iowa on September 18, 1883, he attendd the University of Illinois in 1900-01 and a business college in Quincy, Illinois during the following year. In 1902, Maytag became a factory employee in Parsons Band Cutter & Self Feeder Company, a family business. The company was later renamed the Maytag Company, after his father purchased the interests of the other partners. Maytag advanced through the ranks, eventually obtaining the positions of billing clerk, stock clerk, salesman, general manager, secretary, treasurer and president of the firm.

Under his leadership, the Maytag washers, which were first produced in 1907, were steadily improved. The company added such features as: the first swinging reversible wringer; an electric motor; an all-aluminum tub; and the Gyrafoam washing principle using an agitator and forced water. By 1927, Maytag Company had produced its first million washers, achieving world dominance in the industry. The company work force increased from 1,750 employees in 1926 to 3,200 employees in 1933. Production and sales continued to grow and even during the Great Depression the company saw a profit each year. Branch offices were maintained throughout the United States and Canada.

Maytag's efforts were also directed toward the welfare of his associates and employees. In 1923-24, he assisted many employees in obtaining their own homes when he built 200 residences for sale to them on easy terms. In 1926, he established the E.H. Maytag Trust and each year during 1929 through 1932, he personally set aside $50,000 in trusts for the benefit of employees upon reaching the age of 60.

In addition to his direction of the manufacturing of washers, Maytag was a partner in the Maytag-Smith Company, a home building company; vice president and a director of the Maytag Sales Corporation; treasurer and a director of the Maytag Loan and Abstract Company; and secretary and a director of the Maytag Investment Company. He was also president of the Jasper County Savings Bank in Newton, the Kellogg Savings Bank, and LaGorge Island, Inc., a real estate development company in Miami Beach. Interested in public affairs, he was appointed by Herbert Hoover in 1931 to serve on a national advisory committee organized to deal with unemployment problems. He also took a prominent role in YMCA work. In 1933, Maytag received the Newton Chamber of Commerce's Community Service Award.

Particularly interested in agriculture, Maytag purchased a farm in Iowa in 1918 and added to it until he owned 4,212 acres. He developed a herd of pure-bred Holstein-Friesian dairy cattle and exhibited the animals at leading state fairs across the nation.

Maytag was married to Ora Blanche Kennedy in 1910. The couple had four children. He died on July 20, 1940.

MCCAIN, JOHN SIDNEY, JR., (1911-1981) — Admiral in the United States Navy, was born in Council Bluffs, Iowa, the youngest of three children of Admiral John S. McCain, Sr. and Katherine (Vaulx) McCain. Young McCain was the first full- admiral son of a full admiral in the history of the United States Navy. McCain grew up in Washington, D.C. and entered the United States Naval Academy at Annapolis, Maryland at the age of sixteen. He was rebellious and not a very good student, graduating near the bottom of his class.

McCain served his first tour of duty on the battleship *Oklahoma* and on submarines from 1933 to 1938. In the latter year, he became an instructor of electrical engineering at the Naval Academy. During 1940 and 1941, he was on board the USS *Skipjack* and during World War II, won the Silver Star, the

Bronze Star with Combat "V," and two letters of commendation for his performance in commanding submarines in both the Atlantic and Pacific. He became director of records in the Bureau of Naval Personnel after the war and then in 1949, became a submarine division commander. His successive duties during the 1950's included executive officer of the USS *St. Paul;* director of Navy undersea warfare research and development; commander of submarine Squadron 6; commander of the attack transport USS *Monrovia;* director of progress analysis in the office of the chief of naval operations; commanding officer of the USS *Albany;* and chief of legislative liaison for the secretary of the Navy. In 1959, he was promoted to rear admiral and four years later, to vice-admiral.

From 1962 to 1963, McCain was chief of information and then was a commander of the Atlantic Fleet amphibious force from 1963 to 1965. For his performance during a clash in the Dominican Republic, he was awarded the Legion of Merit. He also received a gold star during his command of the Atlantic amphibious force.

In 1965, McCain became military advisor to the United States Ambassador to the United Nations. He received another Gold Star for "exceptionally meritorious service." In May, 1967, he was promoted to the rank of full admiral as he succeeded Admiral John Smith Thatcher as Commander in Chief of the United States Naval Forces in Europe and in 1968, became commander in chief Pacific after Admiral Ulysses S. Grant Sharp retired.

John S. McCain Jr., married Roberta Wright on January 21, 1933. The couple had three children: Lt. Commander John S. McCain, III, a Navy aviator who

MCCREE

was a P.O.W. in North Vietnam; John Pinckney and Jean Alexandra.

Other awards he has received include the Philippine Legion of Honor and the Republic of Korea's Order of National Security Merit First Class.

McCain retired in 1972 and lived in Washington, D.C. where he served as president of the U.S. Strategic Institute. He died on March 22, 1981 of a heart attack while on a military aircraft returning from Europe.

MCCREE, WADE H., JR., (1920-1987) — judge and solicitor general, was born in Des Moines, Iowa, the son of Wade Hampton McCree, the first black man to own a pharmacy in the state of Iowa and the first black narcotics inspector to work for the Federal Food and Drug Administration (FDA). The McCrees lived successively in Hawaii, Chicago and Boston because of the senior McCree's work with the FDA. Young Wade graduated high school from Boston Latin School and *summa cum laude* from Fisk University in 1941. He then entered Harvard Law School where he graduated with an LL.B. degree in 1944. In between entering and graduating from law school, McCree served a stint as a battalion staff officer during World War II.

After graduating from law school, McCree was ready to embark on his law career in Detroit, Michigan. Unfortunately, racial prejudice smacked him in the face at the first law firm where he applied -- he didn't get the job either. In spite of this first rejection, he practiced law in Detroit, Michigan from 1948 to 1952. In 1952, he was appointed commissioner for the Michigan Workmen's Compensation. He then served as Wayne County's circuit judge until 1961 and in the same year received an appointment by President Kennedy as district judge for Michigan's Eastern district, which he held until 1966. He later received a promotion from President Johnson to the United States Court of Appeals for the Sixth Circuit. In 1977, he received an appointment from President Carter to solicitor general, where he stayed until 1981 and which he described as being "the most exciting lawyer's job in the nation."

Wade McCree, Jr. made it his life's work to be a racial barrier breaker and he faced plenty of barriers. One of the incidences he spoke was one that took place in the court room when a white client asked that Judge McCree be replaced by a white judge because he thought a white judge would be more fair. The incident stuck in McCree's mind for a long time. He said of the incident, "That was one hell of an assumption." Yet McCree did not succumb to racial prejudice himself and was highly regarded among the Supreme Court justices as a man of good character and sound judgment.

In 1981, McCree resigned as solicitor general and joined the staff of the University of Michigan Law School.

In 1946, Wade McCree married Dores B. McCrary, a professional librarian. The couple had two daughters, Kathleen and Karen, and one son, Wade Hampton, III.

Wade McCree received several honors and awards, among them honorary LL.D. degrees from Wayne State University, the Tuskegee Institute, Detroit College of Law, the University of Detroit, Harvard University, Michigan State University, the University of Michigan, and Oakland University. He also received an honorary D.Litt. degree from Centre College in Danville, Kentucky.

MERRILL

Wade McCree, Jr. died on August 30, 1987 from bone marrow cancer.

MERRILL, SAMUEL, (1822-1899) — seventh governor of Iowa (1868-72), was born in Turner, Oxford County, Maine on August 7, 1822, son of Abel and Abigail Hill (Buxton) Merrill. He is of the eighth generation in descent from Nathaniel Merrill who came from Salisbury, England, to Salisbury, Massachusetts, in 1636. Two ancestors, Samuel and Abel Merrill, served in the Revolutionary War, while Thomas, Samuel, and the governor's father served in the War of 1812. Samuel Merrill was brought up on his father's farm, and received only a brief academic education. He began to teach in the common schools at the age of seventeen, and taught successfully for eight years, subsequently becoming superintendent of schools. He moved to Tamworth, New Hampshire, in 1847, and engaged in merchandising. He was a member of the New Hampshire legislature during the exciting years of the repeal of the Missouri Compromise, participating in the celebrated election of John P. Hale and James Bell to the United States Senate.

Merrill moved to Iowa in 1856, continuing as merchant and banker until the outbreak of the Civil War, and later became a member of the Iowa legislature. He was commissioned as colonel of the 21st Iowa Infantry, and served in the western department with General Grant, participating in the battles of Missouri. While commanding the forces in the battle of Hartsville, Missouri, he was severely wounded. He was forced to resign before the end of the war because he was unable to endure the hardships of the service. Being granted a pension for his wounds, he donated the entire proceeds to a hospital in Des Moines, Iowa, for sick and disabled soldiers.

After the war, he was engaged in merchandising and banking until 1868, when he was elected governor of Iowa. In his first inaugural address, he combated the theory that U.S. bonds should be paid in depreciated paper issue, declaring the theory to be in every way vicious and dishonest. In 1868, an amendment to the state constitution was adopted by a public vote, with the word "white" being dropped from the qualification of electors. As governor, he held the plough to break the ground for the state capitol. As chairman of the building commission, he combated speculation and jobbers, and secured the construction of the building by honest day labor. Merrill watched over the charitable institutions of the state, introducing many reforms. Before receiving applications for pardons, he required public notice to be given, and a written opinion of the judge, district attorney and jury before whom the case was tried, while before granting pardon in capital offenses, he had a private interview with the prisoner. He organized a Sunday-school in the chapel of the prison, and secured the services of the justice of the supreme court to superintend the same, which proved to be a success.

Retiring at the end of his second term in 1872, he returned to his occupation as a banker, and in 1889, moved to California, where he spent the last years of his life. Governor Merrill was married three times: to Catherine Thomes, who died in June, 1845; to Elizabeth D. Hill, who died in March, 1888; and to Mary S. Greenwood. Merrill died in Los Angeles on August 31, 1899.

MEZVINSKY, EDWARD MAURICE, (1937-   ) — a U.S. Representative from Iowa; born in Ames, Story County, Iowa, January 17, 1937; attended the public schools; B.A., University of Iowa, Iowa City, 1960; M.A., political science, University of California, Berkeley, 1963; J.D., the same university, 1965; admitted to the Iowa bar in 1965 and commenced practice in Iowa City; legislative assistant to United States Representative Neal Smith (Iowa), 1965-1967; member, Iowa State house of representatives, 1969-1970; elected as a Democrat to the Ninety- third and to the Ninety-fourth Congresses (January 3, 1973-January 3, 1977); unsuccessful candidate for reelection in 1976 to the Ninety-fifth Congress; appointed United States representative to the United Nations Commission on Human Rights, 1977-1979; elected Democratic Party State Chairman of Pennsylvania, 1981-1986; is a resident of Penn Valley, Pa.

MILLER, GLENN, (1909-1944) — bandleader, trombonist and captain in the United States Army Air Corps, was born in Clarinda, Iowa to Lewis Elmer and Mattie Lou (Cavender) Miller. Young Miller attended high school at Fort Morgan, Colorado and later took a two-year course at the University of Colorado from 1924 to 1926. He had learned to play the trombone as a teenager, having bought his first instrument with money he earned by milking cows. His first work as a musician was with Boyd Senter and band in Denver.

After college, Glenn went to the West Coast and worked in small bands. There he joined Ben Pollack while doing arrangements for other bands at the same time. Later he went to New York and worked as a trombonist and arranger for Red Nichols, Victor Young, Jacques Renard, Freddy Rich and others. In the early 1930's, when Ray Noble came to the United States, Miller helped him organize an American orchestra.

Although Miller was quite successful in doing arrangements and playing for other bands, his big dream was to have a band of his own. Finally, in 1935, the time came for him to take the plunge. He was so sure of his ambition that he passed up a $350-a-week job with MGM in order to pursue his dream. After a period of two years, he had his band put together and was ready to go. Their first gig was at the Hotel New Yorker, unfortunately, that was the same night that his percussionist received a better offer. The band was to go through ten months of struggles before Miller dropped it and started over the following year. In 1938, with mostly young, new recruits, and only a couple of the original members, the Glenn Miller Band made a go of it. They faced a lot of hard times but considered it worth it when they were playing to a packed house at the New York theatre, later receiving an offer to play at the famous Glen Island Casino. Miller's desire was that the band would be versatile with its music and able to play different types of music well. The band was however, mostly known for its great rhythm section in spite of the difficulties Miller had with finding good musicians to fill that section.

Songs that Miller and his band were most noted for include their theme song, *Moonlight Serenade,* and *Old Black Joe, Falling Leaves, Johnson Rag, Little Brown Jug, Bugle Call Rag, Tuxedo Junction, Chattanooga Choo-Choo,* and others. In 1940, they were given a spot on national radio with three shows weekly, and in 1941, Miller instituted "Sunset Serenade" in collaboration with the U.S.O., for the men in the armed services. In that same year, Miller and his band were featured in the Twentieth-Century-Fox picture, *Sun Valley Serenade,* with Sonja Henie. They were later seen in the film, *Orchestra Wives* with Ann Rutherford and George Montgomery.

A little known fact about Miller is that before his career took off, he made many small-band records which became collector's items after he became well known. One of those records is an arrangement he did for Benny Goodman and the Charleston Chasers of *Basin Street Blues* and *Beale Street Blues.*

In 1942, Miller announced his intention to break up the band and enter the United States Army Air Force. As a captain in the Air Force, he was given the assignment of putting together a special band which played for marching cadets, troop entertainments, and on a radio recruiting program. In 1944, the band flew to England and played for six months before being scheduled to fly to Paris. Miller went on ahead to make advance arrangements, but his plane disappeared and was never found. The date was December 15, 1944.

Glenn Miller had married his college sweetheart, Helen Burger on October 6, 1928 and had two adopted children, a boy, Steven and a girl, Jonnie. After his death, the band was revived twice, first by Tex Beneke who was succeeded by Ray McKinley, and later by Buddy De Franco. In 1953, a motion picture was made of his life, and entitled *The Glenn Miller Story.*

MILLER, MERLE, (1919-1986) — author, born in Montour, Iowa to Monte M. and Dora B. (Winders) Miller. He attended high school in Marshalltown, Iowa and college at the University of Iowa from 1935 to 1940, except for a year in the middle when he attended the London School of Economics. Miller quit college before completing his degree because he did not want to participate in the ROTC which was a requirement for graduation. He joined the Air Corps in 1942 and worked for the *Yank*publication until 1945. After that, he wrote several articles for various magazines including *Show, Harper's, Esquire, Saturday Review, Reader's Digest, Redbook, Collier's,* and the *New York Times Magazine.* He also wrote several books, fiction and non- fiction, including: *Island 49, We Dropped the A-Bomb, That Winter, The Sure Thing, The Judges and the Judged, Reunion, The Rains Came By, A Secret Understanding, A Gay and Melancholy Sound, A Day in Late September, Only You Dick Darling!; or How to Write One Television Script, and Make $50,000,000, On Being Different: What It Means to Be a Homosexual, What Happened,* and *Marshalltown, Iowa.*

Miller basically had no interests other than writing. He did not do much teaching because he believed that the best way to learn to write is to write. His only real hobby was traveling, but he also liked to drink beer and watch bad movies, when he wasn't writing. He was married for awhile to Eleanor Green, however, that marriage ended in divorce.

Merle Miller died in 1986 of an abdominal infection and peritonitis in Danbury, Connecticut.

MOREY, WALT, (1907-1992) — was an author best known for his children's book, *Gentle Ben.*

Born Walter Nelson Morey in Hoquiam, Washington on February 3, 1907, he struggled mightily with school, describing reading as "a torture for me." Finally, around the age of fifteen he began to make some headway, after which he became a voracious reader. During 1927-28 he attended Benkhe Walker Business College.

Morey worked at several jobs during his adult life including construction, millwork, and also as a professional boxer, winning all of his twenty-three professional matches. He quit boxing after he saw a friend of his, whom he hadn't seen in a while, with his face "all mashed in." Deciding that might eventually be his fate, Morey quit. Other professions Morey was involved in included filbert farming, shipbuilding, deep sea diving, and working as a projectionist manager in a movie house. During 1960-61 he was director of the Oregon Nut Growers Cooperative.

It was during his time as a projectionist that Morey began writing his own stories, eventually joining a freelance writers club and meeting writer John Hawkins, who gave Morey advice and inspiration. Pulp magazines bought his work regularly until they faded out in the 1950s, and Morey went several years without writing another word. It was his wife, according to Morey that "hectored me for the better part of ten years, and to get her off my back--to prove that I couldn't do it--I began the story that became *Gentle Ben.*"

Later writings for young people by Morey included: *Home Is the North* 1967; *Kavik, the Wolf Dog* 1968; *Angry Waters* 1969; *Gloomy Gus* 1970, reprint 1989; *Deep Trouble* 1971; *Scrub Dog of Alaska* 1971, reprint 1989; *Canyon Winter* 1972; *Runaway Stallion* 1973, reprint 1989; *Run Far, Run Fast* 1974; *Year of the Black Pony* 1976; *Sandy and the Rock Star* 1979; and *The Lemon Meringue Dog* 1980.

His adult works included: *No Cheers, No Glory* (1945); (with Virgil Burford) *North to Danger* 1954, revised 1969; *Operation Blue Bear: A True Story* 1975.

Morey's book, *Gentle Ben,* which was translated into several languages, was the catalyst for the film *Gentle Giant,* made in 1967, and for the television series *Gentle Ben,* which aired from 1967 to 1969. Other works by him were adapted for television and film including *Year of the Black Pony,* which was made into the movie *The Wild Pony.*

Considering what a hard time Morey had learning to read, he was happy that he finally had found his calling as a writer, saying: "Nobody can really teach you to write. Not even God can teach you that. But if you're determined to write, not even God can stop you."

Morey was married twice: to Rosalind Ogden, and after her death in 1977, to Peggy Kilburn. He died on January 12, 1992.

MORRIS, MARK, (1956-) — is a highly-respected choreographer.

Born in Seattle, Washington on August 29, 1956, Morris' love of dance and music came at an early age and was encouraged by both of his parents. One of his first major inspirations came at the age of eight when his mother took him to see flamenco dancer Jose Greco. "I adored it," he later told an interviewer, "and it seemed perfectly natural to me that I should start doing that immediately." He learned several styles of dancing from his first dance teacher, Verla Flowers. She remembered her talented student well, telling writer Eric Levin: "He was like a sponge. He could absorb anything just by watching it, even the most complicated rhythms. I never felt I was working with a child." Flowers eventually let him choreograph small portions of her student recitals. After graduating from high school, Morris traveled throughout Europe for several months, and stopped in Madrid long enough to study Spanish dancing. When he returned home to Seattle in 1975, he continued his ballet instruction with Perry Brunson.

MORRIS

Morris eventually went to New York City where he began dancing with the newly-formed Eliot Feld Ballet. Not long after,he decided to go freelance, performing with such troupes as Twyla Tharp's company, as well as the Laura Dean and Hannah Kahn groups. It was during this time that he got to travel extensively to several countries including India and New Zealand.

In 1981 the dancer formed his own Mark Morris Dance Group, and after performing such pieces as *Castor and Pollux* and *Gloria,* for the Dance Theater Workshop, the company got rave reviews. Subsequent works the following year included *Not Goodbye,* choreographed to Tahitian music; *Songs That Tell a Story;* and *New Love Song Waltzes.* Morris then moved back to Seattle for a year, so that he would be "freer to experiment," noting that "you can't be corny in New York anymore."

When he did return to New York, he choreographed such works as *"Tamil Film Songs in Stereo" Pas de Deux; Celestial Greetings; Death of Socrates;* and *Dogtown,* the latter performed to several songs by Yoko Ono. In 1984 his dance troupe performed at the Next Wave Festival, under the aegis of the Brooklyn Academy of Music.

Morris often likes to expand his horizons by choreographing from other sources besides music. His work, *One Charming Night,* was suggested from the Anne Rice novel *Interview With a Vampire,* and he used French writer Roland Barthes's essays to create his *Mythologies,* a trilogy that included: *Championship Wrestling, Soap Powders and Detergents,* and *Striptease.*

In 1986 a number of his works were performed on the Public Broadcasting System's *Great Performances/Dance in America,* and he was also commissioned for a piece to be danced by the Joffrey Ballet, which he called *Esteemed Guests.* The following year, his ballet, *The Red Detachment of Women,* was included in the John Adams opera *Nixon in China,* performed at the Houston Grand Opera. Later works by Morris have included a dance to music based on Hopi Indian chants entitled *Strict Songs.*

In 1988 Morris took a group of his dancers to Brussels, Belgium where they were dancers-in-residence at the Theatre Royal de la Monnaie. In 1990 he was choreographer for the White Oak Dance Project.

In a 1988 *Newsweek* article, writer Laura Shapiro describedMorris's work as "startlingly honest, a quality that often makes his dances more interesting to think about than to watch," but next to the shallowness of most choreography, she noted, it makes his work "stand out dramatically...Morris cultivates his imagination, not his audiences or board of directors, and he does exactly what he wants, not what the dictates of fashion or career bid him to do next."

MOTT, FRANK LUTHER, (1886-1964) — was an historian of journalim, an editor and an educator.

Born on April 4, 1886 near What Cheer, Iowa, he attended Simpsn College; received a Ph.B. degree from the University of College in 1907; and a M.A. and Ph.D. from Columbia University in 1919 and 1920, respectively.

Mott started setting type by the time he was 10 years old. He also worked on newspapers during his high school and college days. Mott was co-editor, with his father, of the *Marengo (Iowa) Republican* from 1907 until 1914, and editor and publisher of the *Grand Junction (Iowa) Globe* from 1914 until 1917. Mott then switched his career to teaching. He held faculty and administrative positions at Simpson College, State University of Iowa, and the University of Missouri. In addition, Mott later served as editor of *Journalism Quarterly* and joint editor of *The Midland.*

Mott began a prolific writing career in 1917, with his first published work, "Six Prophets Out of the Middle West." His short story, "The Man with the Good Face" was later included in "O'Brien's Best Short Stories," anthologized, translated into several foreign languages and used in high school English classes throughout the United States. The complete list of his published materials, both articles and books, is extensive. In 1939, Mott won the Pulitzer Prize for his three- volume "History of American Magazines." His subsequent works earned him a reputation as an noted expert on the subject of American journalism.   Mott married Vera H. Ingram in 1910. The couple had a daughter. He died on October 23, 1964.

N

NAHPOPE, (ca. 1800-) — was Black Hawk's chief lieutenant and one of the vociferous Sauk warriors demanding Indian resistance during Black Hawk's War of 1832. According to some accounts, in fact, it was Nahpope who convinced the hesitant old Sauk chief to take to the warpath. After visiting the British in Canada and the Winnebago prophet Waupeshek in Wisconsin, Nahpope returned to inform Black Hawk that action would win the support of British troops as well as warriors from the Potawatomis, Chippewas, and Ottawas. The Winnebago prophet also assured Nahpope that the British would supply guns, ammunition, provisions, and even a Canadian sanctuary for Black Hawk's followers should they face defeat.

In all of these assurances, Nahpope was deceived. Yet, the promise of such assistance was all that Black Hawk needed to hear. The Black Hawk War, which lasted only about fifteen weeks through the spring and summer of 1832, was really only a series of frontier skirmishes between the Illinois state militia and the small band of Sauk and Fox who refused to surrender their ancestral homeland at the junction of the Rock and Mississippi rivers. During the war, however, Nahpope distinguished himself as a valiant warrior. On July 21, 1832, he commanded a small band of braves in covering the flight of the main body of his people across the Wisconsin River. The outnumbered Indians held off a large militia force, allowing the rest of the tribe to escape.

Nahpope continued to fight the Americans, whom he detested, until he was captured by Keokuk--a fellow tribesman who had found it to his advantage to cooperate with Black Hawk's enemies. Nahpope was sent to Fortress Monroe at Old Point Comfort, Virginia, and was imprisoned there for several weeks along with Black Hawk. President Jackson released them and sent the Sauk warriors back to their people--now living on the west side of the Mississippi River in Iowa.

NAREY, HARRY ELSWORTH, (1885-1932) — a U.S. Representative from Iowa; born in Spirit Lake, Dickinson County, Iowa, May 15, 1885; attended the public schools and Grinnell College, Grinnell, Iowa; was graduated from the State University of Iowa at Iowa City in 1907; was admitted to the bar the same year and commenced practice in Spirit Lake, Iowa; county attorney of Dickinson County, Iowa, 1914-1920 and 1943-1945; city attorney of Spirit Lake, Iowa, 1918-1943; delegate to the Republican State conventions 1916-1960; chairman of the Dickson County Republican Central Committee 1918-1943; elected as a Republican to the Seventy-seventh Congress to fill the vacancy caused by the resignation of Vincent F. Harrington and served from November 3, 1942, to January 3, 1943; was not a candidate for reelection in 1942 to the Seventy-eighth Congress; again practiced law; appointed judge of the fourteenth judicial district of Iowa in 1944 and served until his resignation in 1959; resumed the private practice of law in Spirit Lake, Iowa, until his death August 18, 1932; interment in Lakeview Cemetery.

NEWBOLD, JOSHUA G., (1830-) — tenth governor of Iowa (1877-78), was born in Fayette County, Pennsylvania on May 12, 1830. After receiving a common school education, he moved to Iowa in 1854, settling in Hillsboro, Henry County, where he entered upon a mercantile career. In 1875 he was elected lieutenant-governor of the state of Iowa, and by virtue of this office, succeeded to the governorship upon the resignation of Governor Samuel J. Kirkwood in 1877. Upon the expiration of his term of office in 1878, he moved to Mt. Pleasant, Iowa, and served as mayor of that city in 1901.

P

PARETSKY, SARA, (1947-) — novelist, was born on June 8, 1947 in Ames, Iowa to David Paretsky, a college professor, and Mary Edwards, a librarian.

Her family moved to Lawrence, Kansas when she was still a child. She earned her own way through college, even though her parents paid for her brothers' tuition, and eventually received her Ph.D. from the University of Chicago in 1977. It wasn't until her late twenties, however, that she decided upon writing as a profession.

In the 1970's Paretsky tried a career as a businesswoman, working for Continental National America (CNA) Insurance in the marketing department developing direct-mail campaigns, drafting speeches and writing press releases. In 1977, unfulfilled in her work, she tried writing a mystery novel, which she entitled *Indemnity Only,* but did not complete it until May, 1990. The book is about a female private investigator who Paretsky had created to be somewhat like herself. She has stated that, "...what I really wanted was a woman who was doing what I was doing, which was trying to make a success in a field traditionally dominated by men." Her next two novels, *Deadlock,* and *Killing Orders,* were a continuation of the story of V.I. Warshawski, the female private investigator. In 1985, Paretsky sold the movie rights for $200,000 to TriStar Pictures. However, the film, *V.I. Warshawski,* starring Kathleen Turner, was a big disappointment. Even Paretsky herself conceded that it wasn't very good. The benefits derived from selling the movie rights, however, enabled Paretsky to quit her job at the insurance company and concentrate on writing novels fulltime.

In 1985, Paretsky took on another project, aside from writing novels, and helped to found the Sisters in Crime, dedicated to promoting the work of other female mystery writers who had not received the media attention due them.

Other novels Paretsky has written include *Bitter Medicine, Blood Shot, Burn Marks,* and *Guardian Angel.* She also edited *A Woman's Eye,* an anthology comprising stories written by female crime writers. She was recognized in 1987 as one of Ms. Magazine's Women of the Year and received several awards, including a prize from the Friends of American Writers in 1985 for *Deadlock,* and the Silver Dagger Award from the Crime Writers Association in 1988 for *Blood Shot.*

Paretsky is an activist for abortion rights and has been a member for many years of the board of the Chicago National Abortion Rights Action League. She has been married to Courtenay Wright, an experimental-particle physicist and a professor at the University of Chicago, since 1967. Her husband also acts as her copy editor.

PEPPER, IRVIN ST. CLAIR, (1876-1913) — a U.S. Representative from Iowa; born in Davis County, Iowa, June 10, 1876; attended the public schools; was graduated from Southern Iowa Normal School at Bloomfield in 1897; principal of the Atalissa High School and of the Washington School at Muscatine; secretary for Congressman Martin J. Wade of Iowa 1903-1905; graduated from the law department of George Washington University, Washington, D.C., in 1905; was admitted to the bar the same year and commenced practice in Muscatine, Iowa; served as prosecuting attorney of Muscatine County 1906-1910; elected as a Democrat to the Sixty-second and Sixty-third Congresses and served from March 4, 1911, until his death in Clinton County, Iowa, December 22, 1913; chairman, Committee on Expenditures in the Post Office Department (Sixty-third Congress); interment in Shaul Cemetery, near Ottumwa, Wapello County, Iowa.

PICKETT, CHARLES EDGAR, (1866-1930) — a U.S. Representative from Iowa; born near Bonaparte, Van Buren County, Iowa, January 14, 1866; attended the common schools; was graduated from Iowa State University at Iowa City in 1888 and from its law department in 1890; was admitted to the bar in 1890 and commenced practice in Waterloo, Iowa; vice president of the Pioneer National Bank; regent of the State University of Iowa 1896-1909; elected as a Republican to the Sixty-first and Sixty- second Congresses (March 4, 1909-March 3, 1913); unsuccessful candidate for reelection in 1912 to the Sixty-third Congress; resumed the practice of law in Waterloo, Iowa; chairman of the Republican State conventions in 1899 and 1916; delegate at large to the Republican National Convention in 1920; unsuccessful candidate for the Republican nomination for United States Senator in 1926; died in Waterloo, Iowa, July 20, 1930; interment in Elmwood Cemetery.

PUSEY, NATHAN MARSH, (1907-) — university president born in Council Bluffs Iowa, on April 4, 1907. The youngest of three children of John Marsh and Rosa (Drake) Pusey he grew up in the city of his birth. Pusey attended and graduated from the Abraham Lincoln High School in Council Bluffs, maintaining a practically straight "A" record He was the editor of the school paper, president of the Philomanthian Literary Society and an active participant on the debate and basketball teams.

Pusey held a number of summer jobs including that of messenger for a local savings bank. He was able to attend Harvard University by winning one of two available $450 scholarships established by Mrs. Charles Elliott Perkins. Requirements of the scholarship demanded the recipients remain on the "Dean's List." To assure the necessary high grades Pusey developed methodical work and study habits, placing strict limitations on his extracurricular activities. It was said he was the first student to have held the Perkins scholarship throughout his entire four years of college. The only college sport Pusey participated in was as a substitute on the basketball team during his freshman year. However, in his senior year he took first place in a Harvard-Yale competitive examination in English literature. Majoring in English and comparative literature, Pusey took his A.B. degree *magna cum laude* in June 1928.

He spent a year in Europe and after several unsuccessful attempts to engage employment with a publishing house, he joint the faculty of the Riverdale Country School on the outskirts of New York City. It was over the next two years that Pusey discovered he had an talent for teaching thus began his career in education.

He returned to Harvard in 1931 to prepare for a M.A. degree. In order to qualify for a course taught by Professor William Scott Ferguson, Pusey spent the summer of 1931 studying Greek. As a result, he shifted his major from English to Greek and ancient history. Pusey made a special study of Athenian civilization under Ferguson and took a M.A. with the highest honors in 1932. He took employ at Harvard as a part time assistant in 1933. Pusey was awarded the Archibald Cary Coolidge Fellowship in 1934 which enabled him to continue research in his specialty at the American School of Classical Study in Athens. An essay written under the pseudonym of "Pseudo Politicus. Gent" and entitled "The Political

Theory of Demosthenes brought him a Bowdoin Prize in 1934.

Pusey was invited by university president, Henry M. Wriston in the summer of 1935 to participate in an experimental tutoring program at Lawrence College. The program was a great success and generated student interest in the classics. He was considered by Wriston "without question the most brilliant young teacher he as ever known." Pusey received his Ph.D degree from Harvard in 1937..

Pusey accepted an assistant professorship at Scripps College in Claremont, California in 1938. He taught history and literature for the next two years and in 1940 moved to Middletown, Connecticut to become an assistant professor of classics at Wesleyan University. He was advanced to associate professor in 1943 and was responsible for developing new liberal arts course for freshmen and sophomores. In 1944 Pusey was elected the eleventh president of Lawrence College at Appleton Wisconsin. His nine-year tenure at Lawrence proved successful, he is credited with more than doubling the school's endowment fund, raising faculty salaries and was instrumental in the construction of a new science building, arts building and student union. He also served on the Wisconsin Governor's Commission on Human Rights and as chairman of both the Midwest President's Conference and the commission on liberal education of the Association of American Colleges.

It was announced on June 1, 1953 Pusey would become the twenty-fourth president of Harvard University and the first non- New Englander to earn the honor. The announcement took place on the twenty-fifth anniversary reunion of Pusey Harvard class. Upon taking office Pusey rproclaimed his plans to redevelop the Divinity School and to strengthen the

Graduate School of Education. He retired from Harvard president emeritus in 1971

Pusey's writings include; *The Age of the Scholar: Observations on Education in a Troubled Decade* (Harvard University Press, 1963); *American Higher Education* (1945- 1970); *A Personal Report* (Harvard University Press, 1978); *Lawrence Lowell and His Revolution* (Harvard University Press, 1980).

Pusey married Anne Woodward of Council Bluffs on June 10, 1936. they are the parents of two sons and one daughter.

R

RAWSON, CHARLES AUGUSTUS, (1867-1936) — a U.S. Senator from Iowa; born in Des Moines, Iowa, May 29, 1867; attended the public schools and Grinnell (Iowa) College; engaged in banking and the insurance business and also in the manufacture of clay products; member of the board of trustees of Grinnell College; State chairman of the war work council of the Young Men's Christian Association and served overseas with that organization during the First World War; appointed as a Republican to the United States Senate to fill the vacancy caused by the resignation of William S. Kenyon and served from February 24 to December 1, 1922, when a successor was elected and qualified; was not a candidate for election to fill this vacancy; member of the Republican National Committee 1924-1932; resumed the manufacture of clay products; also interested in banking; died in Des Moines, Iowa, September 2, 1936; interment in Woodland Cemetery.

RAY, ROBERT D., (1928-) — was Governor of Iowa from 1969 to 1983.

Born on September 26, 1928 in Des Moines, Iowa, he attended Drake University, earning a B.A. degree in 1952. He went on to Drake University Law School, receiving his J.D. degree in 1954. Not long after, he passed the bar exam and was given a partnership at the law firm of Lawyer, Lawyer, Ray & Crouch, which later became Lawyer, Lawyer, Ray & Dunn.

In 1956, Ray, a Republican, decided to enter politics, running unsuccessfully for county attorney and state representative. In 1968, he made a bid for the governor's office. His campaign was interrupted when he was involved in a twin-engine plane crash, which caused a six-week stay in the hospital due to his serious injuries. His campaign was kept alive by his staff and friends, and when he was able to get around, he resumed his activities. Although his opponent was supported by incumbent governor, Harold E. Hughes, Ray easily won the election by over 90,000 votes.

A liberal, and supporter of several reforms, Ray was a popular governor and was elected to four consecutive terms. During his administration, a law was passed that prohibited any sort of discriminatory practices concerning housing, employment, or gender. Other measures he supported include: the lowering of the voting age from twenty-one to nineteen; a new "no- fault" divorce law; and the creation of both a Department of Transportation and a Department of Environmental Quality; and a veto to a bill that would have permitted wiretapping. Also, sympathizing with the Native American community, he ordered the state historical museum to eliminate its display of the remains of five Indian graves.

REASONER

Ray retired from office in 1982 and later went into the insurance business. He served in the United States Army from 1946 to 1948. He is married to Billie Lee Hornberger and the couple have three children.

REASONER, HARRY, (1923-1991) — broadcast journalist and author, was born in Dakota City, Iowa on April 17, 1923 to Harry and Eunice (Nicholl) Reasoner. The family moved to Minneapolis and Harry attended West High School there. Desiring to be a writer, he majored in journalism at Stanford University in California and the University of Minnesota, working for the Minneapolis *Times* while he was finishing school.

Reasoner was drafted into the United States Army during World War II and after his discharge, returned to the *Times*. He lost his job, however, after writing an unfavorable review of the musical *Up in Central Park*. In 1946, he published his one and only novel, *Tell Me About Women*, but it did not do well. In 1948, he took a public relations job with an airline for two years, returning to news writing for a Minneapolis radio station in 1950. In 1951, he went to work for the United States Information Agency as writer and editor for its Far East operation for three years. In 1954, Reasoner joined KEYD-TV in Minneapolis as news director in order to gain some television experience so he could eventually work for CBS. In 1956, CBS hired him to work at its network base in New York and in 1958, he received what he considered to be his most important news story, the racial crisis in Little Rock, Arkansas. In 1961, he narrated the *Eyewitness to History* programs, produced by CBS.

One of the programs Reasoner is perhaps best remembered for is his participation in CBS' *60 Minutes,* the magazine-style news program that started up in 1968. The program defied all expectations and became a top-rated television show. Reasoner stayed with the show until 1970 when he went to ABC's nightly news team. He stayed with ABC until 1978 when he left because of the "bad chemistry" between himself and his co-anchor, Barbara Walters. He went back to CBS and *60 Minutes,* until May 1991. He died a few months later after surgery for removal of a blood clot. Harry Reasoner married Kathleen Ann Carroll in 1946 and had seven children: Stuart, Ann, Elizabeth, Jane, Mary Ray, Ellen and Jonathan. He and Kathleen divorced in 1981 and he married Lois in 1988. Reasoner had not received his degree as a young man attending college, but at the age of sixty-six, he went back to school and completed it.

Reasoner received several awards and honors throughout his career including first prize in a Republican Party essay competition, an Emmy for news documentary, a Peabody Award, an honor medal from the University of Minnesota and an Emmy for outstanding news broadcasting. Published works include: *The Reasoner Report,* a collection of essays; and *Before the Colors Fade,* a collection of memoirs. Television broadcasts he narrated aside from those already mentioned include: *Calendar,* "Vote-for What?," *Eye on New York,* "The Fat American," "The Taxed American," "The Teen-Age Smoker," *CBS Reports,* "The Harlem Temper," *Portrait, An Essay on Doors,* "The Catholics and the Schools," *An Essay on Bridges, The Great Love Affair, The National Citizenship Test, The National Health Test,* and *Evening News.*

ROBINSON, THOMAS JOHN BRIGHT, (1868-1958) — a U.S. Representative from Iowa; born in New Diggings, Lafayette County, Wis., August 12, 1868; moved with his parents to Hampton, Iowa, in 1870; attended the public schools and the Hampton High School; engaged in agricultural pursuits; president of the Citizens National Bank of Hampton 1907-1923; member of the Hampton Board of Education and board of trustees of Cornell College, Mount Vernon, Iowa; member of the State senate 1912-1916; delegate to many Republican State conventions; elected as a Republican to the Sixty-eighth and to the four succeeding Congresses (March 4, 1923-March 3, 1933); unsuccessful candidate for reelection in 1932 to the Seventy-third Congress; engaged in the real estate and investment business; died in Hampton, Iowa, January 27, 1958; interment in Hampton Cemetery.

ROSS, LAWRENCE S., (1838-1898) — eighteenth governor of Texas (1887-91), was a native of Bentonsport, Iowa, the son of *Shapley Prince,* an Indian fighter and agent, and *Catherine Fulkerson Ross.* The family moved to Austin, Texas in 1846 and young Lawrence attended public schools until his entrance to Baylor University at Waco. He continued his education at Wesleyan University in Florence, Alabama, from which he graduated in 1859. That year, he also married *Elizabeth Tinsley* and returned to Texas, where he followed his father's example by fighting Comanche Indians along the Pease River with the Texas Rangers. *Governor Houston* made him an aide-de- camp of the state troops, with the rank of colonel. Ross joined the Confederate Army in 1861, beginning as a private and rising to the rank of brigadier general by 1864. He fought in Mississippi and Georgia, 135 battles in all. He returned to Texas and led a quiet life until 1873 when he was elected sheriff of McLennan County. He was a delegate to the Texas Constitutional Convention of 1875. In 1881-83 he was a member of the state senate, serving as chair of the committee on finance, and being nominated for governor in 1886, he was elected by a large majority. Ross was a popular governor, especially since times were getting better in Texas. Railroads were built rapidly; taxes were reduced; immigration was promoted by societies established to attract settlers, and the U.S. government paid into the state treasury nearly $1 million for expenses incurred by the state in defending its borders since annexation in 1846. In May 1888 the new state capitol was dedicated, and new reformatories and asylums were built at that time. Ross also approved new regulations for railroad companies and supported an amendment to the state constitution for prohibition of alcohol. That amendment failed with the voters. Ross left office without trying for a third term, and soon was appointed President of the new Texas Agricultural and Mechanical College at Bryan. He was offered a place on the State Railroad Commission, but turned it down in favor of remaining at the college. He held the post until his death, and was buried at Waco.

ROWE, LEO STANTON, (1871-1946) — political scientist and diplomat, was born in McGregor, Iowa to Louis U. Rowe and Katherine (Raff) Rowe. The family moved to Philadelphia when Rowe was a young boy and he received his high school education from Central High School, graduating in 1887. He went on to earn his Ph.B. degree from Wharton School of Finance and Commerce in 1890 and his

Ph.D. from the University of Halle in 1892. He later studied law at the University of Pennsylvania and received an L.L.B degree in 1895.

The same year he graduated from the University of Pennsylvania, Rowe accepted an assignment there as an instructor in municipal government, becoming an assistant professor in 1896 and a full professor in 1904. He stayed at the university until 1917. In 1900, he had helped found the American Society of International Law, and in that same year, took a two-year leave of absence from teaching and accepted an appointment from President McKinley to the Commission to Revise and Compile the Laws of Puerto Rico. In 1906, President Theodore Roosevelt named him a delegate to the Third International Conference of American States at Rio de Janeiro in Brazil. In 1907, Secretary of State Elihu Root named him chairman of the executive committee of the Pan-American Committee. Later, he accepted appointments as chairman of the United States delegation to the First Pan American Scientific Congress in Santiago, Chile from 1908-1909; as a member of the United States-Panama Land Commission in 1913; and as secretary general of the First Pan American Financial Conference in Washington, D.C. in 1915, and of the United States Section of the Inter-American High Commission created by the conference. He also served as secretary of the United States- Mexico Mixed Claims Commission from 1916-1917.

Rowe became the government's top Latin American expert and in 1919, moved to the State Department as chief of its Latin American Division. In 1920, he was appointed director general of the Pan American Union, where he remained until his death in 1946.

Rowe was fluent in Spanish and Portuguese and was not a very large man. He had never married nor had any children, and in 1946, while he was on his way to a reception at the Bolivian embassy in Washington, he was struck by a car and killed. He left most of his half million dollar estate to the union to foster education in Latin America.

RUML, BEARDSLEY, (1894-1960) — publicist, was born in Cedar Rapids, Iowa, to Wentzle Ruml and Salome Beardsley. He had one sister, Frances, who became dean of Radcliffe College. Ruml was a high achiever even as a child, and completed high school in three years. He went on to attend Dartmouth and received his B.S. degree in 1915. He then earned his Ph.D. in psychology and education at the University of Chicago.

Ruml is best known for his "pay-as-you-go" tax system which he proposed to the Senate Finance Committee in the summer of 1942. The plan would "turn the tax clock forward" and taxpayers would get a break on their 1942 taxes. They then would have taxes withheld on their current wages and salaries with an adjustment at the end of the year for under or overpayment. In 1943, Congress passed the Tax Payment Act, which was a modification of Ruml's plan and would cancel seventy-five percent of a year's income tax liability for taxpayer's whose tax was over $50 and one-hundred percent for taxpayer's whose tax was below $50.

After college, Ruml taught for a few months at Carnegie Tech and then went to Washington to serve on the War Department's Committee on Classifications of Personnel. In 1921, he joined Dr. James R. Angell as his assistant at the Carnegie Corporation. A year later, Ruml became director of the

$80,000,000 Laura Spelman Rockefeller Memorial to promote the welfare of women and children. In 1930 he went to Washington and became lieutenant to Arthur Woods, chairman of President Hoover's Federal Committee on Employment. In 1931, he became dean of the Social Science Division of the University of Chicago, as well as professor of education. In 1934, he went to New York City and became treasurer of R.H. Macy & Company. For Macy's he devised an accounting plan that allowed customers to purchase a product without having to come up with the total purchase amount all at once and which allowed the store to maintain its "six percent less for cash" policy. It was also while at Macy's that he came up with the plan for "pay-as-you-go" taxes.

Ruml was a member of the advisory committee of the Coordinator of Inter-American Affairs and of the State Department's division of cultural relations. He was also an advisor to the National Resources Planning Board of the Agricultural Department, the originator of the domestic allotment plan, the chairman of the Federal Reserve Bank of New York a member of the new Committee on Economic Development, director of the National Bureau of Economic Research, and a trustee of the Museum of Modern Art and of the Farm Foundation.

Ruml married Lois Treadwell, on August 28, 1917 and had three children: Treadwell, Alvin, and Anne. Ruml was six feet tall and weighed approximately two-hundred pounds. He was opposed to physical exercise, but loved to exercise his intellect. He died in Connecticut on April 18, 1960.

RUMPLE, JOHN NICHOLAS WILLIAM, (1841-1903) — a U.S. Representative from Iowa; born near Fostoria, Seneca County, Ohio, March 4, 1841; attended the public schools, Western College, Iowa, and the Iowa State University; enlisted in Company H, Second Iowa Cavalry, in August 1861 and remained in the Army until October 1865, when mustered out as captain; studied law; was admitted to the bar in 1867 and commenced practice in Marengo, Iowa County, Iowa; member of the State senate 1873-1878; member of the board of regents of the State University of Iowa 1580-1886; curator of the State Historical Society of Iowa 1881- 1885; member of the city council; mayor of Marengo, Iowa, in 1885 and 1886; attorney for the city council of Marengo 1896-1900; member of the school board; elected as a Republican to the Fifty- seventh Congress and served from March 4, 1901, until his death in Chicago, Ill., January 31, 1903; interment in the Odd Fellows Cemetery, Marengo, Iowa.

RUTLEDGE, WILEY (BLOUNT, JR.), (1894-1949) — United States Government official, was born in Cloverport, Kentucky, the son of Mary Lou (Wigginton) and Wiley Blount Rutledge. Rutledge, Sr. was a Baptist minister who "rode the circuit" in the Appalachian mountains and young Wiley often accompanied his father on those rides. He attended high school at Maryville College in Tennessee and then attended the College proper for three years after that. In 1913, he transferred to the University of Wisconsin where he received his B.A. degree.

Rutledge taught in high schools in Indiana, New Mexico and Colorado from 1915 to 1922, while he studied law. It was during this time that he also acquire tuberculosis. In 1922, he completed his Bachelor of Law degree from the University of Colorado and passed the Colorado Bar exam. For two years afterward, he practiced law in the law firm of Goss, Kimbrough, and Hutchinson in Boulder, Colorado.

Rutledge became associate professor of law at the University of Colorado in 1924, where he stayed for two years. In 1926, he became professor of law of the Washington University School of Law in St. Louis. In 1930, he became acting dean at Washington University School of Law and dean a year later. In 1935, he became professor of law and dean of the Law School of the State University of Iowa. During his years of teaching, Rutledge had a question that he often asked students: "Of what good is the law if it does not serve human needs?"

In 1939, Rutledge received an appointment by President Roosevelt to the bench of the United States Court of Appeals to the District of Columbia. As the eighth man appointed by Roosevelt to the position of Associate Justice of the United States Court of Appeals, Rutledge displayed a rather liberal point of view. He was not alone, for the court at that time was prone to liberalism, not conservatism. In January of 1943, he was appointed to the Supreme Court after Senate confirmation by voice vote. Although for the most part he was approved, there were some that felt he didn't have enough experience in practicing the law and therefore was not qualified to fill the position. Nevertheless, on February 15, 1943, Rutledge was sworn in as Associate Justice of the Supreme Court. Immediately, he was asked to help decide three cases that were in dead-lock and needed his vote to be the deciding factor. Those cases consisted of whether or not there should be a municipal restraint on pamphlet distribution by Jehovah's Witnesses; whether or not involvement in the Communist Party is sufficient grounds for revoking of American citizenship; and the third case involved a question of jurisdiction of the Federal Power Commission over a utility which claims to operate entirely within one state, but which sells current to a company transmitting it across the state line.

Although Rutlege was among other liberal thinkers, his stay in the United States Supreme Court was marked by his uncompromising, dissenting opinions. In two other cases that he voted on, the Yamashita and the United Mine Workers contempt of court cases, Rutledge stirred up much controversy by voting against the majority. He was a strong individual with a deep interest in people and felt the law should be a servant of the people not the other way around.

Rutledge married Annabel Person, a former teacher of Greek, on August 28, 1917. The couple had three children: Mary Lou, Jean Ann, and Neal. Rutledge was known as a man who liked people and was very hospitable.

Wiley Rutledge died on September 10, 1949.

S

SANDBERG, RYNE DEE, (1959-) — is a baseball player who made his mark with the Chicago Cubs.

Born in Spokane, Washington on September 18, 1959, he was named, somewhat prophetically, after New York Yankees' baseball player Ryne Duren. Talented in all kinds of sports while growing up, he initially thought he might want to pursue football, and although several Pacific Ten Conference schools wanted him, he changed his mind after an offer was made by the Philadelphia Phillies ballclub. Playing in the minors, Sandberg moved up the ranks quickly, and toward the end of the 1981 season, played his first game in the major leagues, getting his first hit, ironically, against his future team, the Chicago Cubs.

Sandberg was brought to the Cubs organization by Dallas Green and Lee Elia, who had been with the Phillies, and who both left to become involved with the Chicago team. Green later told a reporter about the trade that brought Sandberg to Wrigley Field: "I simply wasn't going to make the trade without Sandberg...I said, 'You've got to give us Sandberg. You *have* to.'"

During 1982 Sandberg played third base, but when Ron Cey was hired for that position, the former was moved to second base, and although it took him a little time to adjust to his new position, he made National League history when he became the first player to garner the Gold Glove award in his first year at a base position.

In his first couple of years, Sandberg never considered himself that good of a hitter. However, Cubs manager Jim Frey decided Sandberg had the ability and gave him some pointers on the subject. "I saw an athlete I thought was an extraordinary athlete and better than he was giving himself credit for," Frey told a Chicago *Tribune* reporter.

By the summer of 1984 Sandberg began to hit his stride, hitting .376, along with eight home runs in the month of June. When the Cubs won a June 23 game against the St. Louis Cardinals, in part because of two crucial home runs by Sandberg, longtime Cardinals manager Whitey Herzog exclaimed: "Sandberg is the best player I've ever seen." That year the Cubs secured their first division championship in several years. Although they never made it to the World Series, losing to the San Diego Padres, Sandberg won the most-valuable-player award, the first

Cub to do so since Ernie Banks had won it in the late 1950s.

Although he once complained that he felt he "lacked consistency" in his playing, his batting statistics were quite impressive, especially in 1989 when he hit thirty home runs, and helped steer the Cubs toward another division title in 1989. However, in keeping with the infamous Cubs jinx, the team lost the championship series to the San Francisco Giants four games to one. When he hit forty home runs in 1990, he became the first second baseman in the history of the game to wallop thirty or more out of the ballpark in consecutive seasons. In 1991, after hitting twenty-six home runs and driving in a staggering one- hundred runs, he created another record for his fielding prowess when he became the first second baseman to garner a ninth consecutive Gold Glove.

In March of 1992, before the baseball season started, Sandberg re-signed with the Chicago Cubs for an unprecedented four-year, $28.4 million contract extension, making him the highest-paid player in baseball history. The Cubs organization took some flak for the contract, but chairman of the board Stanton Cook told a *Sports Illustrated* journalist: "It's more money than you'd like to spend, but Ryne's a great athlete in great condition, with a great history in Chicago. Value is in the eyes of the beholder."

Sandberg didn't disappoint in the 1992 season, hitting .304, driving in eighty-seven runs, and batting twenty-six home runs. However, in 1993, sustaining both a dislocated finger on the right hand, and a broken left hand, his game suffered immensely, although he was asked for the eighth year in a row to be in the All-Star Game. The 1994 season wasn't much better for Sandberg, statistically, and by June, having lost his desire to play, Sandberg, with an integrity rare in highly-paid sports figures, retired from the game. At his press conference, he explained: "I am not the type of person who can be satisfied with anything less than my very best effort and my very top performance. I am not the type of person who can leave my game at the ballpark and feel comfortable the future is set, regardless of my performance. And I am certainly not the type of person who can ask the Cubs organization and Chicago Cub fans to pay my salary when I am not happy with my mental approach and my performance."

Sandberg is divorced from Cindy White; the couple have two children.

SCHERLE, WILLIAM JOSEPH, (1923-   ) — a U.S. Representative from Iowa; born in Little Falls, Herkimer County, N.Y., March 14, 1923; graduated from St. Mary's Academy in New York; attended Southern Methodist University of Dallas, Tex., 1945-1947; served in the Second World War, 1942-1946, and in the United States Naval Reserve, 1947- 1954; assistant division manager with George D. Barnard Co., Dallas, Tex., 1947; became a grain and livestock farmer, 1948; chairman, Mills County Republican Central committee, 1956-1964; served in the State house of representatives, 1960-1966; elected as a Republican to the Ninetieth and to the three succeeding Congresses (January 3, 1967-January 3, 1975); unsuccessful candidate for reelection in 1974 to the Ninety-fourth Congress; deputy administrator, United States Department of Agriculture, 1975-1977; president of a consulting firm in Washington, D.C., 1977-1987; is a resident of Henderson, Iowa.

SCHULLER, ROBERT, (1926-) — minister, was born in Alton, Iowa to Anthony and Jenny Schuller on September 16, 1926. He was the youngest of five children and his parents were farmers. He decided at quite a young age to become a minister and after graduating from high school, attended Hope College in Holland, Michigan, majoring in psychology and history.

Schuller received his B.A. degree in 1947 and entered Western Theological Seminary. He earned his B.D. degree in 1950 and became pastor of the Ivanhoe Reformed Church in Chicago, Illinois. The tiny congregation grew from thirty-eight to four-hundred in the five years that Schuller pastored there. In 1955 he was called upon to establish a church in Orange County, California and took the challenge with eager expectations. Going about things some-what differently, and with a goal to reach mostly unchurched people, Schuller rented the Orange Drive-In Theatre near the Santa Ana Freeway and built the altar there with his own hands. His slogan in the local newspaper advertising the church read, "Worship as you are/In the family car." His pulpit was the roof of the refreshment stand and his first service on March 27, 1955 brought in seventy-five cars and an offering of $86.79. Desiring to reach the Garden Grove community with the Gospel, Schuller rang 3,500 doorbells during his first year there.

Schuller's next step was to open a walk-in church, but found it quite a stretch to conduct two services every Sunday, one at the drive-in and one at the walk-in. To solve the problem, he worked with architect Richard Neutra, and in 1961 completed a mostly glass structure which could seat 1,700 people, and an asphalted area nearby where another 1,600 people could hear the service by car radio in the midst of beautiful landscaping complete with fountains and pools. In 1968, he had another structure built called the Tower of Hope which is a fourteen-story office building complete with a chapel on top that is open to the public daily. The structure also contains classrooms where Sunday School is taught to more than 2,000 children and a telephone counseling service which is offered twenty-four hours a day nationwide. There is a neon cross on the top of the building which is visible from the "Matterhorn" in the Disneyland amusement park a short distance away. In 1980, the controversial Crystal Cathedral was dedicated. The structure was designed by well-known architect Philip Johnson and is shaped like star of four points with walls that contain 10,661 different panels of glass. It stands more than 120 feet high, is larger than the Notre Dame Cathedral in Paris, seating around 3,000 people.

Schuller himself bases his ministry on a very positive and uplifting philosophy. When he first came to California he had a very simple motto: "Find a need and fill it, find a hurt and heat it." With that always at the core, he is one of the most positive televangelist of his day. Even in the midst of controversy, Schuller did not lose his nerve, nor his positiveness. In 1983, the California State Board of Equalization ruled that the Crystal Cathedral must forfeit its tax-exempt status and that Schuller must pay more than $600,000 in property tax to the state. The reason was because Schuller was extremely successful at fund-raising and brought in a large amount of money to support his ministry. Schuller contended that he did not do anything different than any other church, except on a larger scale.

Schuller has written several books on positive thinking and has been the subject of two unauthorized biographies: *Robert Schuller: The Inside Story,* and *Mountains into Goldmines: Robert Schuller and the Gospel of Success.* His writings include: *God's Way to the Good Life, Your Future Is Your Friend: An Inspirational Pilgrimage through the Twenty-Third Psalm, Move Ahead with Possibility Thinking, Self-Love: The Dynamic Force of Success, Power Ideas for a Happy Family, You Can become the Person You Want to Be, The Greatest Possibility Thinker That Ever Lived, Your Church Has Real Possibilities, Love or Loneliness, You Decide,* and several others. Awards and honors he has received include: the Washington Honor Medal of the Freedom Foundation; the principle award of the Freedom Foundation; the distinguished alumnus award from Hope College; LL.D. degrees from Azusa Pacific College, Pepperdine University, and Barrington College; a D.D. degree from Hope College; named headliner of the year in Orange County, California and clergyman of the year by Religious Heritage of America.

Robert Schuller married Arvella de Haan on June 15, 1950 and had five children, Sheila, Robert, Jeanne, Carol, and Gretchen.   Schuller is six feet, one and a half inches tall, has grey hair and brown eyes.

SCHWENGEL, FREDERICK D., (1906-   ) — a U.S. Representative from Iowa; born on a farm near Sheffield, Franklin County, Iowa, May 28, 1906; attended the rural schools in West Fork Township and high schools in Chapin and Sheffield, Iowa; graduated from Northeast Missouri Teachers College at Kirksville in 1930, and attended Iowa University graduate school 1933-1935; athletic coach and instructor of history and political science in public schools of Shelbina and Kirksville, Mo., 1930-1937; engaged in the insurance business in Davenport, Iowa, from 1937 to 1954; served in the Missouri National Guard 1929-1936; member of the State house of representatives 1945-1955; member, Iowa Development Commission, 1949-1955; elected as a Republican to the Eighty-fourth and to the four succeeding Congresses (January 3, 1955-January 3, 1965); unsuccessful candidate for reelection in 1964 to the Eighty-ninth Congress; elected as a Republican to the Ninetieth and to the two succeeding Congresses (January 3, 1967- January 3, 1973); unsuccessful candidate for reelection in 1972 to the Ninety-third Congress; founder and president of the Capitol Historical Society, 1982 to present; founder and president, Republican Heritage Foundation; is a resident of Arlington, Va.

SEBERG, JEAN, (1938-1979) — actress, was born in Marshalltown, Iowa. Her mother was a substitute elementary teacher and her father ran a pharmacy where she sometimes helped at the soda fountain. She attended the local public schools and taught Sunday School at the Lutheran church where she and her family attended. At the age of twelve, she became interested in acting because of an admiration for Marlon Brando.

In 1956, Miss Seberg acquired her first acting role as Joan of Arc in the film, *Saint Joan*. She was seventeen at the time and beat out 18,000 other girls from across the nation who were also trying for the part. Seberg, however, was a determined girl. Once, during a screen test, the director and producer, Otto Preminger, screamed at her. She became tearful, but when he asked if she wanted to quit, she replied that she would, "rehearse until you drop dead." Preminger laughed and gave her the part. Unfortunately, Seberg found that her first acting experience was quite demoralizing and what's more, she was considered a failure by critics. In her second and last picture under Preminger's direction, Seberg faired a little better, but still received much negative criticism regarding her acting.

After leaving Preminger who turned the remaining part of her contract over to Columbia pictures, Seberg played minor roles in such films as *The Mouse that Roared* and *Let No Man Write My Epitaph.* On September 6, 1958, she married Francois Moreuil. After being considered a failure in Hollywood, she then started working in France's New Wave film industry in Paris with the help of her husband. Her first success in Paris was a film entitled, *A Bout du Souffle,* which in the United States was released as *Breathless.* The films that followed included, *Playtime, Time Out for Love,* and *The Five Day Lover.* In 1961, she was in Africa filming *Congo Vivo,* and in 1962, began to work on her first American language film since 1959. The film was entitled, *In the French Style.* Her well-done performance in that film earned her a new contract with Columbia Pictures as well as a higher salary.

In 1965, Seberg's career began to gain momentum and she was offered the starring role in one of Universal Pictures big-budget films, *Moment to Moment.* In spite of her new-found success in America, Seberg continued to make France her home although she maintained her American citizenship.

On September 21, 1960, Seberg divorced her first husband and on October 19, 1963, married Romain Gary, a French diplomat and writer.

Seberg was politically liberal and stirred up much controversy because of her support of the Black Panthers. When she became pregnant in 1970, a rumor was circulated, allegedly from the CIA, that the child she was carrying was the product of relations with a black militant. Shocked and upset by the rumor, Seberg went into premature labor and delivery and the child died. She never quite recovered emotionally from the unfortunate circumstances and reportedly tried to take her life several times. In 1979, her body was found in her car in Paris, nine days after she disappeared from her Paris apartment with a supply of prescription barbiturates.

Other films to Seberg's credit include *Lileth, Paint Your Wagon,* and *Airport.* She also wrote a book based on her psychiatric treatment following the death of her child. It was entitled, *Blue Jeans.*

SHAW, LESLIE MORTIER, (1848-1932) — seventeenth governor of Iowa (1898-1902), was born in Morristown, Vermont on November 2, 1848, son of Boardman Osias and Louisa (Spaulding) Shaw. His great-grandfather, Ebenezer Shaw, was one of the earliest settlers of Morristown. In early childhood, his father moved the family to a farm in Stowe, Vermont where Leslie M. Shaw spent his childhood. He received his early education in the common schools of his county and the People's Academy of Morrisville, Vermont, and having moved to Iowa in 1869, graduated from Cornell College, Mt. Vernon, Iowa, in 1874. He was dependent upon his own efforts in obtaining an education, but with characteristic persistence, by teaching school, selling nursery stock, and working in the harvest fields, he earned enough money to complete his college and professional course, and graduated from the Iowa College of Law in 1876. In the same year, he settled in Denison, Iowa, and from the start, took high rank in his profession.

Shaw was the largest contributor towards the establishment of an academy and normal school at Denison and held the position of president of the board of trustees from its organization. He was also a trustee of Cornell College, and for several years, was president of the school board of Denison, Iowa. He was also president of the Bank of Denison, at Denison, and Bank of Manilla, at Manilla, Iowa. Prior to 1896, he was never active in politics, although always prominent in local campaigns, speaking in defense of the principles of the Republican Party.

At the beginning of the memorable free silver controversy of that year, he was requested by the adherents of the gold standard to reply to an address made in his town by William Jennings Bryan. From that date to the end of the campaign, which resulted in the election of President McKinley, he was in constant demand, and proved one of the most efficient speakers in that notable canvass. His speeches brought his name prominently before the state, and when in 1897, Governor Drake declined a renomination because of ill-health, Shaw was nominated by the Republican Party for governor. He had a solid platform, fighting distinctively for the gold standard without equivocation, and was elected by a plurality of 29,975. He was selected by the Sound Money Commission to preside at the Indianapolis Convention of 1898, where his address attracted national attention.

Shaw was married to Alice Crawshaw. He died on March 28, 1932.

SHERMAN, BUREN ROBINSON, (1836-1904) — twelfth governor of Iowa (1882-86), was born in Phelps, Ontario County, New York on May 28, 1836, son of Phineas L. and Eveline (Robinson) Sherman. His father was an axe maker by occupation, and a man of more than ordinary intelligence. Sherman's early education was received in the public schools in his native town, and at the Elmira (N.Y.) Academy. He was admitted to the bar in 1859, and began practice in Vinton, Iowa with Judge J. C. Traer. In the following year, he was admitted to the supreme court of Iowa; in 1875, to the U.S. Circuit Court, and in 1879, to the Supreme Court of the United States. In the interim, he enlisted in the Federal Army at the outbreak of the Civil War, served as second lieutenant, was promoted to captain, and on April 6, 1862, at the battle of Shiloh, was severely wounded, a situation which eventually forced him to resign from the service.

Sherman was the judge of Benton County during 1865-67; served as clerk of the district court from January, 1869, to December, 1874, and in October of the latter year, was elected auditor of the state of Iowa, being reelected twice more, serving until 1881. He was elected governor of Iowa in October, 1881, and was inaugurated on January 12, 1882. He was reelected to that post, serving until January 1886, when he retired from politics. The degree of LL.D. was conferred upon him in 1883 by the University of Iowa.

Sherman was married to Lena Kendall. He died on November 4, 1904.

SMITH, COURTNEY (CRAIG), (1916-1969) — college president, was born in Winterset, Iowa to Samuel Craig Smith, a lawyer and banker, and Florence Myrtle Smith. He had two brothers and one sister and attended Roosevelt High School in Des Moines. In school, he was elected to the National Honor

Society and was made an officer of the student council. After high school, he attended Harvard University, majoring in English. In 1938, he received his A.B. degree *magna cum laude* and was awarded a Rhodes Scholarship. From 1938 to 1939, he attended Merton College, Oxford University, England and studied English literature. He returned to Harvard and earned his M.A. degree in 1941 and his Ph.D. in 1944.

After completing his graduate work, Smith served in the United States Navy from 1944-1946. Later in 1946, he took a position as instructor in English at Princeton University, becoming assistant professor from 1948 until 1953. From 1951 to 1953, he was bicentennial preceptor at Princeton and from 1952 to 1953 was director of the National Woodrow Wilson Fellowship Program. In 1953, Smith succeeded John W. Nason as president of Swarthmore College. Just before accepting this position, he had been named American secretary of the Rhodes Scholarship Trust. In that same year, he became director of the John and Mary R. Markle Foundation of New York and was made a trustee for the Eisenhower Fellowship Program. He was also associate trustee of the University of Pennsylvania, a member of the board of overseers of Harvard University and a Fellow of the Society for American Studies. He was a member of the American Association of University Professors, the Modern Language Association, the Harvard Club of Philadelphia, and the University Club of New York.

Smith, the ninth president of Swarthmore, was also one of the youngest college presidents in the United States. In his new position he devoted himself completely to his work. He worked arduously and made a number of improvements including seeing that the college had a first class faculty by conducting the interviews himself. He also challenged students in their thinking; helped to provide a better dining hall, a number of modern dormitories, an improved social center and the best athletic facilities. He was successful at raising funds from alumni and foundations and helped to get removed from the National Defense Education Act of 1958 the requirement that applicants file a "disclaimer" of belief in the overthrow of the United States. He believed that such a statement was an attempt at "mind control."

In 1968, Smith announced his decision to resign from Swarthmore and become president of the John and Mary Markle Foundation. Unfortunately, he would never fill that position, for during a crisis at the college involving an uprising by black students, Smith died of a heart attack.

Courtney Smith married Elizabeth Bowden Proctor of Boston on October 12, 1939 and had three children: Courtney Craig, Jr., Elizabeth Bowden, and Carol Dabney. Smith was six feet tall, had brown hair and brown eyes. He was considered to have given immeasurably greater strength to Swarthmore College during his years of service there, in spite of the sad ending to his life at the age of fifty-three.

SMITH, JEFF, (1939-) — is the very popular television cooking show host known as "The Frugal Gourmet."

Born on January 22, 1939 in Seattle, Washington, he knew his way around the kitchen from the time he was a young boy, often helping his mother with the cooking. At Seattle's Pike Place Market he went from washing pots and pans at fifteen to managing their Brehm's delicatessen two years later. He attended the University of Puget Sound in Tacoma, earning a B.A. degree in philosophy and sociology in

1962. He then traveled to New Jersey to attend Drew Theological School, graduating cum laude and receiving a master of divinity degree in 1965. Soon after, he was ordained a minister of the United Methodist Church, and after serving in two different churches, he was appointed assistant professor of religion, and also served as chaplain, at the University of Puget Sound between 1966 and 1972.

Smith taught one of the school's most popular courses, "Food As Sacrament and Celebration." Several years later he recalled for an interviewer that the idea came to him when he began to notice that "many of the students involved in the peace movement were starving to death, living on brown rice and telling me they felt great. So I began giving cooking lessons to my students. And, after a while, we just lost control. Everything that's happened, really, has evolved from my experience in the university." During that time he also did "what every responsible clergyman did in those days"--smuggled letters to the conscientious objectors of the Vietnam War who were serving prison time. "Those people went to jail because they thought that war was immoral."

Deciding to leave academics for a while, in 1972 he opened Chaplain's Pantry, "a multipurpose business that served as a delicatessen, restaurant, catering service, cookware store, and cooking school." Injecting his own sense of humor into his venture, he called one vegetarian sandwich "Habeas Corpus"--in other words, he later explained: "You couldn't find a body."

In 1973 Smith began hosting his first cooking show, then entitled *Cooking Fish Creatively,* on *Seattle Today,* which would eventually evolve into *The Frugal Gourmet.* Everything came to a screeching halt in 1982 when he underwent open heart surgery.

In order to pay the subsequent medical bills, Smith sold Chaplain's Pantry. He also paid attention to the lesson from his ordeal, recalling: "When I woke up from open-heart surgery, and I realized that I'd made it, I gave thanks, and I decided that from then on, it would be all kicks, that I'd never 'work' again, that I'd only do things that are joyful."

After appearing on *Donahue,* Smith received over 45,000 requests for his spiral-bound cookbook, *Recipes from the Frugal Gourmet,* which led to his cooking show going national, via Chicago's PBS television station WTTW. Smith's mass appeal was instantaneous, prompting a University of Massachusetts college anthropology professor to surmise: "A lot of cooking shows focus on the upper end--maintaining class differences in an upwardly mobile society. But I think *The Frugal Gourmet* is appealing to middle-class people who aspire to gourmet cooking at a reasonable price." In a *TV Guide* review, Don Merrill noted that Smith "runs a cooking show that is amusing as well as instructive, as good--and certainly as practical--as any we've seen...one of his objectives is to make cooking seem like fun, and his own unrestrained delight in what he's doing is most convincing."

Smith "has set publishing records for having written the only cookbook (his third) ever to warrant an original printing of 500,000 copies and for being the only cookbook writer to have two titles (his first and second) in the top two spots on the New York *Times* bestseller list simultaneously."

Subsequent books by Smith include: *The Frugal Gourmet Cooks with Wine* (1986); *The Frugal Gourmet Cooks American* (1987); *The Frugal Gourmet Cooks Three Ancient Cuisines: China, Greece and Rome* (1989); *The Frugal Gourmet Cooks Your Immi-*

grant Heritage: Recipes You Should Have Gotten from Your Grandmother (1990); *The Frugal Gourmet's Culinary Handbook* (1991); *The Frugal Gourmet Celebrates Christmas* (1991); and *The Frugal Gourmet Desk Diary* (1991).

Closing every show with the comforting and familiar phrase "I bid you peace," Smith never forgets what his life's purpose is-- that he's "primarily a clergyman--theologian-- concerned with the nature and future of our culture, our human community. And the table is the proper place for the communication. Most shows teach cooking--I do not. This is a front--a plot--to try to get people in touch with each other...Food is a catalyst for joy, fellowship, human communication, and meaning..."

Smith has received three Daytime Emmy nominations for his show. He is married to Patricia M. Dailey and the couple have two children.

SMITH, WALTER INGLEWOOD, (1862-1922) — a U.S. Representative from Iowa; born in Council Bluffs, Pottawattamie County, Iowa, July 10, 1862; attended the common schools; studied law; was admitted to the bar in 1882 and commenced practice in Council Bluffs, Iowa; judge of the Fifteenth judicial district of Iowa 1890-1900; elected as a Republican to the Fifty-sixth Congress to fill the vacancy caused by the resignation of Smith McPherson and on the same day was elected to the Fifty-seventh Congress; reelected to the Fifty- eighth and to the four succeeding Congresses and served from December 3, 1900, to March 15, 1911, when he resigned to accept an appointment on the bench; appointed by President Taft to be United States circuit judge for the eighth judicial circuit and served from March 16, 1911, until his death in Council Bluffs, Iowa, on January 27, 1922; interment in Fairview Cemetery.

SPEDDING, FRANK H., (1902-1984) — physicist, was born in Hamilton, Ontario, Canada to Howard Leslie and Mary Ann Elizabeth (Marshall) Spedding. He attended the University of Michigan and obtained a Bachelor of Science degree in 1925 and a Master of Science degree in 1926. He went on to earn a Ph.D. in 1929 from the University of California.

From 1923 to 1925, Spedding was a teaching assistant in Analytical Chemistry at the University of Michigan. From 1929 to 1930, he was an Instructor in Chemistry at the University of California. After receiving a Guggenheim professorship, he traveled to England, Germany and Russia between 1934 and 1935. From 1935 to 1937, he was George Fisher Baker Assistant Professor at Cornell University in Ithaca, New York. He held several other posts before his death in 1984, the most notable of which include Director of the Atomic Project from 1942 to 1947, Director of the Institute for Atomic Research from 1945 to 1968 and Director of the Ames Laboratory of Atomic Energy Commission at Iowa State University from 1968 to 1984.

In 1942, Spedding and his Iowa colleagues were asked to develop new techniques for the purification of uranium which was needed for the development of the atomic bomb. Although Uranium is plentiful, separating U235, the substance needed for the bomb, from the plentiful U238 was a problem. The method that Spedding and his colleagues used was ion exchange chromatography. Through this method, they produced one third of the U235 needed for the first nuclear reaction in Chicago on December 2, 1942. Spedding was invited to witness this and to join the

Manhattan Project which developed the bombs dropped on Japan in 1945.

During his years with the Iowa State University for Atomic Research which later developed into the Ames Laboratory, Spedding concentrated mainly on plutonium rather uranium. Since these two elements are chemically and physically very similar, Spedding and his team once again used ion exchange chromatography for the purpose of separating the two. They were able to obtain the separated "rare earths" in substantial quantities for the first time. Spedding was also a specialist in atomic and molecular spectra, as well as other chemistry associated with atomic energy problems.

Spedding was nominated several times for the Nobel Peace Prize but never received the award. He was, however, awarded several honorary degrees and other awards including, an honorary LL.D. from Drake University in 1946; a D.Sc. from the University of Michigan in 1949; a D.Sc. from Case Institute of Technology in 1956; the Langmuir award from the American Chemical Society in 1933; the Nichols Medal in 1952; the Douglas Medal from the American Institute of Mining, Metallurgical and Petrol Engineers in 1961 and the Francis J. Clamer Medal from the Franklin Institute in 1969. Besides writing 257 articles for various scientific journals, he has written *The Rare Earth,* and with Adrian Daane, *Chemistry of Rare Earth Elements.*

Frank Spedding married Ethel Annie Macfarlane in 1931 and had one daughter, May Ann Elizabeth Calciano.

Spedding died at the age of eighty-two on December 15, 1984.

STECK, DANIEL FREDERIC, (1881-1950) — a U.S. Senator from Iowa; born in Ottumwa, Wapello County, Iowa, December 16, 1881; attended the common schools; graduated from the law department of the University of Iowa at Iowa City in 1906; was admitted to the bar the same year and commenced practice in Ottumwa; during the First World War, served in France as a captain; resumed the practice of law in Ottumwa; successfully contested as a Democrat the election of Smith W. Brookhart to the United States Senate and served from April 12, 1926, to March 3, 1931; was an unsuccessful candidate for reelection in 1930; resumed the practice of his profession; special assistant to the United States Attorney General 1933- 1947; retired; died in Ottumwa, Iowa, December 31, 1950; interment in Ottumwa Cemetery.

STEELE, THOMAS JEFFERSON, (1853-1920) — a U.S. Representative from Iowa; born near Rushville, Rush County, Ind., March 19, 1853; attended the public schools and Axline Seminary, Fairfax, Iowa; taught school in central and western Iowa; studied law at Sheldon, Iowa; engaged in the hardware business and in banking at Wayne, Nebr.; county clerk of Wayne County, Nebr., 1884-1886; moved to Sioux City, Iowa, in 1897 and became a livestock commission merchant; elected as a Democrat to the Sixty-fourth Congress (March 4, 1915-March 3, 1917); unsuccessfully contested the election of George C. Scott to the Sixty-fifth Congress; resumed business as commission merchant; unsuccessful candidate for election in 1918 to the Sixty-sixth Congress; died in Sioux City, Iowa, March 20, 1920; interment in Graceland Park Cemetery.

STEGNER, WALLACE, (1909-1993) — writer, was born in Lake Mills, Iowa on February 18, 1909 to George and Hilda (Paulson) Stegner, Scandinavian immigrants. Wallace's family moved a great deal and he grew up in several different states: North Dakota, Washington, Montana, Wyoming, Utah and Saskatchewan, finally settling in Salt Lake City, Utah in 1921. Wallace finished his high school years there and went on to graduate from the University of Utah with a B.A. degree in 1930. In 1932, he obtained his M.A. degree in English from the University of Iowa, and his Ph.D. in 1935 from the same University.

In 1934, Stegner became an instructor in English at the University of Utah until 1937 when he joined the faculty of the University of Wisconsin. Two years later he became Briggs- Copeland instructor of composition at Harvard University, and stayed there from 1939 to 1945. In 1945, he became a professor of English at Stanford University and in 1946, director of the creative writing program at the same University until 1971 when he retired.

Stegner's first attempt at writing was in the form of his Master's thesis which consisted of several short stories. In 1937, he won his first award for writing a novelette entitled *Remembering Laughter.* His first major work was *The Big Rock Candy Mountain* which was first published in 1943 and again in 1973. All of Stegner's books, fiction and non-fiction, captured the basic nature of the American West. He had a fascination for the West, it's land and people, which came through in his writing. A central issue that all of his work dealt with also was the quest for identity, whether personal or regional. Stegner said of himself that he was a "straightforward realistic storyteller from the West." Some of the more notable books he wrote include; *The Uneasy Chair, Wolf Willow,* and

The Sound of Mountain Water. Others include *The Potter's House, On a Darkling Plain, Fire and Ice, Second Growth, The Preacher and the Slave, A Shooting Star, All the Little Live Things, Angle of Repose, The Spectator Bird,* and *Recapitulation* as well as several short stories and essays. He also wrote critical studies for various journals and contributed to the *Saturday Review,* and the New York *Times Book Review.* He was the editor for Houghton-Mifflin on the West Coast from 1945 to 1953, editor-in-chief of the magazine *American West,* from 1966 to 1968, and honorary consultant in American letters to the Library of Congress from 1973 to 1976. He was a member of the National Institute of Arts and Letters and the American Academy of Arts and Sciences.

Honors and awards Stegner received during his writing career include several O. Henry awards, the Houghton-Mifflin Life-in- America Award, the Anisfield-Wolfe Award, a Guggenheim fellow, a Rockefeller fellow, a Wenner-Gren Foundation grant, a fellow from the Center for Advanced Studies in the Behavioral Sciences, an honorary D.Litt. degree from the University of Utah, an honorary D.F.A. from the University of California and Utah State University, a National Endowment for the Humanities senior fellow, a Pulitzer Prize, and several others.

Wallace Stegner married Mary Stuart Page on September 1, 1934 and had one child, Stuart Page Stegner. Stegner died of injuries following an automobile accident in 1993 at the age of 84.

STEWART, DAVID WALLACE, (1887-1974) — a U.S. Senator from Iowa; born in New Concord, Muskingum County, Ohio, January 22, 1887; attended the common schools; graduated from Geneva College, Beaver Falls, Pa., in 1911; high school teacher and athletic coach 1911-1914; graduated from the law department of the University of Chicago in 1917; was admitted to the bar the same year and commenced practice in Sioux City, Iowa; during the First World War served overseas as a first sergeant 1918-1919; discharged; resumed the practice of law in Sioux City, Iowa; president of the Sioux City Chamber of Commerce in 1925; appointed August 7, 1926, as a Republican to the United States Senate to fill the vacancy caused by the death of Albert B. Cummins, and was subsequently elected November 2, 1926, to complete the unexpired term ending March 3, 1927, and served from August 7, 1926, until March 3, 1927; was not a candidate for renomination in 1926; resumed the practice of his profession; president of the board of trustees of Morningside College 1938- 1962; died in Sioux City, Iowa, February 10, 1974; interment in Logan Park Cemetery.

STONE, WILLIAM MILO, (1827-1893) — sixth governor of Iowa (1864-68), was born in Jefferson County, New York on October 14, 1827, son of Truman and Lovina (North) Stone. His early educational advantages were limited. At sixteen years of age he was a driver for two seasons on the Ohio Canal, and from seventeen until about twenty-three years of age, he was employed as a chairmaker, while studying and reading during his leisure moments. He studied law, and, after being admitted to the bar in 1851, began practice in partnership with his first preceptor, Judge James Mathews, at Coshocton.

In 1854, he moved to Knoxville, Iowa, followed by Mathews, and the partnership continued until the election of Stone to the bench. In 1855, he became the editor of the Knoxville *Journal,* and was a member of the convention, which in February, 1856, organized the Republican Party of the state. He was chosen judge of the 11th judicial district in April, 1857, and when the new constitution went into effect the following year, was elected judge of the 6th district. He was a delegate to the Chicago Convention in 1880, and was an earnest supporter of Abraham Lincoln for the Presidential nomination.

At the start of the Civil War, he enlisted as a private and assisted in organizing Company B of the 3rd Iowa Infantry, becoming captain of the company, and upon the organization of the regiment, its first major. In May, 1861, he was wounded in the battle of Blue Mills, Missouri, and at Shiloh, where he was in command of the regiment, he was taken prisoner. In 1862, he was appointed, by Governor Kirkwood, colonel of the 22d Iowa, and with his command, participated in the battles of Fort Gibson, Champion Hills, Black River, and the charge on the works at Vicksburg, May 22, 1883. At Fort Gibson he commanded the brigade, and at Vicksburg, he was wounded in the left arm. In June, 1863, he was nominated for governor by the Republicans of Iowa, and in August, resigned his commission in the army. In 1864, he was brevetted brigadier-general.

Stone assumed the gubernatorial chair in January, 1864, holding the office for two terms. As one of the war governors, he was called to Washington several times for conference with President Lincoln, and was there for that purpose at the time of the assassination of the President, being a witness of the murder at Ford's Theatre. He was with the President constantly until his death, and was one of the pall bearers who accompanied the remains to Springfield, Illinois for burial. Governor Stone retired from the executive chair in January 1868, and resumed the practice of law at Knoxville, Iowa, having for a partner his brother-in-law, Judge O. B. Ayers. In 1877, he was elected to the lower house of the Iowa legislature, serving for one term.

In 1880, he became interested in mining operations in Arizona, and for several years practiced law sporadically. In 1883, having formed a partnership with Judge T. J. Anderson, they moved to Pueblo, Colorado, but in 1885, Governor Stone returned to Iowa, settling in Des Moines, as a member of the firm of Stone, Ayers & Gamble.

He was elector for the state at large on the Harrison ticket in 1888, and was appointed assistant commissioner of the general land office by President Harrison, becoming commissioner upon the resignation of Judge Thomas Carter. At the close of his official term in 1893, Governor Stone moved to Oklahoma City, Oklahoma Territory, and while engaging in the practice of law, also devoted some time to agriculture. He was married, in 1856, to Caroline Mathews, daughter of his former partner, James. Governor Stone died on July 18, 1893, leaving a widow and one son.

STROUSE, NORMAN HULBERT, (1906-1993) — was chairman of what has been described as the world's largest advertising agency.

Born on November 4, 1906 in Olympia, Washington, Strouse immediately joined the work force after his high school graduation, first becoming a secretary to the State's director of licenses, then working in the same capacity for the advertising director of the Seattle *Post-Intelligencer,* eventually becoming assistant to the national manager of that paper.

In 1929 he got a position as an assistant space buyer in the San Francisco office of the J. Walter Thompson Company, and began what would be a lifelong connection with that advertising agency. He continued to move up the ranks of the firm, being named an account representative in 1936, thenassistant Pacific Coast manager in 1942. When World War II intervened, Strouse became a private in the United States Army Air Forces. Between 1943 and 1945 he was executive officer for the information and education special staff division under General Douglas MacArthur. Strouse was discharged at the rank of major.

After the war, Strouse returned to the J. Walter Thompson · Company and was asked to handle the substantial account of Detroit's Ford Motor Company. The Ford Company was in need of an overhaul regarding its "antiquated" image, and it was Strouse's job to give it a more modern appeal, which he did with his idea of stressing the need for "two Fords in every garage."

Within two years Strouse went from vice-president of the J. Walter Thompson Company to director of the firm, in 1949, then ascended to the presidency of the company in June of 1955, beating out eighty-four company vice-presidents. Strouse, as head of the company, wasted no time in confirming that the J. Walter Thompson Company was the top advertising agency in the world, not only picking up new business, but convincing former clients, such as RCA, that they should come back. The company had so many accounts that a writer once noted "it might be possible to get born, live a complete life, and die, using nothing but J. Walter Thompson advertised products and services."

Strouse served as chairman of the company from 1964 to 1968. When he retired in the latter year, Strouse spent his free time indulging himself in his other passion--collecting rare books. With his wife,

Charlotte Auger, he founded the Silverado Museum, located in St. Helena, which the couple dedicated to Robert Louis Stevenson, and which they filled with over 6,000 books. In addition, Strouse donated 1,500 volumes to the University of California at Berkeley, and also taught antiquarianism at the University of California at Santa Cruz.

Strouse died on January 19, 1993.

STRUBLE, ISAAC S., (1843-1913) — a U.S. Representative from Iowa; born near Fredericksburg, Va., November 3, 1843; moved to Iowa with his parents, who settled in Johnson County; attended the common schools; during the Civil War enlisted at the age of seventeen and served three years as a private in Company F, Twenty-second Iowa Regiment, Volunteer Infantry; attended the University of Iowa in Iowa City; studied law; was admitted to the bar in 1870 and commenced practice in Ogle County, Ill.; settled in Le Mars, Plymouth County, Iowa, in 1872; elected as a Republican to the Forty-eighth and to the three succeeding Congresses (March 4, 1883-March 3, 1891); chairman, Committee on Territories (Fifty-first Congress); unsuccessful candidate for renomination in 1890; resumed the practice of law; died in Le Mars, Iowa, on February 17, 1913; interment in Le Mars Cemetery.

SUCKOW, RUTH, (1892-1960) — author, editor born in Hawarden, Iowa on August 6, 1892, the second daughter of William John and Anna (Kluckholn Suckow. Her father a Congregational minister greatly influenced her early writing. In fact, Suckow herself said her early work was based on the "purity and economy" of her father's sermons Because he changed pastorates frequently, the Suckow family lived in several Iowa towns of various sizes.

Suckow attended Grinnell College, the Curry School of Expression in Boston and the University of Denver, where she earned her A.B. (1917) and A.M. (1918) in English. She first taught as a graduate assistant at University of Denver and after writing her thesis on female novelists, Suckow decided her calling was that of an author. However, to ensure herself a means of support, Suckow studied beekeeping in 1919 and for the next five years ran an apiary in Iowa while she began to spend time writing. Suckow's first short stories appeared in a University of Iowa journal, *Midland* and during the 1920's she had sixteen short stories published. Around mid 1920's having established herself in the literary world Suckow begantp wrote novels. Soon she sold her apiary, moving to New York, and concentrated her efforts on writing novels, eventually spending very little time on short stories. From 1924 through the end of the decade Suckow completed five novels.

At the height of her career, Suckow was one of America's leading novelist. Her realistic fiction received high praise from writers like Sinclair Lewis and Robert Frost. Set mostly in early twentieth-century Iowa, her work was recognized for its sociologically acute character analysis and well-attuned dialogue. An outspoken feminist, Suckow's writing usually examined social issues of the day. Topics ranged from relationships to personal growth and the contrasts of men and women. Many of Suckow's stories such as, *The New Hope* (New York & Toronto: Farrar & Rinhart, 1942); *The Bonney Family* (New York Knopf, 1928, London, Cape 1928); and *The Folks* (New York, Farrar & Rinhart, 1934) explore family relationships, while others probe the feminine struggle for self-realization; *Cora* (New York: Knopf, 1939; London, Cape 1928); *The Kramer Girls* (New York, Knopf, 1930) and *The Odessy of a Nice Girl* New York, Knopf, 1925, London, Cape 1926).

Although Suckow's work was respected and praised, she was considered a regionalist as an author and it was thought by many her topics were to domestic and somewhat boring, appealing more to women than to men. Despite her popularity in the early to mid twentieth century, her work is virtually unknown in current times.

Suckow married a fellow writer and Iowa native Ferner Nuhn on March 11, 1929. She died in Claremont California on January 23, 1960.

SUNDAY, BILLY, (1862-1935) — was a talented baseball player whoeventually found God and gave up the game to become a well-known evangelist.

Born William Ashley Sunday on November 19, 1862 n Ames, Iowa, his father died while serving in the Civil War. Unable to support the entire family, his mother placed William and an elder brother in the Soldiers' Orphan Home. Sunday went to live for a time on his grandfather's farm near Ames, and later at the home of Colonel John Scott, who supervised his early training. While attending Nevada High School, he developed exceptional skill as a runner and baseball player, and in 1883, was asked to join the team of the Chicago Baseball Club where he played for eight years. During this time the Pacific Garden Mission was enjoying a great vogue in Chicago. Sunday went to one of the meetings in the winter of 1886, and was soundly converted. He threw himself into religious work at once, joining the Jefferson Park Presbyterian Church of Chicago where he was elected an elder. He gave up baseball as a profession, and during 1891-93, was assistant secretary of the Young Men's Christian Association in Chicago, an experience which proved of inestimable value in later years. His first efforts in the wider field of evangelism were as assistant to Dr. J. Wilbur Chapman whom he was associated with for three years.

In 1896, "Billy" Sunday began conducting independent meetings, and developed an original and sensational style which, while shocking to some of his hearers, was entirely successful in reaching the class of people he aimed to convert, and it was not long before huge crowds were flocking to hear him. These meetings, begun in the towns of the middle West, extended to all parts of the United States and in the cities of New York, Boston, Philadelphia and Pittsburgh. Special tabernacles, seating from 12,000 to 18,000 people, were erected for his services.

Sunday possessed a magnetic and forceful personality, and an intense enthusiasm, and he preached with all his might, making no pretense to culture and laying no claims to learning. His preaching was the religion which entered his own life. Said one of the publications of his own church: "As a preacher and evangelist, Mr. Sunday is in a class by himself. He has never been a pastor and could not be one...His audiences are never surprised at anything he does or says. He is as likely to sit on top of the pulpit as to stand behind it, and to take off his coat as button it up. It is nothing unusual for him to give directions to his assistants while he is praying or to stop in the middle of a petition to command some enthusiastic brother waxing too loud with 'amens' to 'shut up'. From the time he announces his text until the sermon closes, he storms and rages up and down the platform, whacking the pulpit, and twisting and working his body until we are as much amazed as the physical endurance of the man as at the resources of his tongue. He outrages every rule of church decorum, and slaps in the face all our traditions of dignity and reverence in worship; but not for a moment is he a clown, much less a mountebank. On the contrary he impresses those who hear him as one of the most earnest, serious- minded and deeply spiritual men they have ever listened to."

Charged with making use of "every vulgarity and irreverence of language, addressing his hearers, and the Almighty in the idiom of the saloon, the gutter and the yellow newspaper," he succeeded in attracting the largest revival meetings every held in any country, and is credited with having converted over 700,000 men and women to the Christian faith. He was ordained a minister of the gospel in 1903 by the Chicago presbytery, and the honorary degree of D.D. was conferred on him by Westminster College of New Wilmington, Pennsylvania in 1912. He was married to Helen A. Thompson and the couple had four children. He died on November 6, 1935.

SWANSON, CHARLES EDWARD, (1879-1970) — a U.S. Representative from Iowa; born on a farm near Galesburg, Knox County, Ill., January 3, 1879; in 1890 moved to Iowa with his parents, who settled on a farm in Ringgold County; attended the public schools of Galesburg, Ill., and Clearfield, Iowa; was graduated from Knox College, Galesburg, Ill., in 1902, and from the law department of Northwestern University, Evanston, Ill., in 1907; principal of schools, Altona, Ill., 1902-1904; was admitted to the bar in 1907 and commenced practice in Council Bluffs, Iowa; prosecuting attorney of Pottawattamie County, Iowa, 1915- 1922; elected as a Republican to the Seventy-first and to the Seventy-second Congresses (March 4, 1929-March 3, 1933); unsuccessful candidate for reelection in 1932 to the Seventy- third Congress and for election in 1934 to the Seventy-fourth Congress; resumed the practice of law; chairman, City Board of Tax Review, 1949-1968; died in Council Bluffs, Iowa, August 22, 1970; interment in Walnut Hill Cemetery.

SWEET, BURTON ERWIN, (1867-1957) — a U.S. Representative from Iowa; born on a farm near Waverly, Bremer County, Iowa, December 10, 1867; attended the common schools and the Iowa State Normal School at Cedar Falls; was graduated from Cornell College, Mount Vernon, Iowa, in 1893 and from the law department of the University of Iowa at Iowa City in 1895; was admitted to the bar in 1895 and commenced practice in Waverly, Iowa; city solicitor of Waverly 1896-1899; member of the State house of representatives 1900-1904; delegate to the Republican National Convention in 1904; member of the Republican State central committee 1902-1906; elected as a Republican to the Sixty-fourth and to the three succeeding Congresses (March 4, 1915-March 3, 1923); did not seek renomination in 1922, having become a candidate for Senator; unsuccessful candidate for United States Senator in the Republican primary election of 1922 and again in 1924; resumed the practice of law; died in Waverly, Iowa, January 3, 1957; interment in Harlington Cemetery.

T

TAGGARD, GENEVIEVE, (1894-1948) — was a poet and author.

Born in Waitsburg, Washington on November 28, 1894, the family moved to Hawaii when she was two. Raised by her missionary parents, she loved the multi-cultured environment of her home, and when a friend said to her "Too bad you gotta be Haole (white), she later wrote: "Off and on, I have thought so too, all my life." When she was eleven, the family moved back to Waitsburg due to her father's illness, then lived in Hawaii another four years until finally returning to her birthplace. It was from the latter place that her point-of-view, according to one source, "crystallized into a liberalism she later expressed through leftist poetry and commitment to liberal and proletarian causes." She herself had written in 1934 that those years in Waitsburg had been "the active source of my convictions. It told us what to work against and what to work for."

The family eventually moved to California and Taggard enrolled at the University of California at Berkeley. Because she and her mother had to help support the family by working as servants in a Berkeley student boardinghouse, it took Taggard six years to receive her diploma. During her college years she studied poetry and continued to form views that she carried throughout her life and later described as "left of center."

After her 1920 graduation, she made her way to New York on the advice of writer Max Eastman, who was trying to arrange a job for her on the *Freeman,* which later fell through. Instead she got a job with

TAGGARD

B.W. Huebsch, an avant-garde publisher, then later joined up with two other people to publish *Measure: A Magazine of Verse.* In 1922 Taggard published her first book *For Eager Lovers,* which got high praise from critics like the *Literary Review's* Louis Untermeyer, who wrote: "It is a woman speaking; straightforward, sensitive, intense. Instead of loose philosophizing there is a condensed clarity; instead of rhetoric we have revelation."

Through the years, her poetry evolved from such subjects as nature and love, to the experiences of women, art, and social protest. It was the latter that critics often had a hard time with, as did a *Time* magazine writer who described Taggard as a "worried, earnest, political nondescript." Another journal also described his frustration at her writing about many different things, but somehow not focusing, saying "I think that what I am regretting is the absence of a unified sensibility in these fine poems."

She and her husband, Robert L. Wolf, also a writer, and their new baby daughter, lived in San Francisco during 1922, then the following year, they moved to New Preston, Connecticut. After spending a year in Southern France, Taggard once again settled in New England where she got a position teaching at Mount Holyoke College during 1929-30. In 1931 she was honored with a Guggenheim Fellowship, which she used to travel with. Between 1932 and 1935 Taggard was an instructor at Vermont's Bennington College, then taught at Sarah Lawrence College until 1946.

Other books by Taggard included: *Hawaiian Hilltop* (1923); *Travelling Standing Still: Poems 1918-1928* (1928); *The Life and Mind of Emily Dickinson* (1930); *Not Mine to Finish: Poems 1928-1934* (1934); *Calling Western Union* (1936); *Long View* (1942); *A*

Part of Vermont (1945); *Slow Music* (1946); and *Origin: Hawaii* (1947). Her work was also included in various anthologies.

Taggard was divorced from her first husband in 1934 and she remarried to Kenneth Durant the following year. She died on November 8, 1948.

TAIMAH, (fl. early 19th century) — also known as Taima, Tama, and Taiomah, was a Fox chief and medicine man of the Thunder branch who ruled a village near present Burlington, Iowa. A friend to the white settlers, he was responsible for once saving the Indian agent residing at Prairie du Chien, Wisconsin. With Keokuk and other Sauk and Fox chiefs he signed the Washington August 4, 1824 treaty rescinding all claims to lands west of the Mississippi River in Missouri. Taimah died in his village shortly after 1824. The county and town of Tama, Iowa are named for him.

TAUKE, THOMAS JOSEPH, (1950-   ) — a U.S. Representative from Iowa; born in Dubuque, Dubuque County, Iowa, October 11, 1950; attended the Dubuque County private schools; graduated from Wahlert High School, 1968; B.A., Loras College, Dubuque, 1972; J.D., University of Iowa College of Law, Iowa City, 1974; admitted to the Iowa bar and commenced practice in Dubuque in 1974; served in the Iowa general assembly, 1975-1978; delegate, Iowa State Republican conventions, 1972-1978; delegate, Republican National Convention, 1976; elected as a Republican to the Ninety-sixth and to the four succeeding Congresses (January 3, 1979-January 3, 1989); is a resident of Dubuque, Iowa.

THOMPSON, SADA CAROLYN,, (1929-) — actress born in Des Moines, Iowa on September 27, 1929, the oldest of the three children of Hugh Woodruff and Corlyss Elizabeth (Gibson) Thompson. Around 1934 the family moved to Fanwood, New Jersey where Thompson's father became the Eastern editor of four poultry magazines of the Watt Publishing Company. She married Donald E. Stewart on December 18, 1949, they had one daughter.

First bit by the acting but at an early age, Thompson was enchanted and totally consumed by the stage upon her first encounter. Thompson's parents took her to see Cole Porter's Broadway musical *Red, Hot and Blue* a 1936-37 season hit and she was soon attending acting classes in nearby Plainfield.Thompson was active in high school productions at Scotch Plains High School (New Jersey), she attended and earned a B.F.A in 1949 from Carnegie Institute of Technology Drama School.

During her college years, her efforts focused on the theatre. In the summer of her sophomore year, Thompson and a number of her classmates formed a stock company in Mashpee, Massachusetts, the University Playhouse. It was here that she made her first professional appearances in a wide variety of challenging roles, both classic and contemporary. Her stage debut occurred 1945 as Nick's Ma in William Saroyan's *The Time of Your Life*. While still a student she performed professionally at the Pittsburgh Playhouse, The Playhouse in Erie (Pennsylvania) and in a number of summer stock productions at the Henrietta Hayloft Theatre in Rochester, New York. Her early roles included Mrs. Higgens in *Pygmalion,* Mrs., Montgomery in *The Heiress,* and Emily Webb in *Our Town.*

Continuing her apprenticeship in stock, Thompson was invited to join the Brattle Theatre Company of Cambridge Massachusetts, but was informed on her, the company had folded. Thompson found work in New York as a speech teacher at the Ninety-second Street YMHA where she met Dylan Thomas. He asked her to participate in a reading of a radio play in verse form that he was writing, *Under Milk Wood*. On May 14, 1953, Thompson made her New York debut at the YMHA, reading several of the sixty-three parts in *Under Milk Wood*. She later performed in two other productions of the verse play; a 1961 Off-Broadway revival at the Circle in the Square Theatre, and the National Education Television presentation in 1966.

Following her appearance at the Ninety-second Street Y, Thompson returned to summer stock working for companies in Connecticut and Pennsylvania and in Ontario, Canada. Her first professional job in New York City was the part of Mrs. Heidelberg in *The Clandestine Marriage* at the Provincetown Playhouse in 1954. This was followed in 1955 by appearances at the Phoenix Theatre as Cornelia in *The White Devil* and Feng Nan in *The Carefree Tree*.

Thompson earned a Drama Desk Vernon Rice Award for her performance in Off Broadway's, Theatre East presentation of the newly translated *The Misanthrope* in 1956. She netted her second Vernon Rice award for her portrayal of an English girl mourning the war-time death of her half-brother in *The River Line*. The production opened January 1957 at Carnegie Hall Playhouse.

Thompson was invited in the summer of 1957 to join the newly formed American Shakespeare Festival at Stratford, Connecticut. This began a long association with a highly-regarded company and extended

Thompson the opportunity to perform in wide variety of roles. Her Broadway debut came in 1959 at the Winter Garden. Thompson played the part of Mrs. Coyne in *Juno.* Despite the play's elaborate production, lavish investment and a cast of stars that included Shirley Booth and Melvyn Douglas, the play was a commercial failure. Thompson returned to the American Shakespeare festival in July 1959 and appeared in all three Stratford productions the following year.

Thompson continued to work the stage receiving not only recognition for her performances but several awards as well. Her role in *The Effect of Gamma Rays on Man-in-the-Moon* brought her critical acclaim, an Obie and a Drama Desk Award.. She also received an Obie for her performances in *Marigolds* and *Tartuffe.* Her first Broadway hit brought a long overdue public acclaim by critics and not only a Tony, but the *Variety* New York Drama Critics Award for best actress. The play was *Twigs* which opened at the Broadhurst in November 1971. Thompson played four roles in that production and confirmed her stardom as many times. The story is one of three sisters and their contrasting lives. Thompson not only performs the parts of all three sisters, but the mother as well who is introduced in the final act.

Despite the fact that the stage has been her true love, Thompson has appeared on film and television. Her movie credits include *You Are Not Alone* (1961), *The Pursuit of Happiness* (Columbia 1971), and *Desperate Characters* (Paramount, 1971). Among her television appearances are the role of Kate Lawrence in *Family* (ABC, 1976-1980), for which she won a 1978 Emmy. and a variety of specials and guest appearance. Her television credits include *Carl Sandburg's Lincoln* (ABC), *The Entertainer* (1976) *Marco*

Polo (1982), *Princess Daisy* (1983), *The Goodyear Playhouse,* (NBC), *Kraft Theatre* (NBC), *The Big Story* (NBC), *The Nurses* (CBS), and *Owen Marshall* (ABC).

Thompson is a member of Actors' Equity Association (former council member), American Federation of Television and Radio Artists, and the Screen Actors Guild.

THURSTON, LLOYD, (1880-1970) — a U.S. Representative from Iowa; born in Osceola, Clarke County, Iowa, March 27, 1880; attended the public schools; during the Spanish-American War enlisted on June 13, 1898, as a private in Company I, Fifty-first Regiment, Iowa Volunteer Infantry, and served with this company during the Philippine Insurrection, and was honorably discharged on November 2, 1899; was graduated from the law department of the University of Iowa at Iowa City in 1902; was admitted to the bar the same year and commenced practice in Osceola, Clarke County, Iowa; captain in the National Guard of Iowa 1902-1906; prosecuting attorney of Clarke County 1908-1910; during the First World War served with the rank of captain in Company C, Twenty- sixth Battalion, United States Guards, at Fort Crook, Nebr.; member of the State senate 1920-1924; elected as a Republican to the Sixty-ninth and to the six succeeding Congresses (March 4, 1925-January 3, 1939); was not a candidate for renomination in 1938, but was an unsuccessful candidate for the Republican nomination for United States Senator; resumed the practice of law in Osceola, Iowa; died in Des Moines, Iowa, May 7, 1970; interment in Maple Hill Cemetery, Osceola, Iowa.

TOWNER, HORACE MANN, (1855-1937) — a U.S. Representative from Iowa; born in Belvidere, Boone County, Ill., October 23, 1855; attended the public and high schools of Belvidere, the University of Chicago, and Union College of Law; was admitted to the bar in 1877 and commenced practice in Prescott, Adams County, Iowa; moved to Corning, Adams County, Iowa, in 1880, having been elected county superintendent of schools, in which capacity he served until 1884, when he resumed the practice of law; elected judge of the third judicial district of Iowa in 1890 and served until January 1, 1911; lectured on constitutional law in the University of Iowa 1902-1911; elected as a Republican to the Sixty-second and to the six succeeding Congresses and served from March 4, 1911, to April 1, 1923, when he resigned to become Governor of Puerto Rico, in which capacity he served until his resignation on September 29, 1929; chairman, Committee on Insular Affairs (Sixty-sixth and Sixty-seventh Congress); resumed the practice of law in Corning, Iowa, until his death on November 23, 1937; interment in Walnut Grove Cemetery.

TURNER, DANIEL W., (1877-1969) — twenty-fifth governor of Iowa (1931-33), was born in Corning, Iowa on March 17, 1877, the son of Austin and Almera (Boher) Turner. He attended Corning Academy in 1898, and was a member of the Iowa Volunteer Infantry during 1898-99. In the latter year, Turner turned to farming to make a living.

Turner's first foray into politics was when he was elected to the state senate in 1904, serving in that body until 1909. Several years later, in 1930, he secured the governorship of Iowa on the Republican ticket. While in office he had to face issues having to do with the Great Depression, and worked on tax reduction for the state. Another problem Turner had to deal with was dubbed the "Cow War," during which he had to ask the National Guard to protect veterinarians from angry farmers as the vets tried to test cows for tuberculosis, which had become an epidemic.

In a show of support for his state's citizens, Turner tried to persuade President Herbert Hoover to stop forclosures on farms; however, his efforts did not garner him a second term as governor--he lost to Democrat Clyde Herring by over 50,000 votes. Turner ran against Herring once again in 1934, but lost a second time as well.

Turner returned to public life in 1941 when he served on the War Production Board during World War II, a post he held until 1945. He was married to Alice Sample and the couple had three children. Turner died on April 15, 1969.

U

UTTERBACK, HUBERT, (1880-1942) — (cousin of John Gregg Utterback), a U.S. Representative from Iowa; born on a farm near Hayesville, Keokuk County, Iowa, June 28, 1880; attended the rural schools and Hedrick (Iowa) Normal and Commercial College; was graduated from Drake University, Des Moines, Iowa, in 1908; studied law; was admitted to the bar in 1906 and commenced practice in Des Moines, Iowa; instructor in the law department of Drake University 1908- 1935; lecturer on law, Still College, Des Moines, Iowa, 1911- 1933; judge of police court of Des Moines 1912-1914; judge of the ninth Iowa judicial district 1915-1927; member of the Iowa State Conference of Social Work and served as chairman of the legislative committee 1923-1925; served as an associate justice of the State supreme court from December 5, 1932, to April 11, 1933; elected as a Democrat to the Seventy- fourth Congress (January 3, 1935-January 3, 1937); was not a candidate for renomination but was an unsuccessful candidate for nomination as United States Senator in 1936; chairman of the State parole board 1937-1940; State Democratic National committeeman 1937-1940; died in Des Moines, Iowa, on May 12, 1942; interment in Glendale Cemetery.

V

VAN BUREN, ABIGAIL, (1918-) — author of syndicated newspaper column, "Dear Abby," and broadcaster of daily radio show, "Dear Abby." She was born Pauline Esther Friedman on Independence Day of 1918 in Sioux City, Iowa. Her parents, Abraham and Rebecca (Rushall) Friedman, were Russian emigrants. Abigail has a twin sister, Esther Pauline, who writes a column under the pen name of "Ann Landers." Abigail Van Buren graduated with honors in 1936 from Sioux City's Central High School and attended Morningside College in Sioux City, majoring in psychology and journalism. She did not, however, complete her degree even though she received high grades. After marrying Morton Phillips and having two children, Jeanne and Eddie, Ms. Van Buren became active in philanthropic causes and in the Democratic party. Then around 1955, she submitted some sample articles to the San Francisco *Chronicle* who was at that time publishing an advice column by Molly Mayfield. She arranged for an interview and the editors enjoyed talking with her so much that they dropped Ms. Mayfield and gave Ms. Van Buren the column. She created the pen name of Abigail Van Buren and started writing her "Dear Abby" column in January of 1956. Within a month she had signed a ten-year contract with the McNaught Syndicate and within a year, her column was appearing in over eighty newspapers.

Part of the attraction to "Dear Abby's" column is perhaps her quick-witted one liners. She has dealt with a number of topics including pornography, teen sex, bed-wetting and unwanted pregnancies. She employs eight secretaries and receives over 12,000 letters a week. For those that request a personal reply to their letters, she accommodates them, and sometimes will honor an urgent problem with a phone call. Wanting to help those when help is really wanted, she has advised those with very difficult problems to seek help with psychiatrists, clergymen, or social workers. Her readers are grateful for her advice as evidenced in one man's letter, who wrote: "Thanks, Abby, for giving me a kick in the pants when I needed it. It woke me up." Along with her columns, she has also written several booklets including "How to Be Popular," "How to Have a Lovely Wedding," and "How to Write Letters for All Occasions." Books she has authored include, *Dear Abby, Dear Teenager, Dear Abby on Marriage,* and *The Best of Dear Abby.* She has also received many honors and awards including: the *Los Angeles Times* Mother of the Year Award; the Golden Kidney Award; the Sarah Coventry Award; the Woman of the Year

Award from the International Rotary Club; an honorary Litt.D. from Morningside College; the National Conference of Christians and Jews Award; the Good Samaritan Award from the Salvation Army; and the list goes on.

Abigail Van Buren is a slight woman, standing only five feet two inches and weighing only about 108 pounds. She has black hair and greenish-blue eyes. Her hobbies include playing the piano, violin and electric organ and stamp collecting with her children. She has many celebrity friends and once took a small role in the film *At War with the Army.* She has strong convictions that her family -- her husband and children -- come first in her life.

VAN DUYN, MONA, (1921-) — poet, was born in Waterloo, Iowa. She obtained her B.A. at the University of Northern Iowa in 1942 and her M.A. at the University of Iowa in 1943. In that same year she became an instructor in English at the University of Iowa until 1946. She left that institution and became an instructor of English at Washington University in St. Louis from 1950-1967. In 1973 she was lecturer for the Salzburg (Austria) Seminar in American Studies. She has also served as poetry consultant for the Olin Library Modern Literature Collection at Washington University and from 1947 to 1967, she was co-editor of the *Perspective: A Quarterly of Literature.* In 1943, she married Jarvis A. Thurston, a professor of English.

Mona Van Duyn started writing at a young age and has chosen as her subjects ordinary people and ordinary, every day events. Although her poetry has been tagged as "domestic," Van Duyn has said that it's a label that irritates her. Her poems, although seemingly domestic, centered around subjects such as birthdays, cocktail parties, gardening, and relatives, are often metaphors for subjects such as death, the possibility of atomic destruction, the nature of the human imagination, unsettling scientific experiments, etc. Her acceptance speech for the National Book Award in 1971 contained these statements about her perspective on poetry: "Poetry honors the formed use of language particularly, being concerned with both its sound and its meaning, and a poet spends his life's best effort in shaping these into a patterned experience which will combine an awareness of earlier patternings with the unique resonance of his own voice. He tries to do so in such a way that the experience may be shared with other people. This effort assumes a caring about other human beings, a caring which is a form of love." She has put together several collections of her poems including *Valentines to the Wide World: Poems, A Time of Bees, To See, To Take, Bedtime Stories, Merciful Disguises: Poems Published and Unpublished, Letters from a Father and Other Poems, Near Changes: Poems,* and *Lives and Deaths of the Poets and Non-Poets. To See, To Take,* is her strongest collection of poems and perhaps her most notable.

Van Duyn has won several awards for her poetry including the Eunice Tietjens Memorial Prize; the Helen Bullis Prize ; the National Endowment for the Arts grants in 1966-67 and 1985; the Harriet Monroe Memorial Prize; the Hart Crane Memorial Award; first prize, Borestone Mountain Awards; the Bollingen Prize from the Yale University Library; the National Book Award for Poetry; the John Simon Guggenheim Memorial fellowship; the Loines Prize from the National Institute of Arts and Letters; the Academy of American Poets fellow; the Sandburg Prize from Cornell College; the Shelley Memorial Award from the Poetry Society of America; the Ruth Lilly Poetry Prize from the Modern Poetry Association; the Pulitzer prize; and honorary D.Litt degrees from Washington University, Cornell College and the University of Northern Iowa.

VAN VECHTEN, CARL, (1880-1964) — author, critic, photographer born in Cedar Rapids Iowa on June 17, 1880, the son of a banker and insurance agent and his wife, Charles Duane and Ada Amanda (Fitch) Van Vechten.

Van Vechten entered the University of Chicago in 1899. He graduated in 1903 with a PH.B and began working for the *Chicago American* covering spot news, locating photographs and writing a society column. Moving to New York in 1906, Van Vechten was commissioned by Theodore Dreiser, then editor of *Broadway* magazine to write an article on Richard Strauss's opera *Salome*. In 1906 he secured a position as assistant to Richard Aldrich, *New York Times* music critic. Thus marking him a journalist-critic-essayist in music and the arts.

A trip abroad in 1907 netted him wife and employment. He married a long time acquaintance from Cedar Rapids, Anna Elizabeth Snyder in London on June 1907. They divorced in 1912. Van Vechten was a Paris correspondent for the *New York Times* from 1908-1908. He returned to New York and resumed critical writing for the *Times* and served a brief stint as a drama critic for the *New York Press* . He married actress Fania Marinoff on October 21, 1914. The long-lasting union produced no children.

Van Vechten met Mabel Dodge and joined her celebrated salon groups. She introduced him to Gertrude Stein and for decades he championed Stein's work with publishers and the public. He actually handled her manuscripts and acted as her unofficial agent. He served as her literary executor after his death in 1946 Throughout his career, Van Vechten continued to service, in a number of ways, those artists for which he held respect and admiration. The list included experimental composers such as Satie, Schoenberg and Stravinsky as well as a number of performers. A number of Van Vechten's favorable essays on such figures were collected in *Music After the Great War* (1915), *Music and Bad Manners* (1916), Interpreters and Interpretations (1917), *The Merry-Go-Round* (1918), *In the Garret* (1919) and *Red* (1925). In addition, these volumes contained essays on ragtime, jazz, musical comedy, the blues and music for the movies. In *Excavation* (1926) he called attention to unusual and overlooked literary figures like Edgar Saltus, Ronald Firbank, and Ouida. As early as 1921 when it was still a neglected piece, Van Vechten enthusiastically applaued *Moby Dick* as a great work of literature and called due notice to Herman Melville.

Van Vechten cultivated a particular interest in black culture, literature and art which appeared to have an early start in his life. Not only had he been exposed to black entertainers in his youth, but a black washerwoman and gardener were the first adults he knew outside his immediate family. His upbringing taught him respect of all adults regardless of race. Van Vechten wrote a series of articles on black subject for *Vanity Fair* in 1925. The series focused on singers Bessie Smith and Ethel Waters, spirituals, black theater, and the blues (the first serious considerations given this kind of music). He was a major financier of singer Paul Robeson's first spiritual programs and similar musical performances of Taylor Gordon and J. Rosamond Johnson.

VAN VECHTEN

A partial list of other discoveries and enthusiasms of Van Vechten's is impressive. He endorsed the first performances in America of Isadora Duncan, Anna Pavlova, Mary Garden, Fyodor Chaliapin, Vaslav Nijinsky, Sergei Rachmaninoff and the operas of Richard Strauss. He greatly admired the music of George Gershiwn and advocated, musical scores by classical composers for motion pictures. He was a pioneer in reviewing Spanish music and considers jazz and ragtime as fervently as he considered music of contemporary performers and composer.

Van Vechten first novel. *Peter Whiffle: His Live and Works* (1922) is a semiautobiography featuring the scenes in Europe and New York in which he took part. Contemporary artists, aesthetes, and intellectuals were the characters often under their own identities and sometimes thinly disguised. Several novels followed in which the author presented, with a mock decadence befitting the times, a perverse and exotic comedic tone capitalizing on popular issues. The *Blind Bow-Boy* (1923) and *Firecrackers* (1925) portrayed restless sophisticates seeking sensationalism and running from boredom, while the *Tattooed Countess* (1924) fell in with "the revolt from the village," *Spider Boy* (1928) satirized Hollywood's movie madness. *Nigger Heaven* (1926), was one piece that brought controversy and criticism. The novel deals with the complex layers of Harlem life. It is thought by some that instead of offering insight to the black culture of Harlem, Van Vechten depicted a fragmented scandalous society. Nonetheless this novel did not appear to alienate him from the black community, but instead strengthened his ties.

Through the remainder of his long career, he devoted his energies to a wider recognition of black achievement, primarily through photography, a longtime hobby and belated career interest. Van Vechten produced a wide range of unretouched documentary portraits of both famous and little-known personalities. He was the founder and major contributor of Yale University's James Weldon Johnson Memorial Collection of Negro Arts and Letters. Not only did donate his own vast collection of black literature and memorabilia, including many of his photographs, he contributed financially to the cause during his lifetime and afterwards through special provision made in his will.

Van Vechten died in New York City on December 21, 1964

W

WADE, MARTIN JOSEPH, (1861-1931) — a U.S. Representative from Iowa; born in Burlington, Chittenden County, Vt., October 20, 1861; moved to Iowa with his parents at an early age; attended the common schools and St. Joseph's College (later Columbia University), Dubuque, Iowa; was graduated from the law department of the University of Iowa at Iowa City in 1886; was admitted to the bar the same year and practiced in Iowa City, Johnson County, Iowa, 1886-1893; judge of the eighth judicial district of Iowa 1893- 1903; lecturer in the law department of the University of Iowa 1891-1903 and professor of medical jurisprudence 1595-1905; president of the Iowa State Bar Association in 1897 and 1898; elected as a Democrat to the Fifty- eighth Congress (March 4, 1903-March 3, 1905); unsuccessful candidate for re-election in 1904 to the Fifty-ninth Congress; resumed the practice of his profession in Iowa City, Iowa; delegate to the Democratic National Conventions in 1904 and 1912; appointed judge of the United States District Court for the Southern District of Iowa in 1915 and served until his death April 16, 1931, in Los Angeles, Calif., while on a visit in that State; interment in St. Joseph's Cemetery, Iowa City, Iowa.

WALLACE, HENRY AGARD, (1888-1965) — was an agricultural scientist,secretary of agriculture, and vice-president under the administration of Franklin D. Roosevelt.

Born near Orient, Iowa on October 7, 1888, his father and grandfather were both prominent in the agricultural field and owned the newspaper, *Wallaces' Farmer,* a popular journal at that time. Following in his family's footsteps, he studied agriculture at Iowa State College, earning a B.S. degree in animal husbandry in 1910. He then worked as a writer and assistant editor of *Wallaces' Farmer,* taking over as editor after Warren G. Harding chose the elder Wallace to be his secretary of agriculture. Later, instead of continuing on to graduate school, Wallace decided to strike out on his own. His first major success was a hybrid of corn he produced which became a popular product and made him wealthy. That led to the establishment, in 1926, of the Hi-Bred Corn Company, which was also highly successful.

When a surplus of crops in the 1920's led to a depression in the agricultural market, Wallace suggested to farmers that they cut back on their output by concentrating specifically on domestic needs. However, the suggestion was not adopted and his next plan, what was called export "dumping," became known as the McNary-Haugen bill. However, President Calvin Coolidge refused twice to pass it, and Wallace was so enraged that he switched political parties from the family's long-time Republican affiliation.

After the start of the Great Depression, Wallace was a supporter of more world trade, along with a newly suggested voluntary domestic allotment plan which gave farmers a stipend for cutting back on their crop production. Wallace was not impressed with the way Herbert Hoover was handling the nation as it was reeling from the Depression, and in 1932, he became a strong supporter of Franklin D. Roosevelt who appointed Wallace as secretary of agriculture after his Presidential win.

After Congress passed the Agricultural Adjustment Act in 1933, which gave Wallace more authority, he wasted no time in implementing programs he felt were crucial, the first being the voluntary domestic allotment plan. In addition, Wallace was a suppoter of Secretary of State Cordell Hull's plan to remove trade restrictions which increased international commerce and greatly helped the farmers. Besides crop control, other policies Wallace was responsible for included soil conservation and food stamp assistance.

Wallace was an early advocate of a spiritual path that is now the mainstay of the current New Age movement. His view of the Great Depression was not limited to the political aspect, but instead, he saw a larger picture, which he felt should entail a change in attitude by Americans, in which they would set aside some of their personal or selfish needs and devote their time and energies toward social justice and the common good, following a "higher law of cooperation," an objective he never stopped believing in.

WALLACE

President Roosevelt respected Wallace enough to choose him as his running-mate in the 1940 Presidential election. The Presidentfelt that his presence would be an advantage in the Midwest where Roosevelt's popularity was at its weakest. However, other Democrats were not as impressed with Wallace and there was infighting among them before Wallace was ultimately accepted. While the vice-presidency is usually known as a thankless job, Wallace was highly visible in his new position and traveled extensively throughout Latin America, Asia and China. Right before the start of the Second World War, Wallace was appointed as chairman of the Board of Economic Warfare. However, he was soon involved in several heated disputes, mostly with Secretary of Commerce, Jesse H. Jones, with the end result being the dissolving of the Board by the President.

After the war ended, Wallace continued speaking out regarding his views on the importance of unity, on both an economical and spiritual level. Believing it was the "century of the common man," he felt it was the responsibility of the United States to help improve the living standards of underdeveloped nations by encouraging education and supporting industrialization. He held the unswerving belief that war and angry rebellion would continue if poverty and hunger were not alleviated. His utopian vision of the world was often criticized by others of a more cynical nature, and he was dubbed as one of the "Post War Dream Boys." However, Wallace, never at loss for words himself, retorted that his critics were nothing more than "American fascists."

Unfortunately, the Democrats who were against his initial vice-presidential nomination, dug in their heels and convinced President Roosevelt, who was running for a fourth term, that there were others more fitting for the position. Although Roosevelt told Wallace that he was still his first choice, privately the President let it be known that other possibilities for the position might be Senator Harry S. Truman or Supreme Court Justice William O. Douglas. Roosevelt's lackadaisical attitude toward Wallace tipped the scales against him, and the Democratic Party chose Harry Truman for vice-president.

Although deeply hurt by the President's betrayal, Wallace still believed that Roosevelt was the best man to lead the country, and campaigned for him zealously. A grateful and possibly guilt-stricken Roosevelt named Wallace as his secretary of commerce. Wallace delved into the new position with his usual passion, putting his energies into helping small businesses, and also worked at extending the 1934 Trade Agreement Act in hopes of building economic balance globally, which he felt would create world peace.

One of Wallace's strongest beliefs concerned relations between the United States and the Soviet Union. While a member of Roosevelt's cabinet, he worked closely with the President, who agreed with Wallace that the way to handle the potentially explosive situation was to work at conciliation in order to win Russia's trust. However, after Roosevelt's death, President Truman took the opposite position, feeling that the U.S. had to show strength in their dealings with the Soviet Union. Wallace went so far as to write a twelve-page letter to Truman, outlining what he felt would alleviate the friction, including the offer of economic assistance to Russia. However, Truman held his ground, and Wallace, in a show of rebellion, gave a speech in September of 1946 in which he offered his opposition to the President's policies, a decision that prompted Truman to immediately fire him.

Wallace, however, would not be silenced, and announced that he would continue to "carry on the fight for peace." His termination left him free to publicly denounce Truman's policy toward Russia, which he was often able to do in his new position as editor of *New Republic*. Angered even further by the Truman Doctrine, he accused the President of "whipping up anti-Communist hysteria," with his warmonger attitude. He continued to strongly feel, as he always had in the past, that better living standards, prompted by American monetary and technical assistance to Russia (or any other underdeveloped nation), would prevent wars. Unfortunately, Wallace was the lone voice in a country that was gripped by anti-Communist fervor, although he clung to the belief that eventually the American people would come around to his way of thinking. However, when he ran for President on the Independent ticket in 1947, he received less than 3 percent of the total vote, partially due to the support he had received during his campaign from the American Communist Party, an association that did not sit well with the voters, liberals included.

Wallace spent his remaining years on his farm in South Salem, New York. He still spoke out occasionally, as when he opposed the Korean conflict, and he never renounced his previous views on American foreign policy.

Wallace was married to Ilo Browne and the couple had three children. He died in near obscurity on November 18, 1965, in Danbury, Connecticut.

WAYMACK, WILLIAM WESLEY, (1888-1960) —
was one of the first mebers of the Atomic Energy
Commission.

Born on October 18, 1888 in Savanna, Illinois,
he earned his BA. degree at Morningside College in
Sioux City, Iowa, where he was a member of the
journalism fraternity Sigma Delta Chi. He began his
journalism career as a reporter on the Sioux City
Journal. Three years later, he was promoted to city
editor and chief editorial writer. In 1918, he moved
to Des Moines to write editorials for the *Register* and
Tribune. Waymack became managing editor of these
newspapers in 1921. He eventually became editor in
chief of both papers, a position he held for more than
20 years. Waymack was a runner-up for the Pulitzer
Prize in distinguished editorial writing in 1936,
achieving the award from Columbia University in the
following year.

Waymack's extensive work on governmental advisory committees throughout the years led to his
appointment in 1946 by President Harry S. Truman to
the newly established Atomic Energy Commission
(AEC). Control of the United States Army's $2 billion
atomic energy project, under the code name of Manhattan District, passed into the hands of the AEC.
Waymack and his fellow commissioners were vested
with complete control and responsibility for all
atomic energy work in the United States and all
source materials, even to the power of expropriating
all newly discovered deposits of such ores. Inasmuch
as the United States had a relative monopoly of the
facilities and techniques for releasing atomic energy,
these five men stood as "trustees of the world" of the
vast new power.

Waymack married Elsie Jeannette Lord in 1911. The couple had one son. Waymack died on November 5, 1960.

WAYNE, JOHN, (1907-1979) — actor, was born Marion Michael Morrison, in Winterset, Iowa, with the nickname "Duke," after his pet airdale. His parents were Clyde L. Morrison, a druggist, and Mary Margaret Brown. The Morrisons moved to southern California when Duke was six, settling first in Lancaster and then Glendale. Duke attended Glendale High School and helped his father in his drugstore in his spare time.

After high school, Duke attended the University of California on an athletic scholarship from 1925 to 1927. He worked as a stuntman at the Fox Film Corporation in Hollywood and had small parts in a couple John Ford's silent movies. His first full acting part was in a movie entitled *The Big Trail,* a western produced by Raoul Walsh which was a box office flop. It was Raoul Walsh that gave Duke the name John Wayne. Wayne spent hours perfecting the walk, bar room brawling techniques, and stunt riding which became part of his identity later in his career. Wayne also was a singing cowboy in the early days of his career but stopped doing those types of roles when he received constant requests for personal singing appearances. It wasn't that he didn't like personal appearances, but the music had always been dubbed into the film, since Duke neither sang nor played the guitar.

After a series of low rated films in the 1930's, Duke was cast by John Ford as Ringo Kid in the western, *Stagecoach.* The film won three Oscars and made Wayne a star. Although he became most well-known for his roles in a great many westerns,

Duke Wayne also accepted roles in movies such as *The Long Voyage Home,* in which he played a young Swede working on a British tramp steamer and *The Wake of the Red Witch,* in which he played a tough captain. He also made a bunch of World War II films including *They Were Expendable,* and a comedy entitled, *No Reservations.* His most notable films include *Hondo, The Searchers, Stagecoach* and *Rio Bravo.* He also made outstanding appearances in the 1960's in *North to Alaska, Hatari, El Dorado, The Man Who Shot Liberty Valance,* and the Academy Award winning *True Grit* in which he played Rooster Cogburn, a rough and tumble, gutsy, one-eyed gunfighter. Probably one of his biggest disappointments during Wayne's career in film making was a picture he invested $1,200,000 of his own money into. *The Alamo,* in which Wayne himself played the part of Davie Crockett was a failure both critically and commercially. In the late 1970's, after a personal battle with lung cancer, Wayne played a dramatic role as an aging gunfighter dying of cancer in *The Shootist.* The picture made several best film lists for 1977 and was especially noted for Wayne's outstanding performance.

John Wayne was married to Josephine Saenz on June 24, 1933 and divorced. His second marriage to Esperanza Baur, actress and dancer, also ended in divorce. He was separated from his third wife, Pilar Palette in 1973. Altogether, he had seven children: Michael, Toni, Patrick, Melinda, Aissia, John Ethan, and Marisa.

Wayne died on June 11, 1979 in Los Angeles, California. In his more than forty years in the movies, he had made more than two hundred films, some of them under his own production company, Batjac Productions Inc. He is now esteemed as one of the great heroes of American cinema along with Humphrey Bogart and Errol Flynn.

WEAVER, JAMES BAIRD, (1833-1912) — was a soldier and statesman.

Born in Dayton, Ohio on June 12, 1833, he was graduated from the law school at Ohio University in 1856. He practice law in Iowauntil the outbreak of the Civil War when he enlisted in the Federal Army as a private. He moved up through the ranks until he was brevetted brigadier-general in 1865.

After the war, Weaver returned to the practice of law. He was prosecuting attorney of the Iowa 2nd Judicial District from 1866 until 1870 and assessor of internal revenue for the 1st District from 1867 until 1873. Subsequently, he became one of the editors of the *Iowa Tribune*.

Weaver was instrumental in the organizing of the Greenback Party and was elected to Congress as its representative in 1878. In 1880, he was a delegate to the national convention of the Greenback Party in Chicago and was nominated as its candidate for president. He was reelected to Congress in 1884 and 1886.

Many of the issue for which he fought in the legislature were very significant to the American political life. Key actions included: the introduction of a resolution for an amendment to the constitution to secure the direction of senators; the advocation of opening the Oklahoma Territory to settlers; and the introduction of a bill to establish the department of labor. He also proposed to equalize the pay of soldiers to make up for the depreciation of the currency they were paid during the war.

In 1892, he was nominated by the People's Party as their candidate for president. He made a good showing, capturing 21 electoral votes and more than one million popular votes.

Weaver married Clara Vinson in 1858. The couple had seven children. He died on February 6, 1912.

WILCOX, FRANCIS (ORLANDO), (1908-1985) — educator, political scientist, public servant, administrator, editor and author. He was born on April 9, 1908 in Columbus Junction, Iowa to Francis Oliver and Verna Wilcox. Wilcox grew up in Montrose, Iowa and graduated from Montrose High School in 1925. In 1930, he graduated from the State University of Iowa with a B.A. degree in political science. He earned his M.A. degree in 1931 and his Ph.D. in 1933 from the same institution. In 1934, he received a Carnegie Fellowship grant and was able to attend the University of Geneva in Switzerland. There he earned the Docteur is Sciences Politiques degree. He has also studied at the University of Chicago and the Hague Academy of International Law.

From 1931 to 1933, Wilcox taught American government as a teaching assistant at the State University of Iowa. In 1935, he was assistant professor of political science at the University of Louisville in Kentucky. He became associate professor, then chairman of the division of Social Science. He has also taught at the University of Michigan and was consultant for a time for the American Council on Education.

Starting in 1942, Wilcox held several positions in the United States government. He began as associate chief of the division of inter-American activities in the Office of the Coordinator of Inter-American Affairs. From 1947 to 1955, he was chief of staff of the Senate Committee and attended most of the meetings of the U.N. General Assembly. In 1951, he was also a delegate to the Japanese Peace Conference.

WILCOX

In 1955, he received an appointment by Dwight D. Eisenhower as Assistant Secretary of State for international organizational affairs. He was later delegate to the tenth session of the U.N. General Assembly. In 1956, he was delegate to the World Health Assembly in Geneva, to Minneapolis in 1958, and to International Labor Organization Conferences in Geneva in 1957 and 1958.

In 1961, Wilcox accepted the position of dean of the School of Advanced International studies in Washington, D.C. which is part of the Johns Hopkins University in Baltimore, Maryland. In this new position, he brought about various changes such as the construction of a $1,500,000 building on Massachusetts Avenue in Washington as part of a $4,247,000 development program for the school.

In the early 1970's, Wilcox served President Nixon's Commission to the United Nations and beginning in 1975 was director general of the Atlantic Council, an organization that promotes close ties among NATO nations.

In addition to his work activities, Wilcox was an executive committeeman of the American Society of International Law from 1948 to 1949, and was chairman of the committee on under-graduate instruction for the American Political Science Association from 1946 to 1948. He was also president of the Washington branch from 1948 to 1949. He received honorary degrees from the University of Louisville and Hamline University.

Wilcox wrote and collaborated on several articles on international relations including, "Treaty Making in Post-war Germany," "Geneva's Future," and "Localization of the Spanish War."

Francis Wilcox married Genevieve C. Byrnes on July 23, 1933 and had one daughter, Carol Lenore.

Mrs. Wilcox died on August 19, 1946. Mr. Wilcox died on February 20, 1985.

WILLIAMS, ANDY, (1930-) — singer, was born in Wall Lake, Iowa, to Jay E. and Florence Bell. He has four siblings: Richard, Robert, Donald, and Jane. When he was young, Andy sang with his family sang in the choir of the local Presbyterian church. When he and his brothers got a little older, they teamed up and made their professional debut on radio. Andy was eight at the time. After appearing on several radio stations in Des Moines, Chicago and Cincinnati, the boys were signed to a motion picture contract with Metro-Goldwyn Mayer in Los Angeles. After Andy graduated from high school in 1947, the brothers both together with comedienne Kay Thompson and created a night club act. In 1953, the group disbanded and the brothers each went their separate ways.

Williams recorded his first song in 1954, and went to New York to market it. While he was there, he started working with Steve Allen's *Tonight* show, where he stayed for two-and-a- half years. After his job with the *Tonight* show ended, Williams signed a contract with Cadence records. Some of the albums Cadence released for him include, *Andy Williams Sings Steve Allen, Andy Williams sings Rodgers and Hammerstein,* and *Two Time Winners.* Some of the singles released during that time include, "Babie Doll," "Butterfly," "I Like Your Kind of Love," "Lips of Wine," "Are You Sincere?," and others.

In 1957, Williams appeared on *The Dinah Shore Chevy Show.* The producers of the show were so impressed with him, that they gave him his own show to replace *The Pat Boone Chevy Showroom. The Chevy Showroom with Andy Williams* ran for thirteen weeks in 1958. After the show ended, he hosted *The Andy Williams Show* which substituted for *The Gary Moor Show,* on CBS. In 1959, he made several one-hour video specials.

Williams' music is a more relaxed, ballad style than the trendy rock 'n' roll. He felt the need to steer clear of rock 'n' roll and lean toward a more easy listening style because, in his opinion, it was better received on television.

Something about his music was well received because Williams won many top awards for it including, seventeen gold albums, two Emmy awards, and six Grammy awards. He also received the annual Personality of the Year award in 1959 from the Variety Club of Washington, D.C. and was later was named Number One Male Vocalist Top Artist on Campus Poll in 1968. His hobbies include collecting oil paintings, traveling, golf, tennis, spectator sports, and reading.

WILLSON, MEREDITH, (1902-1984) — was a musician, composer and lyricist, best known for his effervescent work, *The Music Man.*

Born in Mason City, Iowa on May 18, 1902, he played piano ata very young age, then took up the flute while in high school. After graduating in 1919, he headed for New York and enrolled at the Institute of Musical Art (which later became the famed Juilliard School of Music). While there, he auditioned as a flutist for John Philip Sousa's band and got the job. As a memberof that group, he traveled extensively, visiting Mexico, Cuba and cities throughout Europe. In 1923, he became a member of the Rialto Theatre Orchestra led by Hugo Riesenfeld, and heard his first composition performed by them, entitled *Parade Fantastique.*

Willson continued to work with prestigious musical companies such as the New York Philharmonic-Symphony Orchestra, where as first flutist, he was led by several famous conductors such as Arturo Toscanini. He also worked with the New York Chamber Music Society, conducted the Seattle Symphony in 1929, was the musical director of the American Broadcasting System during 1929-30 and two years later, moved to San Francisco to work as musical director at the western division of the National Broadcasting Company. During the 1930's Willson continued to conduct the Seattle Symphony, along with orchestras in Los Angeles and San Francisco. The latter group performed his first symphony, *San Francisco* in 1936, with Willson at the helm. A year later, he went to Hollywood and became the musical director of the *Maxwell House Coffee Time* radio show.

In 1940, the Los Angeles Philharmonic Orchestra, conducted by Albert Coates, performed Willson's second work, *The Missions of California* No. 2 in E minor. That same year, he met and teamed up with actor/director Charlie Chaplin to score one of Chaplin's best films, *The Great Dictator,* and the following year, he composed the score for the film version of Lillian Hellman's *The Little Foxes.*

After the start of World War II, Willson was given the rank of major in the U.S. Army and was assigned to lead the music division of the Armed Forces Radio Service. Some of the songs he wrote during that time include "America Calling," "Mail Call March," and "Centennial." After his discharge in 1945, Willson once again joined the Maxwell House organization, and along with his music, began to include his own comic material in the form of homely philosophy.

In July of 1949, Willson made his first appearance on television in the *Meredith Willson Show*. He also continued his radio work in the *Big Show* which starred Tallulah Bankhead. It was for that show that Willson wrote the song "May the Good Lord Bless and Keep You." It was a tune that became a huge hit for him, selling over 500,000 copies of sheet music due to its sentimental message that touched many Americans, including most of the soldiers stationed in Korea during that time. Some of his other hits included "You and I," "Iowa," "Two in Love," and "I See the Moon."

In 1948, Willson began working on a musical play which would later become the popular show, *The Music Man*. Willson wrote the music and lyrics, and co-wrote the book with Franklin Lacey. It made it's debut on December 19, 1957, starring Robert Preston and Barbara Cook, and was a solid hit, with critic Brooks Atkinson raving: "Willson's River city folks, circa 1912, are innocent, good-natured, excitable, individual, and entertaining...*The Music Man* has the comic touch; it provides a rousing holiday for everyone." Willson later told an interviewer: "I didn't have to make up anything for *The Music Man*. All I had to do was remember." The show later went on the road in national tours, and won five Tony awards, as well as the Drama Critics Circle award for best musical. It was turned into a popular film in 1962, featuring its original star, Robert Preston and actress Shirley Jones, and won an Academy Award for Best Musical Score.

Willson's next show, also a big hit, was *The Unsinkable Molly Brown,* which was produced for Broadway in 1960, with Debbie Reynolds and Harve Presnell appearing in the 1964 film version. Other plays he wrote were "Here's Love," which debuted in 1963, and "1491," which debuted in 1969.

Willson also authored several books including: *What Every Musician Should Know* (booklet), 1938; *Who Did What to Fedalia,* a novel, 1952; and *The Music Man* (novel based on the musical), 1962. In addition he wrote three volumes of his autobiography: *And There I Stood with My Piccolo,* 1948; *Eggs I Have Laid,* 1955; and *But He Doesn't Know the Territory,* 1959.

Willson was married three times; to Elizabeth Wilson, Ralina Zarova, and Rosemary Sullivan. He died in Santa Monica, California on June 15, 1984.

WILSON, GEORGE ALLISON, (1884-1953) — twenty-eighth governor of Iowa, and United States Senator, was born on April 1, 1884 in Menlo, Iowa, the son of James Henderson and Martha Green (Varley) Wilson. From 1900 to 1903, Wilson was a student at Grinnell College. He subsequently studied at the University of Iowa where he received an LL.B. degree in 1907, and after being admitted to the Iowa bar, Wilson went into private law practice.

Wilson was first exposed to politics when, in 1898, at the age of fourteen, he spent time in the Iowa State Senate as a page. Eventually aligning himself with the Republican Party, he served in several different political posts, including assistant secretary of the State Senate from 1906 to 1909, and secretary, in 1911. After serving some time as assistant Polk County attorney, he was elected to the attorney's position in 1914. In 1917 he was appointed to the post of district court judge, resigning in 1921 to once again take up private law practice, this time as a partner in his own firm, Wilson & Shaw.

WILSON

Wilson returned to politics in 1926, serving in the Iowa State Senate until 1935. Three years later he was elected to the governorship, and with an interim reelection, served until 1943. His next political post was as a U.S. Senator, a seat he held until 1949, during which time he served as a member of the small business, armed forces, and agriculture committees. When his last term was finished, Wilson teamed up with his son George to create the law firm of Wilson & Wilson.

During his tenure as governor, one of the first decisions Wilson made was to eliminate the three-man State Board of Control, due to that department's neglect of the state's fifteen penal institutions, a situation which had caused inhumane conditions for the inmates. New departments Wilson created included the Tax Commission, the Department of Public Safety, and the State Industrial and Defense Commission. In addition, he also reorganized the Board of Social Welfare, and helped pass the Teacher-Tenure Law.

Wilson was married to Mildred E. Zehner and the couple had four children. He died on September 8, 1953.

WILSON, MARGARET WILHEMINA, (1882-1973) — author, missionary born in Traer, Iowa on January 16, 1882. She was the fourth child born to a farmer and livestock trader and his wife, West and Agnes (McCornack) Wilson. The family moved from Traer to Ames, Iowa then to Chicago, Illinois in 1897. Wilson attended Englewood High School in Chicago from there she went to the University of Chicago from which she received an associate degree in 1903 and a B. Phil. in 1904.

In the fall of 1904, just after graduating from University of Chicago, Wilson, much to the amazement of friends and acquaintances enlisted as a missionary in theJservice of the Untied Presbyterian Church of North America.. Her service was confined to the Punjab region in northern Indian where she performed a variety of tasks including teacher and supervisor in the Gujranwala Girls School. It was from these experiences, that she drew upon for two of her later novels, *Daughters of India* (1928) and *Trousers of Taffeta* (1929). Although missionary service was fulfilling for Wilson, it was also stressful and emotionally draining . Due to ill health, the result of a bout with typhoid, and the strain of the mission work, Wilson returned to the United States in 1910, and officially resigned in 1916

Wilson began writing at a young age, her early efforts were poems, a genre she eventually abandoned. Her first poem was published when she was twelve under the pseudonym Elizabeth West, it was entitled "Pain." Encouraged by her parents who both wrote poetry Wilson continued to express herself through poetry, then began to write short stories before eventually progressing to novels. Her first short stories were written under the pseudonym, An Elderly Spinster. Although most of her work was fiction, its content dealt with current social issues, such as the rigidity and adsurdity of domestic law, as well as Christion concerns and the plight of women in a male-donminated society.

Wilson entered the divinity school of the University of Chicago in 1912 as a degree student and completed the academic year. For the next five years she taught at Pullman High School and continued working on her short stories. She returned to divinity school in 1917 remained only two quarters. Her father's health was failing and much of her time was spent caring for him. and the rest spent on writing. It was during this period that she wrote several short stories and two novels, *The Able McLaughlins* (1923) for which she won the 1924 Pulitzer Prize and the *Kenworthys* (1925). Her father died in 1923 and Wilson traveled to Europe, where she married George Douglas Turner in Paris on Christmas Eve 1923. The Two had met in India, where Turner had been secretary of the Young Men's Christian Association in Lahore.

During her early years of marriage, settled in England, Wilson wrote *The Painted Room* (1926), and her two novels based on India he time spent in India., *Daughters of India* and *Trousers of Taffeta* Wilson was, by her upbringing, a firm believer in punishment and was reared to subscribe to the eye for an eye philosophy. However, Turner spent most of his career employed by the prison system and possessed very different ideas on criminals and their punishments. His views on the penal system, crime and prison began to influence Wilson and her writing. Turner had held a number of positions in British prisons and maintained that often laws make the criminal and prisons are generally ineffective in producing rehabilitation.

With ill-health plaguing Turner, he retired in 1938 but continued his cause through writing and public appearances. In the meantime, Wilson wrote a non-fiction piece, *The Crime of Punishment* (1931), and three novels, *The Dark Duty* (1931), *The Valiant Wife* (1933) and *The Law and the Mclaughlins* (1936).

The pair had moved to the English country side upon Turner' retirement, but the onset of World War II brought a disruption the couples' life. Despite his retirement, the British government called upon Turner for a number of duties. Their home was often the site of shelter for a number of soldiers and refugees. Wilson's final novel, a children's story, *The Devon Treasure Mystery* (1939) was written to pay for the installation of central heat in their country home. Tuner died in 1946 and Wilson never resumed writing Her health was not the best and she was cared for, until they died, by her step daughters (from Turner's first marriage). She died on October 6, 1973 in Droitwichm Worcester, England.

WOOD, GRANT, (1892-1942) — painter, was born on a farm near Anamosa, Iowa on February 13, 1892. His father died when he was ten and his mother moved the family to Cedar Rapids, Iowa where Grant completed high school and taught himself to draw. After graduation, he attended the Minneapolis School of Design and Handicraft and later, for a short time, took evening classes at the University of Iowa. He then moved to Chicago to study art at the Art Institute and tried unsuccessfully to become a silversmith. In 1917, he went into the army and was assigned to camouflage work in Washington. While there he made sketches of the soldiers and sold them for 25 cents to one dollar each.

After the war, Wood taught art in the public schools in Cedar Rapids. For awhile he traveled through Europe, studied at the Acadimie Julian in Paris in 1923, and adopted a bohemian life- style for a period of time. After awhile he went back to Cedar Rapids from where, he realized, came all his best ideas for art. He sold his art work to friends for small amounts of money and even earned a little money giving advice to people on how to improve their homes. Wood's techniques using glazing on his paintings was extremely time consuming, and even though he was able to sell pieces for $1,000 each when his art gained maturity, he often took months to complete each one. Because of this he had to supplement his income by taking lecture tours throughout the country. His first important piece of work, *John B. Turner, Pioneer,* was a portrait of his friend in whose mortuary Wood held his first art exhibition. He then did several pieces of work depicting his own Iowa people, such as *Woman with Plants,* a picture of his mother; *American Gothic,* which made him famous; *Dinner for Threshers; The Midnight Ride of Paul Revere; Birthplace of President Hoover; Young Corn; Spring Turning;Death on Ridge Road; Parson Weems' Fable;* and others. Although several of his works contained satire, his one and only completely satirical work, *Daughters of the American Revolution,* almost got him arrested. The painting took a jab at the Cedar Rapids Daughters of the American Revolution who had once attacked Wood with what he considered misdirected patriotism for having a stained glass window, commissioned by the war memorial committee of Cedar Rapids, manufactured in Munich, Germany.

In 1934, Wood was appointed state chairman of the federal Public Works of Art Project and in that same year accepted the position of assistant professor of art at the University of Iowa. His method of teaching was unconventional in that he did not believe in lecturing but rather in allowing the students to get right to work painting and developing their own individual techniques using brown wrapping paper for canvasses. He was promoted in 1941 to full professor after having taken a year off just to paint. Wood was generous with his time and money in helping young artists and was also the founder of the Stone City Art Colony which each year brought together artists of many schools. In 1936, he was awarded an honorary D.Litt from the University of Wisconsin; in 1940, an honorary M.A. from the Wesleyan University; an honorary Dr. of Fine Arts from Lawrence College in 1938 and one from Northwestern University in 1941.

Wood married Sara Sherman in 1935, and after a short, childless marriage, divorced in 1940. Grant Wood died on February 12, 1942.

WOODS, FRANK PLOWMAN, (1868-1944) — a U.S. Representative from Iowa; born near Sharon, Walworth County, Wis., December 11, 1868; attended the public schools and the Northern Indiana Normal School, Valparaiso, Ind.; moved to Estherville, Emmett County, Iowa, in 1887 and worked in a newspaper office for two years; engaged in the mortgage-loan business and private banking; chairman of the Republican State central committee in 1906 and 1907; elected as a Republican to the Sixty-first and to the four succeeding Congresses (March 4, 1909-March 3, 1919); unsuccessful candidate for renomination in 1918; chairman of the Republican National Congressional Committee 1913-1918; resided in Altadena, Calif., until his death there April 25, 1944; interment in Mountain View Cemetery.

Y

YOUNG, LAFAYETTE, (1848-1926) — a U.S. Senator from Iowa; born near Eddyville, Monroe County, Iowa, May 10, 1848; attended country schools and night school in St. Louis, where he learned the printing trade; founded and published the Atlantic (Iowa) Telegraph 1871-1890; member, State senate 1874-1880, 18861888; established the Des Moines Capital in 1890 and was editor until his death; during the Spanish-American War was in Cuba as a war correspondent in 1898; presidential elector on the Republican ticket in 1908; appointed as a Republican to the United States Senate to fill the vacancy caused by the death of Jonathan P. Dolliver and served from November 12, 1910, to April 11, 1911, when a successor was elected; unsuccessful candidate for election to fill this vacancy; war correspondent for four months in Europe in 1915; Chautauqua lecturer in 1915; chairman of the State council for defense for Iowa during the First World War; was made a knight of the Order of Leopold II of Belgium in recognition of his work in raising funds in Iowa for the children of Belgium; died in Des Moines, Iowa, November 15, 1926; interment in Woodlawn Cemetery.